canyouhearme?

canyouhearme?

Tuning in
to the God
who speaks

Brad Jersak

MONARCH
BOOKS

Oxford, UK & Grand Rapids, Michigan, USA

Originally published by Fresh Winds Press 2003.
This edition by agreement.
First published in the UK and USA in 2006 by Monarch Books
(a publishing imprint of Lion Hudson plc),
Mayfield House, 256 Banbury Road, Oxford OX2 7DH
Tel: +44 (0) 1865 302750   Fax: +44 (0) 1865 302757
Email: monarch@lionhudson.com
www.lionhudson.com

ISBN-13: 978-1-85424-756-8 (UK)
ISBN-10: 1-85424-756-5 (UK)
ISBN-13: 978-0-8254-6116-3 (USA)
ISBN-10: 0-8254-6116-2 (USA)

Distributed by:
UK: Marston Book Services Ltd, PO Box 269,
Abingdon, Oxon OX14 4YN
USA: Kregel Publications, PO Box 2607,
Grand Rapids, Michigan 49501.

Not for sale in Canada.

British Library Cataloguing Data
A catalogue record for this book is available from
the British Library.

Printed in Malta.

·····Dedication·····

The king said,
"Find out whose son this young man is."
1 Samuel 17:56

For my dad and mom,
Lloyd and Irene Jersak

·····Thanks·····

Special thanks to

Jesus Christ for being so relentlessly kind.

Eden, Stephen, Justice, and Dominic: my living proof.

Thanks also to

Patrick White: the credible witness and watchman who opened my gate to the Shepherd's voice.

Fresh Wind: the little church that could and still does.

To the Peggs, the Dycks and the MacPhersons: our fearless leadership team.

My spiritual fathers: Kit Mitchell, Eric McCooeye, Glenn Runnalls, Peter Bartel, Barrie J. Palfreyman, and Carl Hinderager.

Brian and Sue West, Brian and Della Headley for training me in prayer ministry.

Charles and Colleen, Lorie, Jodi and all the intercessors that prayed and believed and suffered my learning curve.

Kevin Miller: my editor and friend: *www.kevinwrites.com*.
Colleen, Heidi, Alan, and Paul for proofreading.
Dwight Friesen (Big Sky Design) for cover art.

Kim and Darlene Unrau, Brita and Peter Miko, Murray Dueck, Andy MacPherson, Karin Dart and the other prophets who told me it was time. More recently to Ron Dart, Archbishop Lazar, and Mike Stewart, more iron with which to sharpen iron.

Agora (Sean, Sam, Andre, et al): for testing everything.

The staff at Ethical Addictions.

····· Contents ·····

·····*Introduction*·····

WHERE I'M COMING FROM

It started out innocently enough, even virtuously. I learned to love God's Word from my mother's knee. Before I could read, I was memorizing typical Sunday school Bible verses: "God is love." "We love him because he first loved us." "For God so loved the world..." "Seek first the Kingdom..." As I began to read on my own, I asked my parents if they would buy me my own Bible if I would memorize thirty verses. I was very proud of this accomplishment, and I suspect that's when a little darkness crept in. My next self-given task was to go through my father's Bible and duplicate all of his highlighting into my new Bible. I noticed how those observing my efforts approved. Shortly after that, an early and meaningful baptism combined with a grade three reading level gave me a voracious hunger for Scripture. The first books that I read for myself were Acts followed by an autobiography of David Livingstone, then Acts again. Thus, a strange mixture of spiritual joy, pride, and a need for approval attended my life in the written Word throughout my childhood.

Bible College amplified these issues exponentially. I committed not only to reading the entire Bible but also to studying it until it literally fell apart in my hands. I privately puffed myself up for having the most weathered Bible on campus. I also prided myself on having jotted personal comments in the margins of every single page. But this was not enough. I also determined to take every single Bible and theology course the school offered either in the classroom or by correspondence.

Ironically, as I excelled academically, I was drifting farther and farther from an intimate relationship with God. I despised those who claimed to "hear from God" or anyone who seemed more spiritually devoted than me. I found myself hardening into a deluded objectivity that reduced Scripture to something worthy of dissection with my analytical scalpel but nothing more. Seeking to appear wise, I had ascended in my own mind to a theological high tower where theory was everything and practical matters, especially compassionate care for others, was a great discomfort. I lapsed into a bibliolatry that was far away from the heart of God.

If that weren't enough, I went on to seminary, where I was able to improve my marks and further feed my pride. On top of two master's degrees, I added five semesters of Greek to my tool belt. (Although I really only learned enough Greek to become dangerous.) I enjoyed learning theological terms that others had no clue about, and I filled my mind with the entire works of Christian authors from L. S. Chafer to Francis Schaeffer. Very satisfying! (Picture Tolkien's Gollum here.) I lived for the approval of my instructors, reveling in deep self-satisfaction whenever they suggested that my papers were publishable. A general haughtiness had set in.

I do not hold my parents, my teachers or the schools I attended responsible for my attitude. Nor do I regret those years of training in the Word. The people were not the problem, neither was the scholarship. And I'm not about to discard the Bible! No, the problem was hidden deep within my own heart. Behind my need to perform spiritually were deep issues of insecurity about God's love and an effort to compensate for feelings of inadequacy and rejection. But God was about to expose all that.

As I sat in the lofty balcony of self-noted biblical expertise, God finally challenged the stronghold of spiritual pride. He did so in the person of Patrick, a dear friend and credible witness who, as a type of John the Baptist, prepared my ears for a divine confrontation. And so God spoke a living Word through his written Word to my heart. I'll never forget the way his truth pierced my soul. He said, "Brad, you have a form of godliness but deny its power" (2 Timothy 3:5). Ouch. I knew what he meant. My spirituality was loveless and powerless. It was an empty structure. He continued, "You are in error because you do not know the Scriptures or the power of God" (Matthew 22:29). That hurt. If anything, I was all about knowing the Scriptures and getting my theological ducks in a highly structured row. But even as he exposed my blindness towards real truth, I knew he was right. Facts without love are not truth; they are merely impotent words. This was difficult for me, a prospective teacher, to face. But there was more. "You diligently study the Scriptures because you think that by them you possess eternal life. Yet you have never [even once] heard the voice of my Father, nor does his word dwell in you" (John 5:36–40). How was this possible? How could I be so diligent in biblical studies yet never hear God's voice? Jesus' sharp words against the religious leaders who would finally crucify him were now targeting me with alarming precision. The sandy foundation upon which I had built my spiritual house began to wash away from beneath my feet. I had accumulated Bible facts but ended up bankrupt because I didn't know the Living Word, Jesus. I worshiped the map but had missed the journey and forgotten the destination. The first step to recovery was that I was finally able to recognize and repent of this fact.

I returned to the Bible with different, humbler eyes. I read that Paul's message and preaching were not with wise and persuasive words but with a demonstration of the Spirit's power so that our faith might not rest on men's wisdom but on God's power (1 Corinthians 2: 4–5). I read that his gospel came not simply with words but also with power, with the Holy Spirit and with deep conviction (1 Thessalonians 1:5). And I knew that this sort of teaching was entirely foreign to me. As I returned to my cherished book of Acts, I recognized none of the early Christian experiences or ministry in my own life. I did not know God's voice or his power. In fact, my version of the Christian faith would likely have been unrecognizable to the first apostles.

The Lord had brought me low indeed, shattering my rationalistic "mastery of divinity." It was quite a stripping. Now perhaps he would take my hand and teach me from scratch who he is, what his voice sounds like, and how to walk in the Spirit. I took up Moses' prayer from Exodus 33: "God, I don't just want to know *about* you. I need to know *you*. From now on, if you won't lead me, I'm not proceeding. But if you are pleased with me, teach me your ways so that I may know you. Above all, show me your glory."

I believe the pages that follow reflect God's answers to that prayer, and they reflect my prayer for you, the reader. None of my studies, experience, degrees or credentials will open your ears to the voice of God or open your eyes to see his face. They don't establish me as an authority in your life or authorize me as a spokesman for God's heart. I simply come as a witness and ask you to weigh the testimony herein for yourself. I expect that as you do, God himself will begin to speak to you.

DID I WRITE THIS BOOK FOR YOU?

This book is written for *anyone* who wants to hear God's voice.

It is written for disillusioned churchgoers and "prodigals" who are searching for more reality than western church culture generally offers. It is for the stale and the wounded Christian in exile—for those who've left church but haven't left God.

It is written for spiritually hungry, "unchurched" people who want to hear God's voice but find the pop gurus unsatisfying (too much self--not enough God). It offers an alternative that appeals to those mystical cravings yet demystifies the process. It introduces a path to inner peace that allows them to keep their feet on the ground.

11

It is written for Christian pastors and leaders who want to equip their people with "ears to hear." They will be prepared to train their congregations to hear God without fear of producing prophetic flakes. Christian leaders will become "watchmen" who open the door to the voice of the Good Shepherd.

It is written for Christian lay people who want to hear God for themselves. Those who have depended on church leaders to be God's voice to them will be challenged to tune in to the God who speaks to ordinary people. Their faith will be stirred to encounter and respond to God as he asks, "Can you hear me?"

◀)) *Tuning In* • • • • • • • • • •

The "**Tuning In**" sections in this book are "listening prayer" exercises. They are highly adaptable to your preferred devotional method. They can be practiced in the privacy of your heart, across the pages of a journal, in the intimacy of close friends, or together in large corporate settings. I hope these exercises will serve to tune you in to the voice and the heart of God for you.

..... *Part I* .....

The Simplicity of Listening Prayer

..... *1* .....
"My Sheep Hear My Voice"

"The Sovereign LORD has given me an instructed tongue, to know the word that sustains the weary. He wakens me morning by morning, wakens my ear to listen like one being taught. The Sovereign LORD has opened my ears and I have not been rebellious, I have not drawn back."

- Isaiah 50:4–5

WAKENED EARS

Eden awoke suddenly, her heart pounding and the images from a dream still fresh in her mind's eye. The nightmare was a dreadful premonition of our three-year-old son Dominic hanging with a rope around his neck. It threatened to haunt my wife with sleeplessness for the remainder of the night, so she prayed urgently: "Lord, I cannot watch over that active little boy ALL of the time! I cannot live life in fear of every potential accident that could happen when I'm not looking! What am I supposed to do with this terrible nightmare?"

The answer came quickly and quietly: "Trust me. Ask me to be the all-watching parent and protector. Release his care into my hands, and I will guard his steps." As Eden prayed this prayer, a deep peace came over her, and, surprisingly, she was able to fall back to sleep immediately.

The next day, she and our oldest son, Stephen, fell ill. They struggled with a nasty flu for the next few days. Stephen missed several days of school, and Eden spent much of her time bed-ridden. Neither our prayers nor any medicine seemed to have any impact on the disease.

Things finally began to return to normal over the weekend, and we all worshiped together on Sunday. However, on Monday morning, Stephen complained once again that he was feeling sick. Since Eden had to leave Dominic at the neighbour's house while she fulfilled some responsibilities at the local school that day, she decided to let Stephen stay there as well until she returned. After Eden left, the neighbour went upstairs to do some baking, leaving the boys by themselves in the basement rec. room.

As Stephen rested on the couch watching TV, Dominic played quietly behind him. Suddenly, Stephen heard a muffled cry. He turned quickly and saw Dominic dangling by his neck at the end of a rope, his toes just out of reach of the floor. It turns out Dominic had found an exercise rope attached to a pulley in the ceiling. Thinking that he might try to fly, he climbed up on the couch, wrapped a loop of rope around his neck, and took his first leap of faith! Stephen threw his arms around Dominic's body and lifted him high enough to create slack in the rope so that he could remove the makeshift noose. Phew!

When Eden returned to find Dominic with deep rope burns around his entire neck, she held him tightly and had it out again with the Lord.

Eden: What was that?

God: That was me, saving your son's life. I warned you in a dream about the impending danger, I gave you the prayers that would avert that danger, and I allowed Stephen to be sick so that he would be here to save Dominic's life. You asked me to watch him and protect him when you can't. I am faithful to my promise, and I answered those prayers.

Eden: Okay, but there's one thing I don't understand: Why did I have to be sick too?

God: Ah! It was necessary that you were sick so that you would sympathize with Stephen and believe that he needed to stay home today. If you hadn't experienced this flu, you may have sent him to school this morning in spite of his complaints!

As parents, Eden and I will never forget that experience or its many lessons—the loudest and clearest being the necessity of having ears that are awake to God's voice. That is exactly the thrust of this book: *to open our spiritual ears to listen to the voice of God and to open our spiritual eyes to see his face.*

When we meet with God in prayer, when we behold his face, when we hear his voice, just who or what are we actually encountering? My belief, based on Scripture, Christian tradition and personal experience, is that in listening prayer, we meet none other than Jesus Christ, *the voice of the living God.*[1] To those for whom hearing God is a new experience, I hope to bring you to meet this Jesus. To those who already recognize the voice and face of Christ, I hope to fan the flame of faith within you, to let you know that he has much more to show you, to tell you that *the best is yet to come.* But let us start at the beginning.

My Sheep Hear My Voice

Have you ever heard or made this statement: "You know what bothers me? People who go around claiming 'God told me' as if they have a direct line to God." All of us could probably share a story about someone who said, "God told me," yet got it completely wrong or even flipflopped his or her message within days. We can also recall those who shared virtually every thought and opinion as though it came straight from heaven. Their own desires and whims are somehow distorted into "divine directives" that need to be obeyed upon threat of God's wrath. Some self-proclaimed prophet may have even wounded you directly—or worse, *proposed to you* in the name of God.

When teaching about protocol for sharing alleged "words from the Lord," John Wimber, author of *Power Evangelism,* was fond of recalling how the worship leader at his church told "God told me that you are to marry me" by four different young ladies on the same Sunday! Oddly, my own wife once received a "God told me" marriage proposal from a pastor who otherwise claims that God doesn't speak today. I'm very thankful for her reply: "When God tells me that too, I'll get back to you."

With such people in our churches and communities, is it any wonder that Paul encountered believers for whom prophecies had become contemptible (1 Thessalonians 5:20)? How easily and thoroughly cynicism becomes the grid through which we approach the subject of God's voice!

In direct contrast, Jesus Christ's approach to hearing God is simple and unjaded. He presents this crystal clear message to those who have ears to hear:

> The man who enters by the gate is the shepherd of his sheep. The watchman opens the gate for him, and the sheep listen to his voice. He calls his own sheep by name and leads them out. When he has brought out his own, he goes on ahead of them, and his sheep follow him because they know his voice. But they will never follow a stranger; in fact, they will run away from him because they do not recognize a stranger's voice... I am the good shepherd; I know my sheep and my sheep know me—just as the Father knows me and I know the Father—and I lay down my life for the sheep. (John 10:2–5, 14–15)

The Lord is making a point here about his voice: he has one. He uses it. He speaks. His sheep—those who have ears to listen—hear it, know it, and follow it.

"My sheep hear my voice." What do these words mean? Will we take them seriously? Our hope-stealing cynicism may seem justified, even fashionable, but before the Good Shepherd's voice, it is painfully inappropriate.

"My sheep hear my voice." The words create expectation, sponsor hope, and build faith. They cleanse attitudes and inform theologies. "My sheep hear my voice." In these last days, God has indeed spoken to us through his Son (Hebrews 1:2). And so God's own voice echoes through the centuries, "This is my beloved Son... listen to him."

Note that Jesus did not say, "My prophets hear my voice." He didn't say, "My pastors hear my voice." And he did not say, "Only the spiritual people hear my voice." But rather, "My *sheep* hear my voice." According to Jesus, his voice is not reserved for the spiritually elite, the priest, or the guru. Any "sheep" can hear his call. That means you can hear it too!

Note also that Jesus did not say "might hear," "could hear," "should hear," or "would hear, if only..." "My sheep *do* hear my voice," he asserts. It's just a fact. Jesus claims to be the Good Shepherd who speaks and his people to be the flock that hears his voice. This claim may present a deep challenge to our natural inclination towards cynicism and skepticism. But it is also tremendous news in a world—and a church—that thirsts for a word from the Lord.

Answering Machine Prayers

For much of my Christian journey, I was totally unaware of the Shepherd's voice. For me, prayer amounted to leaving phone messages on God's answering machine. Faith was akin to hoping that God would eventually check his messages. The fruit of this attitude was terrible. It isolated me from personal friendship with God and instilled a hopeless fatalism into my prayer life.

I once served as a summer counsellor at a children's Bible camp. One day, one of the kitchen-helpers lost track of her toddler for a few minutes, only to find that the child had ingested a fatal dose of some poisonous cleaning agent. As they rushed the little one to a distant hospital, the entire camp gathered to pray. I remember watching faithful prayer warriors crying out to God on behalf of the child's life. But in that crucial hour, I could not connect to God in any meaningful way. I struggled to identify with these people who seemed to hear God's voice, feel his heart, and know that their prayers were drawing the healing will of heaven down into this crisis. By contrast, I stood there, dry-eyed and cold, thinking nothing more than, "I guess if he dies, he dies. If God saves him, he saves him."

I now believe that God heard those prayers and acted in power to rescue the child. But I know that I had no active part in it. For me, even when dialing God's 911 number, I expected nothing more than the same old answering machine.

As I complained about how boring and cold prayer of this nature had become, I now realize that God was crying out to my deafened ears, "You think *you're* bored?" Imagine the grief of a passionate God who longs to be Father, Friend, and Lover to a people who will not listen to him. We tend to discard his intimate messages by abruptly "hanging up" the prayer-phone with a quick "amen" as soon as we've got everything off our chests. Picture God sitting on the other end of the line saying, "But you never gave me a chance to get a word in!"

The disparity between the promise of John 10 and the poverty of my testimony begs the question, if his sheep hear his voice, why didn't I? Why didn't he talk to me? Why didn't he answer me? You may be asking the same thing yourself: Why can't I hear him right now? Why doesn't he talk to me? Why doesn't he answer me when I pray? Such questions can lead to despair. But to those who will hear, good news awaits!

The "Silence" of God

God's servant Job voiced the same questions after going through a series of brutal personal catastrophes. His family, his wealth, and finally his health were taken away from him. He was destitute, living on a filthy trash heap and scratching at his sores with a piece of broken pottery. He became so depressed that he was tempted to follow the advice of his wife when she said, "Curse God and die." Finally, Job challenged God on the same perceived silence that I have often complained about.

Enter Elihu. Bear in mind that Elihu was *not* one of the three foolish counsellors who had spoken out of turn. He was a man of true wisdom sent by God just prior to God's own entrance. In a sense, Elihu was God's opening act. In the following speech, Elihu answered Job's accusation (and mine) in regard to God's apparent silence.

> Why do you complain that God answers none of man's words? For God *does* speak—now one way, now another— though man may not perceive it. In a dream, in a vision of the night; when deep sleep falls on men as they slumber in their beds; he may speak in their ears and terrify them with warnings; to turn man from wrongdoing and keep him from pride, to preserve his soul from the pit, his life from perishing by the sword. (Job 33:13–18)

19

As you can see, Elihu confronts Job with this truth: God *does so* speak. He is speaking *all the time*. He speaks in *many* ways. The problem is not with God's voice. The trouble is with our ears. We do not hear or perceive what he is saying. We might even go one step further to say that we *do* hear him—we are just not *aware* that we hear him. Or perhaps we're not willing or ready to listen.

Contact

At this moment, even if the room you are sitting in seems completely silent, the air all around you is saturated with voices and sounds. For example, radio waves flood past your ears carrying music, voices, and commercials of all types. These waves envelop you, penetrating your body and bouncing off your eardrums at this very moment. But unless you turn on a radio and dial into one of these many frequencies, you will not perceive them at all.

In the same way, Elihu is telling us that God's radio station is always on. He's broadcasting loud and clear, 24 hours a day, seven days a week. The trouble is, we are not dialing it in. Our radios aren't working.

Hard to believe? According to David, God's thoughts about you not only surpass all of earth's radio stations combined, they even out-number the sands on the seashore (Psalm 139:17–18). He is thinking about you constantly. And he is willing—no, *longing*—to share those thoughts with you. How can you know this? In John 16, Jesus shares a secret with his disciples, and by extension, with all of us:

> Oh there is so much more I want to tell you, but you can't bear it now. When the Spirit of truth comes [and he has, Acts 2], He will guide you into all truth. He will not be presenting his own ideas; he will be telling you what he has heard. He will tell you about the future. He will bring me glory by revealing to you whatever he receives from me. All that the Father has is mine; this is what I mean when I say that the Spirit will reveal to you whatever he receives from me. (John 16:12–15)

Eavesdropping on Heaven

We can unpack this passage to discover even more claims regarding God's voice. Jesus told his disciples that even after we consider everything he told them, both that which is recorded in the gospels and all that was not, he still had much more to say. But he withheld it, because they could not handle it yet, remembering of course that his thoughts would have filled beaches upon beaches with "truth-sand." Yet, the disciples were not to worry. The Holy Spirit would come and continue sharing that which Jesus had left unsaid. He would guide them into *all* truth (John 16:13). If you want to personalize this message, what Jesus is really saying is, there is *so* much more he *wants* to share with *you*. Were you to memorize every word of the Scriptures, the Lord would still not be satisfied. There is still more. And this "more" is what the Holy Spirit was sent to deliver.

Exactly what is it that the Holy Spirit needs to say? Specifically, Jesus declares that it has to do with truth and with things to come. But perhaps more importantly, his task is to share "whatever he hears." What does the Spirit hear? And *whom* does he hear? The Spirit hears the Father and Son. He eavesdrops on their conversations—on the innumerable thoughts they exchange with one another. Remember: a myriad of those thoughts are about you and for you. Picture it: the Father and the Son are talking about you. The Spirit overhears them and then comes over to say, "Do you know what they're saying? I want to tell you. I am free to reveal *whatever* they are saying, and I do it for this one reason: to bring glory to God."

Downpour

In Acts 2, we begin to see this flood of *revelation*, defined simply as that which God reveals about himself, his ways and his will. Peter describes the coming of the Spirit in this way:

> This is what was spoken by the prophet Joel: In the last days, God says, I will pour out my Spirit on all people. Your sons and daughter will prophesy, your young men will see visions, your old men will dream dreams. Even on my servants, both men and women, I will pour out my Spirit in those days, and they will prophesy. (Acts 2:16–18)

Each manifestation of the Spirit mentioned here—prophecies, visions, and dreams—is a version of God's voice established as long ago as Job himself. The age of the Spirit is not meant to be a famine or trickle of hearing. Rather, we're to experience a roaring downpour of God's voice on *everyone*: every age, gender, and caste. The voice of the Lord is like the sound of *many* waters (Psalm 29). Pentecost released a virtual Niagara Falls of revelation!

I am not advocating for a fuller revelation of God beyond Christ himself. Rather, the Revealer of the Father continues to reveal the Father in the power of the Spirit in existentially fresh ways for every generation of believers.

In the Old Testament era, the voice of God seemed rare, sporadic, and exclusive. It belonged to a few patriarchs, judges, priests and prophets who spoke to the nation on God's behalf. There was always an intermediary between God and humankind. But as Jesus ascended back into the presence of the Father, I imagine he turned to prophets like Isaiah, Ezekiel, and Joel and said, "Watch this. I am about to do something on the earth and *nothing will ever* be the same." And with that he began to *pour out* the Spirit—the Spirit of revelation in particular—on every believer. When the flood from heaven came, it was generous, continuous, and all-inclusive.

Curious George

It is always precious when God demonstrates his willingness to speak to and through what society (and too often the church) regards as "the least of these." He loves to bypass the flashy, the important, and the impressive in favour of the children, the disabled, and the poor (Luke 10:21–24). Those with ears to hear the Lord through the little ones are in for a kingdom feast.

On one occasion, I was at a prayer retreat with a group of prayer ministers from a ministry called Elijah House. To conclude our time together, they were gracious enough to gather around to bless me in listening prayer. Della, one of my dear friends and mentors, shared a fun little picture as an encouragement from God. She saw me as Curious George, the little cartoon monkey. The Lord spoke to her that this would be my new nickname because of my curiosity. He was blessing the many questions that I ask and letting me know that he enjoys childlike inquisitiveness.

I drove home that day full of joy, because I truly believed that Della's message was from God. I respect her integrity and maturity and listen with care when she believes the Lord is showing her something.

When I arrived home, I asked my wife how her day had been. She told me that she had gone to her prophetic class (called "Samuel's Mantle," led by Murray Dueck). She had taken our son Dominic along, who was four years old at the time. On the way home after class, Dominic turned to her and announced out of the blue, "Daddy is getting a new nickname today. It's going to be 'Bradley Curious George Jersak.'" Dominic made this declaration two hours *before* Della had prayed for me!

I was so thrilled that I called Deana, one of my intercessors, on her cell phone to tell her about this neat bit of synchronicity. We laughed at the good bit of fun that Jesus was having with me and then hung up. Within a minute, my phone rang. "It's me again," she said. "You won't believe this. When you just phoned me, I was standing in the video store. While you were telling me about Dominic's 'word', Jakie (Deana's three-year-old son) was yanking on my leg saying 'Rent this! Rent this!' Guess what the video was! 'The Adventures of Curious George.'"

As you can see, when we become like children, we enter the kingdom realm where both mature mentors and little children deliver delicious invitations from the King himself.

Kit

On another occasion, Fresh Wind, our wonderful little church, had gathered for worship outside in a local park. We were sending off a family to the Philippines for a stint with Youth With a Mission (YWAM). Although all of their tuition was covered, we knew they still needed $6,000 for all of their airfares. We decided to ask the church to spend one week listening to God about how much to give in the offering on the following Sunday, then we would contribute that entire offering toward the flights. This was quite daunting since our average offering that summer was about $1,000 per week. I was in the midst of explaining that when we listen, we should do so with open and generous hearts when all of a sudden Kit nudged his way to the front.

Kit is one of our most blessed members. He lives in full-time supportive care for those with disabilities. Although he cannot speak words that we understand, Kit is able to demonstrate his feelings with loving hugs and vocalize heartfelt prayers. To those who can hear, his speech is a beautiful soundtrack of the kingdom. To those who cannot, it sounds like a series of inflected grunts. He can't read, but he is able to print one word, "KIT."

While I continued to wax eloquent, Kit approached and gave me a gentle bump, knocking me aside from the music stand where my Bible was perched. He flipped open the Bible, apparently at random, and began poking the page. I asked if he wanted me to read it. He nodded and grunted with enthusiasm. So I began to read aloud from the exact spot where his finger came to rest:

> Then King David turned to the entire assembly and said, "My son Solomon, whom God has chosen to be the next king of Israel, is still young and inexperienced. The work ahead of him is enormous, for the Temple he will build is not just another building—it is for the LORD God himself! Using every resource at my command, I have gathered as much as I could for building the Temple of my God... Now then, who

23

will follow my example? Who is willing to give offerings to the LORD today?" Then the family leaders, the leaders of the tribes of Israel, the generals and captains of the army, and the king's administrative officers all gave willingly. For the construction of the Temple of God, they gave almost 188 tons of gold, 10,000 gold coins, about 375 tons of silver, about 675 tons of bronze, and about 3,750 tons of iron. They also contributed numerous precious stones, which were deposited in the treasury of the house of the LORD under the care of Jehiel, a descendant of Gershon. The people rejoiced over the offerings, for they had given freely and wholeheartedly to the LORD, and King David was filled with joy. (1 Chronicles 29:1–2, 6–9)

As I read the last verse, my heart was so filled with joy that I began to laugh. Then Kit began to laugh, and then most of our little group began either laughing, crying or cheering. God touched a deep spot in our hearts because we knew that the Lord Jesus had clothed himself with Kit to personally deliver that offering appeal. The Lord of Glory had come down to speak through the "least of these."

The following Sunday I looked around at offering time. There were perhaps sixty of us. I did the math: Twenty-five percent were children. Twenty-five percent were disabled residents and their workers. Twenty-five percent were the working poor. The remainder seemed to be college students. I could count the people with middle-class incomes on one hand. But when we counted the offering, it came to just over $6,000. I made a mental note to remind myself to invite Jesus to take the offering more often!

Even Them? Even Then? [2]

One might object, "If children and the disabled can hear God, it is only because they are so pure in heart. But I am not so innocent. I'm not a very strong Christian and I don't obey very well. I stumble and struggle along, so why should I expect God to speak to me?"

In theory, those who are most repentant, most obedient, most holy should hear God's voice most clearly and most often. Those who live to please God and submit wholly to his Lordship should get the best "reception" as they tune in to his voice.

Oddly, neither Scripture nor experience support that theory. God's *voice* calls us to repentance, obedience and submission; those who hear and obey are blessed. But these are the *results* of hearing him, not the *pre-conditions*. If I can't hear his voice until I'm obedient, what am I obeying? And how obedient do I need to be for him to talk to me? Or how disobedient before he stops talking? If hearing God's voice was conditional upon my behaviour, the relationship would be a formula revolving around me and my performance: "Good people hear—bad people don't." That's the very religion Jesus opposed. Getting right with God is always and only a response to the grace-gift of his voice.

Certainly there can be a famine of hearing when hearts are unrepentant, but that doesn't mean God is not speaking. As a band called "Out Of The Grey" once wrote, "He is not silent, we are not listening."[3] But the Lord has ways of catching our attention, even while we're plugging our ears.

The danger of refusing to heed God's voice is *not* that he will resort to the silent treatment. Rather, we are warned that he will begin to speak *more* clearly and *more* forcefully, which is not always a pleasant experience (remember Jonah?). You can hear his voice as an ointment that heals or as a sword that pierces. In either case, it will bring freedom and life when we finally listen.

While the prodigal son was still wallowing in the pigpen of his rebellion, he came to his senses and resolved to repent (Luke 15:17–18). Why? It was only because the voice of God graciously *spoke* to his heart. When Hosea's unfaithful wife had left her husband, forgotten the Lord and chased after multiple lovers, God said, "Therefore I am now going to allure her; I will lead her into the desert and *speak tenderly* to her" (Hosea 2:14). In fact, most of the prophetic words in Scripture are negative, not because God is generally grumpy, but because his love compels him to keep *speaking* to his wayward ones until they return home. If I read men like Jonah and David right, whether we are following God perfectly or running away feverishly, he graciously, relentlessly, even indiscriminately, continues to speak! No wonder the poet Francis called him "the Hound of Heaven."[4]

I've met a number of men in prison Bible studies who shared that it was while they were still in the stupor of a heroin trip or in the despair of prison lock-up that God visited them, spoke to them and saved them. I've heard the testimonies of women who, while still working the streets of East Vancouver, heard God's voice inside, warning them about which men would beat them and which were safe. God spoke to them even then, even there.

Does this offend you? Why not let the scandalous kindness of God hearten you instead? On your very worst days, while you are still kicking against his will (Acts 26:14), God continues to broadcast his words of love, comfort, warning and promise in your direction. You *will* hear him. When you do, just see to it that you don't harden your heart (Hebrews 12:25).

If Jesus can speak through children and the disabled, to prisoners and prostitutes, then he *will* speak to you. In fact, I am certain that he already has. Have you perceived it? It's time to dial in to God's station. In fact, I believe that God is saying to you today, "Maybe you should check *your* messages."

God's Phone Number: Jeremiah 33:3

Before I demonstrate how well and how often you already hear God, try this warm-up exercise. Hold a Bible at arm's length. Look at it. Turn it over in your hand. Think about what this book shows us about God. Then ask yourself:

- Is this book about a God who speaks or a God who is withdrawn and silent?
- Is this book about a people who couldn't hear or a people who wouldn't listen?
- Is this merely a history text about an ancient religion, or does it contain centuries of firsthand testimony that God continually communicates with his people?

According to Paul, our God is no speechless idol. He is a God whose Spirit speaks to and through his people (1 Corinthians 12:2–4). He "spoke to our forefathers through the prophets at many times and in various ways, but in these last days, he has spoken to us by his Son" (Hebrews 1:1–2). This word confirms an earlier message given right in the thick of Jeremiah's prophecies of the new covenant:

> This is what the LORD says, he who made the earth, the LORD who formed it and established it—the LORD is his name: 'Call to me and I will answer you and tell you great and unsearchable things you do not know.' (Jeremiah 33:3)

As we call out to God, let us rehearse this straightforward promise. God does *not* say, "Call to me and the devil will answer and deceive you." Nor does he say, "Call to me and I might answer you when I feel like it." Nor does he say, "Call to me and I will answer you if..." Rather, he promises us (upon the life of his Son), "*I* [the Lord and no other] *Will* [most certainly] *answer* [respond to, converse with] *you* [not just the prophets or the priests, but *you* my children]. Even Moses rejoiced when he realized this: "What other nation is so great as to have their gods near them the way the LORD our God is *near us whenever we pray to him?*" (Deuteronomy 4:7).

LISTENING SURVEY

This is such good news! In truth, the Spirit of Christ *is* speaking. His voice is constant and clear. But the news gets even better. You already hear him *well* and *often*. You can confirm this through a simple survey of your "listening experiences." I believe you'll find that regardless of your previous assumptions, you will be "proven guilty" of hearing from God, whether you identify yourself as a Christian right now or not.

1. Invitation: *Has God ever invited you into his family?*

Did you know that it is impossible to enter God's family unless God himself issues an invitation? Jesus said, "No one can come to me unless the Father who sent me draws him" (John 6:44). This invitation is your introduction to the voice of God. It comes in innumerable ways. Your initial hearing of the gospel may have come through a parent, a Sunday school teacher or a camp speaker. You may have heard a reasoned presentation or felt an unexplainable hunger in your heart. Perhaps you've felt compelled to walk to the front at some gospel meeting, all the while wondering, "Why am I doing this?" Others experience a silent call in the privacy of their hearts. Regardless of how it comes, what ultimately draws a "yes" from our hearts to the kingdom invitation is always and only God's voice.

In *Life After God,* author Douglas Coupland states his "yes" so beautifully:

> The water from the stream above me roars.
>
> Oh, does it roar! Like a voice that knows only one message, one truth—never-ending, like the clapping of hands and the cheers of the citizens upon the coronation of the king, the crowds of the inauguration, cheering for hope and for that one voice that will speak to them...
>
> Now—here is my secret:
>
> I tell it with an openness of heart that I doubt I shall ever achieve again, so I pray that you are in a quiet room as you hear these words. My secret is that I need God—that I am sick and can no longer make it alone. I need God to help me give, because I no longer seem to be capable of giving; to help me to be kind, as I no longer seem capable of kindness; to help me love, as I seem beyond being able to love.
>
> I walk deeper and deeper into the rushing water... The water enters my belly button and it freezes my chest, my

arms, my neck. It reaches my mouth, my nose, my ears and the roar is so loud—this roar, this clapping of hands.

These hands—the hands that heal; the hands that hold; the hands we desire because they are better than desire... These hands—the hands that care, the hands that mold; the hands that touch the lips, the lips that speak the words— the words that tell us we are whole.[5]

When you hear God's call and feel compelled to respond, it is a simple matter of saying a wholehearted "yes" to his invitation. When you do this, you are saying "yes" to your own healing and "yes" to his destiny for you. You say "yes" to the one who forgives and cleanses, restores and renews. You say "yes" to his ability to meet your deepest needs. You say "yes" to the merciful, wounded hands of the crucified Healer. And you say "yes" to the tender voice of the living Lord who calls to us saying, "Follow me" (John 1: 37–51).

Have you heard the invitation yet? Have you said your "yes" to God? If so, you might just ask him, "What did I say yes to?"

Let me ask you another question: How many people do you think answer that invitation the first time? Many of us need to hear that call two or three or perhaps even twenty times before we say "yes" to God's voice. We are on a journey after all. While a delayed response to God's call is often viewed as stubbornness, the flip side is that when resistant people finally do become believers, they are well practiced in hearing from God.

2. Scripture: *Have you ever heard God through Scripture?*

Do you sometimes recall scriptures in important moments? When you read the Bible, do verses or phrases ever "jump out" at you? Does there seem to be a "Holy Spirit highlighter" on some words when you read the Bible? Do some passages impact your heart with conviction or emotion? These are just a few of the ways that God speaks through his written Word.

When my firstborn son Stephen was eight years old, he asked to be baptized. The immediate fruit of that decision included a voracious hunger for Scripture. He began to read the gospels at bedtime, polishing off Matthew in just a couple of days. Some nights we would hear him chuckling in his bedroom. When we asked why he said, "Oh, Jesus makes a good point. Like why would he be casting out demons if he had a demon? That's a good one!" Stephen loved reading Scripture, but he also grasped its message quite easily for such a young boy. We believed God was speaking to him through the Bible.

One evening during his reading time, Stephen called to us from the bedroom. He sounded alarmed. When Eden and I came in he said, "While I was reading the Bible, my legs started shaking from my toes to my hips. And I could feel electricity going up and down my spine." We asked him what he thought it was. He said, "I think it was the power of God." After that, we noticed that whenever Stephen read Scripture, God would highlight some verses for him as if there was light on them. On other verses, Stephen would feel mild doses of God's power at the base of his neck. This was most helpful when he read from a chapter I was preparing to preach. Sometimes he would zoom right into the text on which God wanted me to focus.

One day, I was to preach from Daniel 9, so I asked Stephen to check the chapter for me. After reading it, he pointed to verse 26, "After the sixty-two 'sevens,' the Anointed One will be cut off and will have nothing. The people of the ruler who will come will destroy the city and the sanctuary. The end will come like a flood: War will continue until the end, and desolations have been decreed." He said that there was a *lot* of power on it. This made no sense to me since my theme had nothing to do with that text. I sent him back to reread the chapter (I know—overdoing it!). He returned and said, "Same verse. *Lots* of power."

"Why?" I asked.

Stephen shook his head. "I don't know."

"Would you please ask God?"

He agreed. After a while, he came back and said, "God says that I am going to meet the One will destroy the person in that verse."

I was thinking, of course he will; we will all meet Jesus when he finally returns. I decided to leave it at that and ended up preaching from a different passage.

Two weeks later while visiting friends in Tumbler Ridge, BC, Stephen had just gone to bed and was saying his evening prayers. He mentioned to the Lord that it would be "really neat" to see him. Suddenly, a man materialized in the middle of the room. He was dressed in modern clothing, sported the expected beard, and began asking my son what he planned to have for breakfast! This was the meeting the Lord had foretold. Stephen arose from his bed to approach the "stranger," who then vanished into thin air. Our son raced directly to our room to report the visit. I asked him (oh me of little faith!), "Are you sure you didn't fall asleep and dream it?" He replied, "I don't know if I fell asleep, but I know I didn't wake up!" I had personally prayed for such a visitation for ten years. Now my ten-year-old had received that very honour. All of this began by simply listening attentively to God's voice in the pages of Scripture.

Theologian Jeromey Martini states it beautifully:

> Like the enchanted armour of the Knight that gives him the power to defeat the dragon, the Bible is a book of Magic and Power and Mystery. It is a collection of words, but of words that have been breathed from Beyond and carry with them the weight and authority of that Breath. These are words with power to penetrate and interrupt lives and to alter people for all Eternity... These are words that reach in from another world and imbed themselves in places more sacred and secret than the heart or the mind or the psyche. The Bible is a magical book, but it is not a book of magic. Its words are not incantations and its power is not derived from some wizard's spell. It is so much more than that. It is a magical book because its words are the breathing words of God. They are read and they are spoken so that the reader and the hearer are confronted with the very voice of God. They are the words of a God who is so in love with His creatures that He has condescended to lisp as an infant in order to be understood in the confines of limited human language. The Bible is a gateway to another realm... a portal that seeks to transport people from this world to another and to point from this reality to a better Reality—a Reality that is Way and Truth and Life. And when that portal has been opened the power of that world is loosed onto this one so that it begins to effect its influence within it. The Bible is a magical book, and as such it can only be read by those with ears to hear and eyes to see. And the reader cannot be left the same after a genuine encounter with it.[6]

3. Teachers: *Has God ever spoken to your heart through a minister, priest, or teacher?*

When listening to a sermon, do you ever get the feeling you're the only person in the room, that perhaps the sermon was directed at you, as if the preacher had been reading your journals—or your mind? This can be very unnerving. Sometimes I wonder if entire conferences haven't been organized as a conspiracy to confront the secrets of my heart.

I remember a camp speaker from twenty years ago whose ministry baffled me. Where I put a high value on mixing with the campers, he would sit out in the field all day by himself, just praying and reading. While I stressed the need for teen camp speakers to be dynamic and relevant, this preacher would read pre-typed notes, peeking up only briefly as he preached. He seemed so dry and unappealing on the surface. But I shall never forget that first evening when he spoke. I don't even remember *what* he said. I just recall this awful feeling that he had free run of my heart and unimpeded access to my head. The conviction of sin and the irresistible call to total commitment were awesome and heavy. I remember wondering how this meek and unremarkable man could know the thoughts of my heart. Had he been reading my journal? Listening to my whispered conversations? I realize now it was the voice of the Lord speaking to my heart as the eyes of the Lord peered at my naked soul.

It reminds me now of Jonathan Edwards' preaching. Like this camp speaker, Edwards was notorious for reading his sermons with a monotone voice and a rigid body. Yet when he preached his famous revival sermon, "Sinners in the hands of an angry God," on July 8, 1741 in Enfield, Connecticut, the spiritual impact of God's voice shook the entire town. Women fainted and strong men clung to the church's pillars and pews, fearing lest they slip into the flames of hell on the spot.[7] Those who tried to stand ended up prostrate (even rolling) on the floor, their weeping drowning out Edwards' voice. Throughout the night, men, women, and children cried out to God for mercy in nearly every house in Enfield. God answered them with the revival now known as America's "Great Awakening." As with this camp speaker, when Edwards preached, each individual heard it as God's voice *directly to the heart.*

A more humorous version of this phenomenon is the feeling that some person other than yourself *really needs* to hear the message you are hearing. I often think to myself, "I sure hope so-and-so is listening carefully right now," or "I sure wish so-and-so were here." What is happening in that moment? God is speaking to *your* heart and rather than keeping it to yourself, you'd like to share it. This is a generous way of saying, the message is hitting too close to home. It's time to deflect it to someone else who surely needs to hear it.

If you've experienced some aspect of this—even if it's not as dramatic as what happened in Edwards' time—then you've heard God speak as his Word was preached.

4. Worship: Has God spoken to your heart through worship?

Has your hair ever stood on end as you've participated in worship? Has a song echoed through your head that was pertinent to your spiritual walk? Did it ever bring you to tears or establish heart knowledge about some important truth in your life? God often uses worship to take information from your head and transform it into revelation in your heart.

I was a youth pastor throughout much of the nineties. During that time, we had wonderful worship leaders who led from the heart and loved to woo the presence of God. Youth would become so passionate for Jesus and aware of his nearness that they would invite friends from school saying, "You need to come to youth tonight. God is going to show up!" As worship would begin, first-time visitors like Desiree would often begin to weep. Our youth leaders would watch for that and ask them, "What's happening?" Desiree answered, "I don't know. I can't stop crying." We asked if it felt like something good or something bad. She replied, "It feels like love."

"That was Jesus," our leaders replied. "How do you like him so far?" Desiree burst out: *"I love him!"* And so it would continue, the voice of Christ speaking life and hope, love and salvation through the worship—winning, healing, and delivering young people into freedom.

5. Conviction of Right and Wrong: *Does God ever address issues you need to make right with God or others? Does he ever affirm areas where you truly please him?*

> When he comes, [the Holy Spirit] will *convict the world of guilt in regard to sin and righteousness and judgment.* In regard to sin, because men do not believe in me; in regard to righteousness, because I am going to the Father, where you can see me no longer; and in regard to judgment, because the prince of this world now stands condemned. (John 16:8–11)

Even if you were unable to admit that you hear the Lord through the first four questions, you will no doubt admit to experiencing conviction of sin. Genuine conviction of sin *is* the voice of God speaking to the heart about what grieves him. Of all the ways God chooses to speak, people have most developed their ability to sense guilt. In fact, with our own penchant for condemnation and the devil's "ministry" of accusation, we have boundless faith for hearing God in this area. By way of experiment, you might just pause now and ask the Lord, "Have I done anything today that grieves your heart or misses the mark?" Listen for a moment. That didn't take long, did it? The Lord *loves* to convict us of guilt because he so enjoys removing that heavy yoke and replacing it with his peace. He loves to silence hearts that condemn and demons that accuse. He loves to cleanse our hearts of sin and its ugly effects.

But might I suggest that since we are so proficient at dialing into conviction, it would be useful to *stay* on that station and hear what else God would like to say. Every time you ask God what has displeased him, why not also ask what pleased him? When you let God point out sin in your heart, why not also wait on him to affirm righteousness? The church has often asserted that God is not just an angry judge waiting to point out our every fault. But it is hard to say so with much authority when our daily practice in prayer contradicts us. The vast majority of Christians may have never even asked the Lord if he is pleased with them or what he likes about them. Why not take a moment right now to do that? You may notice a powerful phenomenon. When you began with a negative conviction, you may have believed firmly that God was speaking. Yet when God spoke words of affirmation, the strongest temptation was to discard those impressions as "just my imagination."

To show you how little sense that makes, consider this example: Imagine if every time your spouse paid you a complement or give you a gift, you refused to receive it. Imagine listening intently only when he or she pointed out flaws or demanded apologies. You would see such a relationship as abusive and dysfunctional. Yet so often our prayer lives model this exact sickness and project these negative images on God. It grieves God when unbelieving hearts spurn his blessings. We would do well to give him *at least* as many opportunities to encourage us as we do to correct us. He is more than willing to do so!

6. A Burden for Others: *Have you ever felt a strong urge to pray for someone?*

As you pray, do faces or names come to mind that God wants you to present back to him in prayer? This is such a common occurrence that we diminish it as something less than God's voice. A coincidence maybe, and we rarely follow up on it. But if we take Jeremiah 33:3 seriously, then we know that when we call on the Lord, he will answer us. You can call on him right now and ask, "Is there someone who you would like me to pray for right now?" As you wait and listen, begin to bless those who come to mind, because it is the Lord himself who brings them to mind at your request—just as he promised! It can't be that simple, can it? That depends on whether you believe in your heart the simple promise of Christ that his sheep hear his voice.

As people come to mind, you might ask God *what* to pray for. Ask him about their needs, about how he sees them, and about how you might encourage them. As you listen for answers, begin to trust that

33

what you are hearing *might* be God's voice. As you step out in faith, his answers become more specific and more frequent.

For example, late one night, my friend Paul and his wife Toni realized together that they were both lying awake in bed. They wondered if perhaps the Lord had woken them to pray for someone. They went to prayer and independently had the same name and face come to mind: Leigh-Ann, a friend. They began to pray for her, asking the Lord what he wanted them to say.

They each got the impression that Leigh-Ann's car had broken down and that she was stranded on a road somewhere. This seemed odd, given that it was roughly 1:00 A.M. Paul and Toni decided to ask Jesus what he wanted them to do with this information. They each heard the same message: "Call her cell phone and tell her not to be afraid. A van will be along shortly to help." They stepped out in faith and called. Leigh-Ann answered. Her car had indeed broken down on the side of the road, and she was feeling a great deal of anxiety. Before they had even hung up, a van pulled up and offered to help.

What I love about this incident is that Paul and Toni assumed in child-like faith that when they called on the Lord, he would answer. They responded in obedience and were blessed with even more confidence in the Shepherd's voice. The fact that this is a normal part of their lives and marriage is a wonderful model for us in intercession.

7. Prompting: Has God ever prompted you to encourage someone?

Have you ever felt compelled to share a word of encouragement or present the gospel to a particular person? Has God nudged you to make a call or send a note that turned out to be timely? Those who follow up those promptings soon find out that God did not develop laryngitis after the first century!

My parents are notorious for sensing these nudges and obeying at the critical moment. I can't count how many so-called "deathbed conversions" have resulted as they answered God's urgent challenge to go and visit the sick and the elderly. On one occasion, my mother had to miss out on her duties with the local girls' club because she was sick in bed. The Lord began to press upon her the urgent need to go visit a particular senior citizen in the hospital. She fought with God briefly over this, first because she was so ill and second, because the fellow in question had been in a coma for several days. But the Spirit would not relent, so mom dragged herself down to the hospital and entered the patient's room. As she began to pray for him, he rose up out of his coma, fully alert. He confessed that he was not ready to meet the

Lord and would like to make things right with God. My mother prayed with him to receive God's gift of salvation. He lay back down in bed, re-entered his coma, and never regained consciousness. I'm so thankful for parents who taught me that God continues to send his people to deliver important messages right on time.

Do Not Despise the Day of Small Things

In this chapter I have tried to model how "normal" it is to hear God's voice. We tend to believe that God will only speak in grandiosity to the mighty and important ones. Yet our faith that God speaks to the "common people" about daily concerns suffers under a mentality that it's beneath him. My friend Brita expressed the perspective perfectly:

> Most Christians have faith that God speaks in "big" ways and *not* in common, everyday ways. They believe God does speak through dreams, but when he does it would be unlike any regular dream. It would be a *DREAM*. Or they believe that God could speak to your mind, but it wouldn't be just like a passing thought. If it were God, it would be a *SPECIAL VOICE* totally different from any regular thought. Or they believe that God gives people visions, but it is not like just something you picture or your wandering imagination, it would be *A VISION*.

The point is: When God speaks to you about your life, it *counts*. He is mindful of the falling sparrow, the hungry raven, and the hairs you leave in your brush. How much more is he concerned about you? And if he's concerned about you, don't you think he'd want to tell you about it? Thankfully, this isn't merely a matter of thinking logically. We stand on Jesus' own promises.

◀)) *Tuning In* • • • • • • • • •

Take a moment to review the previous questions recognizing that to him, they matter precisely because *you matter*:

- *Invitation:* Has God ever invited you into his family? Ask him to remind you of the time and place where it happened. Ask him what he was saying to your heart at the time.
- *Scripture:* Has God ever spoken to you through his Word? Ask him what book he would like you to read from today. Ask him to highlight a verse that will nourish your soul. As you read, take note of

any phrases that jump out at you. Ask God why he wants you to know that.

- *Teachers:* Has God ever spoken to your heart through a minister, priest, or pastor? Ask God to remind you of a messenger that he sent to speak to you. What message was he sending you through him or her? Did you believe the message? Did you act on it? What was the result?

- *Worship:* Has God ever spoken to your heart through worship? Ask God to bring to mind a particular song for today. Consider the lyrics. Which lines really jump out at you today? Why?

- *Conviction:* Has God ever pointed out sins for which you needed to seek forgiveness from God or others? Ask God if you've grieved his heart this week in any way. Ask him if he would forgive you. Does he ever affirm areas in you that truly please him? Ask him to show you some.

- *Burdens:* Has God ever brought people to mind for prayer? Ask God to give you the name or show you the face of someone he wants you to pray for today. How does he see and feel about that person? How would he like to bless him or her? Release that blessing in prayer.

- *Prompting:* Has God ever prompted you to share something with someone? Ask God to help you compose a written prayer of blessing for someone you know well. Ask him what spiritual blessings you should include. (Omit references to winning a lottery if at all possible!) After listening, and then writing this prayer, rewrite it as a message from the Lord to that person. E.g., where you wrote, "Dear God, please bless my friend with your peace," rewrite it to say, "My child, I will bless you with my peace." Send them this message in a card.

The truth is that you already hear God well and often. Realizing this truth will help you to nurture that gift and to recognize God's messages more frequently. Based on Scripture's clear promises and on typical Christian experience, let's agree to reaffirm Jesus' claim, "My sheep hear my voice."

Awakened Hearts:
How We Hear and See God

I slept but my heart was awake. Listen! My lover is knocking!
— Song of Songs 5:28

Blessed are the pure in heart, for they shall see God.
— Matthew 5:8

WHAT DOES GOD SOUND LIKE?

As God wakes up our hearts to the truth that he speaks, we become hungry to hear his voice. When we learn that the pure in heart will see God, we become desparate for his face. We want to know this God who would reveal himself to us. Who is he? How can we meet him? Where do we begin?

God's voice is heard primarily through the Scriptures. People of every faith testify that the surest route to hearing God is by learning to hear him in his holy books. Written oracles like the Bible have stood the test of time because they have a track record of providing clarity and sound counsel to those who heed their inspired wisdom. David dedicates his longest Psalm to the Hebrew Scriptures, calling them a "lamp for our feet and a light for the path" (Psalm 119:105). Isaiah urges us to compare every fresh dream, vision, and revelation with what God has already spoken in these great written works. "To the law and to the testimony!" he cries, "If they do not speak according to this word, they have no light of dawn." (Isaiah 8:20)

Sometimes we wonder why it is so hard to hear the Lord's direction, so difficult to see the path ahead. We strain to hear the promised voice that says left or right, stop or go (Isaiah 30:21). Yet our ability to hear God's voice directly and accurately depends on how well we've filled our hearts with the light of Scripture. So often when the neglected flashlight of the written Word is switched back on, the answers to our queries become obvious.

Menu Versus Meal

But did you know that you could carefully study and faithfully memorize the Scriptures all your life and still never once hear the voice of God? Given what was said in chapter one, this seems impossible. Yet listen to the word of Christ to the Pharisees,

> And the Father who sent me has himself testified concerning me. You have never heard his voice nor seen his form, nor does his word dwell in you, for you do not believe the one he sent. You diligently study the Scriptures because you think that by them you possess eternal life. These are the Scriptures that testify about me, yet you refuse to come to me to have life. (John 5:37–40)

These men had diligently searched the Scriptures, not for the sake of scholarship, but honestly expecting to find life in them. But because they gave no ear to the Living Word, Jesus indicts them as never once hearing the voice of God. We ought to take heed that we don't succumb to this tragedy ourselves. How then shall we approach God's written word?

When we open the Bible without any expectation that God will speak a living word to us, what are we looking for? Apart from the Shepherd's voice, the knowledge, wisdom and guidance of Scripture is reduced to information—mere data that fills the head without penetrating the heart. Apart from the Spirit, we can read about the living God without encountering him. Thus, the Bible is diminished from a nourishing meal of milk (1 Peter 2:2), bread (Matthew 4:4), and solid food (Hebrews 5:12) to a titillating menu. It tempts our appetite but never fulfills it. We may study the menu, memorize it, have menu studies, and open menu colleges, but it is the voice of the Lord that makes Scripture a banqueting table of delights. Reading it with a listening heart should be a spiritual experience, evoking a first-hand encounter with the God who speaks.[1]

You need never open the Bible again without expecting God to speak through it and to meet you in it. In fact, I would insist on this before the Lord. "God, I want to know you—not just *about* you. I am not interested in scanning this book like some menu or historical document or someone else's mail. You promised that this word would bring life. But it *will not* unless you come and speak it into my heart as a message from your heart. Now speak, Lord—your servant is listening."

Beyond the Bible

Not so long ago, much of the church considered it offensive and even heretical to suggest that God might speak outside the bounds of Scripture. The notion of extra-biblical revelation was suspect, maybe even cultic. The doctrine of cessationism taught that once the canon of Scripture was complete, God had delivered his final word; when the last word of the book of Revelation was written, God ceased to speak. Modern-day prophets were said to have crossed the line of orthodoxy. Worse, they were just plain weird. And of course, some of us being threatened with these verses:

> I warn everyone who hears the words of the prophecy of this book: If anyone adds anything to them, God will add to him the plagues described in this book. And if anyone takes words away from this book of prophecy, God will take away from him his share in the tree of life and in the holy city, which are described in this book. (Revelation 22:18–19)

Over the history of the church, cessationists have used John's warning as a hammer to lock God into a Bible-sized box in which his voice is forever confined. They have created a doctrine that God only speaks from within that box. I was convinced of this myself until I started to believe and seriously seek after what the Bible itself proclaims.

The turning point came for me when I encountered a genuine, modern-day prophet for the first time. I had been praying earnestly for a breakthrough in our youth ministry, asking God what it would take to bring revival to our group. Even then I was hoping to "hear" his voice.

As I sat in my back yard waiting for an answer, the word "Styx" came to mind. My first thought was "uh oh," because I had spent a decade diligently collecting all of the LPs from my favourite rock band of that name. The sense I had was that the collection was an idol and that revival would tarry until I gave it up. I argued with God for a good thirty minutes and then finally dug out all of my old albums. One at a time, they went into the garbage. I especially lamented over the *Equinox* album, with its distinctive cover picturing an ice cube on fire. File that image in your memory for a moment.

That night, our youth group met to hear a testimony from a guy named Michael Rempel. Michael is my wife's cousin, and he has a remarkable story of God's saving grace. What I didn't realize was that he is also a profoundly gifted prophet. After sharing about his journey with God, Michael began to pray with each member of my youth group individually. One after another, he accessed and delicately addressed the secrets of their hearts in remarkable detail and with amazing accuracy. Each one received a word of blessing and promise from the heavenly Father. I was awe-struck as Michael addressed believers and unbelievers alike in perfect context without ever having met them before.

For example, with no prior knowledge of her, Michael approached a girl who was inquisitive about God but also extremely tentative about taking any further steps towards him. I cringed, fearing that Michael might overstep her comfort zone and scare her away. Instead, he spoke tenderly to her: "I see a picture of you as a timid, hungry fawn. Jesus is standing quietly at a distance, holding out his hand and offering you some grain. He wants you to know that he's not going to force-feed you. He's patiently waiting for you to come to him at your own pace. He won't startle you. When you are ready, he will satisfy your hunger." Her eyes filled with tears and her heart softened, because she knew it was not really Michael speaking but the Lord through him.

At the end of the evening, Michael turned to me and said, "The Lord gave me a message for you too, but I don't remember what it was." (Even prophets aren't perfect!) Then he added, "But I brought you something you might want to read." He handed me an issue of *Equipping the Saints* magazine, the official publication of the Vineyard church. The title on the cover was "Revival Fire." The cover photo was God's answer to my prayers: a picture of an ice cube—on fire! That evening triggered a new era for our youth group, but even more so for my own life. Cessationism behind me (in revival flames!), I returned to the Scriptures with new ears to hear the truth concerning God's voice.

The Bible testifies and models how God's voice may be heard via at least three broad avenues: messengers, circumstances, and direct messages to our hearts.

I. MESSENGERS

◀)) *Tuning In* · · · · · · · · · ·

Can you recall examples of each of the following types of messengers who delivered the voice of God in Scripture.

- Authors (e.g. Jeremiah):
- Teachers (e.g. Paul):
- Prophets (e.g. Deborah):
- Evangelists (e.g. Philip):

- Musicians (e.g. David):
- Testimonies (Mary):
- Angels (Gabriel):
- Children (Samuel):
- The occasional donkey or shrubbery (hint: Numbers 22:21–41, Exodus 3):

Looking back, has God ever delivered the same message to you through more than one of these messengers at a time? By the time we hear the same message through two or three messengers, we begin to establish in our hearts that God has spoken. (Deuteronomy 19:15 establishes this as a precedent.) We do well to be alert when God borrows someone's mouth to reveal his will.

Blayne Greiner, an apostolic friend of mine from Monroe, WA, received an invitation to speak at a youth leaders' conference in Jakarta, Indonesia. The hosts couldn't afford to cover his expenses at all, but Blayne assured them that God would provide if he was meant to come. Two days later, he was filling his car with gasoline when Larry, one of his intercessors, bumped into him.

"This is odd," Larry said, "my wife and I had you on our hearts this morning in prayer. Do you have any needs right now?" Blayne explained the need with regard to Indonesia. He discovered then that Larry and his wife had desired to go to Indonesia as missionaries and prayed daily for that nation for years. Within minutes, the cost of the trip was covered.

As Blayne prepared to go, three different intercessors called him (these three don't know each other) with this type of message: "I don't quite know how to say this, but there is an assignment of death on you for this trip. Satan will try to kill you. But go anyway. Just be alert and listen to the Lord." Blayne was taken aback, even more so when he received a warning from the U.S. State Department warning him not to go. But he believed that God had called him and was not about to shrink back.

Blayne arrived in Indonesia and had a wonderful time with the pastors there. One of them invited him to visit a secret radio station in the jungle from which they broadcast gospel messages to the Muslim world. The trip was complicated and would begin with a nine-hour train trip into the interior. On the night before his trip, Blayne had a vision-dream in which he saw himself getting killed by members of Al-Qaeda while on the train. He didn't sleep at all for the remainder of the night. In the morning, he shared the dream with the pastors there. They unanimously agreed that he should not board the train.

That day, members of Al-Qaeda boarded the train and searched each car for Americans. They found two and without warning, killed them on the spot. Had Blayne not been alerted through God's messengers and his confirming dream, he would have been on that train. God spoke up to spare his life.

II. LIFE CIRCUMSTANCES

A. Coincidences

Someone once said that coincidences are the winks of God which, when followed, draw a treasure map into the blessings of God. We can spot important coincidences (or better, "God-incidences") in Scripture wherever it says "just then." The most common just-then moment is what we have called "divine appointments." These well-timed encounters range from dramatic exchanges to neat little reminders (winks) that "I am with you always."

For example, Boaz and Ruth met in a just-then moment (Ruth 2:4), Rebekah became Isaac's wife by divine appointment, and many of the biblical encounters with Yahweh or Jesus were literally divine appointments. The most important just-then moment for Gentile Christians comes from the story of Peter and Cornelius in Acts 10.

Just Then...

Peter had just received a vision in which the Lord told him to kill and eat a sheet full of unclean animals. The Lord's point was that Peter should not call anything unclean that God has made pure, meaning the Gentiles, whom Peter would have considered unclean because he was a Jew. *Just then* three Gentiles knocked at Peter's door, inviting him to come to the [unclean] house of Cornelius the [unclean] Gentile, who also happened to revere God. Putting two and two—the vision and the coincidence—together, Peter accepted the invitation. He invited the Gentiles to stay in his home that night, and the next day went to Cornelius's house. As Peter preached, he realized that God shows no favouritism and began to preach that *everyone* who believes in Jesus can be saved, whether Jew or Gentile. *Just then* the Holy Spirit fell upon these Gentiles. Peter saw immediately that this coincidence was really no coincidence at all. God had just welcomed Gentile believers into the family of faith. Now they were ready for baptism.

In Acts 11, Peter had to account for his actions to the Jews in Jerusalem. How was it that their premier apostle had made such a radical doctrinal shift? What could account for his drastic violation of their traditions and even of the Jewish Law itself, which had been hand-delivered to Moses by God? On what basis was Peter asking them to cross this point-of-no-return? A vision, a coincidence, and an experience! To our amazement, the apostles do not even confirm Peter's experience with Scripture until Acts 15:16, thus displaying their implicit trust in him.

◀)) *Tuning In* • • • • • • • • •

Most believers can relate a "God-incidence" such as a well-timed knock on the door, phone-call or song on the radio. How about you? See if you can recall one or two God-incidences you have experienced.

God on the Phone

My friend Chad heard the phone ring one afternoon. He picked it up to hear Sherry on the line. She was a troubled teenager living with her cousin's family while she tried to straighten out her life.

"Hello?" she said.

"Hello?" Chad answered. An awkward silence was followed by "So how are you?"

"Okay, I guess," Sherry replied. Another awkward silence. Chad began probing to find out why Sherry may have phoned him. The conversation continued to stumble along until she began to open up about some of her struggles. Chad tried to encourage her over the next half hour. He felt he was making progress until she interrupted in irritation, "Oh great! Now my cousin is home." Chad asked what was wrong.

"I didn't tell you, but I had packed my bags and was about to run away before my cousin could get home. But then you called and kept me on the phone so long that she's arrived. Now I won't be able to leave."

Confused, Chad said, "I didn't call you; you called me."

Sherry was stunned, "No, I didn't."

As it turns out, through divine coincidence, and because of his great love for Sherry, Jesus had apparently arranged to have the phone ring at both homes simultaneously.

God on the Radio

Blayne (the friend who went to Indonesia) was sharing Christ with a resistant teenager. As they drove along in Blayne's car, he challenged the teen with the message that all he really needed was the love of Jesus. "In fact," Blayne said, "I'm so sure that God wants you to know this that the next song on the radio will be 'All you need is love.'" Blayne turned on the radio and, sure enough, the very next song was the Beatles classic. The young man exploded, banging his fists on the dashboard! He knew that he was "busted." His excuses were futile before a God who loved him enough to convey his message in such an odd and powerful way. He finally gave in to that love.

I was chuckling about this story while on my way to a forum for recreation students at a community college. I knew that there would be an opportunity to share my faith with the class at some point, but I wasn't sure whether I should really "go for it" or not. Sometimes the Lord would have us gently build relationships. At other times he wants us to speak out boldly and directly.

"What about today?" I asked him. "At first I thought I should go for it. Now I'm having these butterflies. Should I back off a bit?" Then the story of Blayne came back to mind. Laughing, I thought, "If it's good enough for Blayne..." and turned on the radio. Loud and clear, Tom Petty sang God's answer back to me: "I won't back down, no I won't back down! You could stand me at the gates of hell, but I won't back down!"

So God *does* wink and speak—now this way, now that—but too often we pass it off as mere coincidence.

An odd phenomenon occurred when I became alert to divine coincidences. I didn't just *notice* them more often. They also began to *happen* more often. I believe that when God sees faith in us to hear him through a certain channel, he initiates an outpouring of his voice through it. He rewards those who seek him with a proliferation in the areas where we are attentive.

B. Symbols

A symbol, as I am using it here, is a tangible thing (noun) or action (verb) that we use to represent an intangible concept because of something the two have in common. Symbols are especially helpful when God uses a physical reality to illustrate a spiritual reality. This is why some have called symbolism the language of God. Others identify symbols as the language of the heart.

Scripture is saturated with symbols that are pregnant with meaning. Entire books are dedicated to cataloguing and defining the types and symbols of the Bible.[2] The images and pictures that God draws for us throughout his Word function to simplify, explain, obscure, create wonder, and even to terrify. They convey information and evoke strong emotion much more than plain words would. They lure us closer for a better look and trigger new questions in our minds. God also uses symbols to sneak important truths past our rational defences and to get in behind faulty paradigms. Most of all, God has revealed much of his own character through symbols in order to help us know what he is like.

◀)) *Tuning In* • • • • • • • • • •

Try this simple exercise: Jot down your first reactions to these basic biblical symbols:

- Fire/burning:
- Light/shining:
- Darkness/blindness:
- Rain/raining:
- Snow/snowing:
- Mountain/climbing:
- River/flowing:
- Rainbow/raining:
- Lion/roaring:
- Lamb/wandering:

This exercise serves to activate symbolism in your mind. You likely didn't even need to come up with something new in every case. Your mind may have already registered most of those items and actions as symbols—you just needed to remember what they usually mean to you. Others may have taken a little more thought.

The Bible is *usually* clear about what certain symbols represent. For example, a serpent normally represents Satan (Genesis 3:1; Isaiah 27:1; Revelation 12:9). But wait a second: in John 3, doesn't Jesus compare himself to the bronze serpent Moses held up for the Israelites in Numbers 21? On a similar note, Isaiah 14:12 uses the "morning star" (Venus) to symbolize Satan. "How you have fallen from heaven, O morning star, son of the dawn! You have been cast down to the earth, you who once laid low the nations!" But in Revelation 22:16 we read, "I, Jesus, have sent my angel to give you this testimony for the churches. I am the Root and the Offspring of David, and *the bright Morning Star*." Thus, we should never assume we know what a particular symbol means. Rather, we should always go back to God and ask him to explain its meaning to us.

God may continue to use standard biblical symbols, but he also tends to develop personal symbols that have particular meaning to us. Sunflowers, killer whales, coyote pups, and wheelchairs have all become part of God's vocabulary with me. He uses such symbols both in my dream life and in the waking realm as I go about my day. In fact, they often work in conjunction with one another.[3]

45

Re-digging Ancient Wells

Last year, I spent time praying that God would unlock some of the blessings of my spiritual heritage. I began asking God if he would "re-dig the ancient wells" of that spiritual inheritance.[4] The imagery of re-digging family wells comes from Genesis 26: 18–19: "Isaac reopened the wells that had been dug in the time of his father Abraham, which the Philistines had stopped up after Abraham died, and he gave them the same names his father had given them. Isaac's servants dug in the valley and discovered a well of fresh water there." This was symbolic of how God's covenant with Abraham was being renewed in the next generation with his son Isaac (Genesis 26:1–5).

As I asked God for the blessings of my family tree, my roots in the Czech Republic came to mind. Closing my eyes, I saw the face of John Amos Comenius, a 17th century bishop and educator whom I also knew to be a spiritual father to my family clan. I sensed that I was to ask for fresh water from the well of Comenius.

I also began to have repeated dreams and visions about labyrinths at that time. I drew them, studied them, and read about them. Then one of my intercessors approached me, saying, "I'm not sure why, but I think you're supposed to have these." She handed me three toy mazes that looked identical to the ones I saw in my mind. I knew that both Comenius and the labyrinths were connected to my request for generational blessings, but I could not put two and two together. That night, I called my father and told him about my family prayers, our spiritual fathers, and this puzzle concerning the labyrinth. What could this symbol mean?

He solved the puzzle for me. In the early 1600's, Comenius became the last bishop of the Unity of Bohemian Brethren and was exiled into Poland. The Jersak and Marek clans (both sides of my dad's family) were displaced along with Comenius and the rest of the Hussites. When they returned 300 years later, my grandparents met and settled in Suchdol, Moravia—right near the tree where Comenius had done much of his preaching before his expulsion! Tradition tells us that when the family was exiled, the only books they could take along were the Bible and "the Labyrinth." The Labyrinth refers to Comenius' book, *Labyrinth of the World and Paradise of the Heart,* a visionary narrative of his spiritual journey. It is very similar to Pilgrim's Progress, including a main character called "Pilgrim," but it was actually written five years *before* John Bunyan was born.

To honour my discovery, my dad decided to send me a transla-tion of *the Labyrinth* for my birthday. Imagine my surprise when I discovered that the theme of *The Labyrinth* is the very truth that I

46

had already planned to write in this work—encountering Jesus in the meeting place of our own hearts! I wasn't thinking new thoughts at all: rather, I was inheriting forgotten truths, re-digging ancient wells.[5] God used the synchronicity of the inner and outer labyrinth symbol to lure me into this spiritual treasure-trove.

C. Parables

Parables are simple spiritual lessons taken from common life occurrences. God creates a parable by stringing symbols together to make a point. For example, Jesus loved to use wedding symbols (e.g., bride and bridegroom, invitations, the banquet, etc.) to teach us about God's kingdom. He would weave tales about a wedding banquet in which he is the Bridegroom and you are an honored guest. He would use these stories to raise questions:

- Did you receive your invitation? Are you willing to come?
- Do you have the right spiritual attire? What does he require?
- Will you be ready when he comes? Will you be awake?

Such a parables carry vitally important messages designed to be discovered by the true seeker. A parable is really a series of symbols that unlock the truth piece by piece as we puzzle over them. Though Jesus' parables were meant to make us scratch our heads a bit, interpreting them becomes even more difficult when the symbols he used are no longer in popular use or have changed with time. But God's use of parables is not locked down to the four gospels. He continues to speak to us symbolically through daily events as if they were parables.

Murray Dueck (of Samuel's Mantle) encourages us to take note of daily occurrences that strike us as odd, whether in our own lives or in the major news items from around the world. If the Holy Spirit highlights an event in our minds, Murray suggests that we ask, "If this were a dream, what would it mean?" The various elements of the natural event take on symbolic meaning, and God speaks to us through it in a way similar to those we see in biblical parables and dreams.

This is not so esoteric as it may sound. The most common parable events happen right beneath my nose. My children mirror my behaviour in such a way that God has an endless supply of illustrations with which to confront me. I hear myself telling them, "You wouldn't have fallen down and hurt yourself if you had listened to me and obeyed the first time!" Then I lift my face to heaven and tell the Lord with some annoyance, "Yes, I caught that one!" Again, as we waken our hearts to hear and see God's parable-messages, they seem to multiply themselves all around us.

Traffic Tickets, Forts, and Old Furniture

Allow me to illustrate how naturally God speaks in our daily lives through three very simple parable-events. While driving home one day, I was talking to God about some of my failures in terms of obedience. I struggled with a sense of dread and condemnation that I couldn't seem to shake. Fear of punishment was troubling me. I was carried away in my thoughts, the car-stereo was blaring, and I just wanted to get home. Suddenly, my rear-view mirror was flashing red and blue. Busted!

Sheepishly, I admitted to the police officer that I was not paying attention and had no idea how fast I was going. He took my license and registration for a while and left me to ponder while he wrote up a ticket. I thought to myself, "If this were a dream, what would it mean?"

When he returned, the officer said, "Because you were honest with me and didn't give me attitude, I'm only giving you a warning this time. Do you know how much money I just saved you?"

Whew.

I thanked him profusely. As I drove away, I felt that God was saying, "When you are honest with me and don't give me attitude (no blame-shifting, no self-justifications), then I can give you warnings rather than discipline. As for punishment, don't you know that I have generously saved you from that? The penalty of sin has been fully paid."

When my son Stephen was barely old enough to swing a hammer, we decided to build a backyard playhouse. While I assembled our little fort, he would take a spare piece of 2x4 and bend nails into it all day. Although his "help" consisted mainly of getting underfoot and slowing the construction down, we found great joy in doing it together. When it was complete, he took great pride in what "we" had built, and I got a kick out of his sense of accomplishment. The Lord didn't miss his opportunity to drive home a lesson. All he needed to do was say, "Son!" and smile at me. I knew what he meant. As God invites me to join with him in building his kingdom, I often just bend nails, get in the way, and slow the whole process down. But he allows it because he loves my company and even enjoys my ownership in his project. He's not even offended when I pretend "we" did it or that it's "our" kingdom. Why not? Because he built it for us.

During a recent vacation to my parents' home in Manitoba, I felt compelled to learn how to refinish antique furniture. I found it relaxing and therapeutic (for a few days). As my mother taught me how to strip, stain, and finish each piece, Eden watched and wondered, "If this were a dream, what would it mean?" Since then, we've listened to the great Refinisher as he shares how he repeatedly takes our brokenness, and then strips, stains, and finishes us into something valuable—indeed, priceless—to him.

◀)) *Tuning In* • • • • • • • • •

Ask God to remind you of a parable-event from your own world. Recall each symbol in the story. Whether it was a mundane event or something that struck you as odd, take note of how each physical image and action highlights a spiritual truth.

III. DIRECT MESSAGES TO OUR HEARTS

Even though we have been talking about hearing God's voice, the Bible actually refers to all the faculties in perceiving God's messages. John Donne, the pre-modern preacher and poet put it this way:

> Every sense is called sight, for there is "taste and see" how sweet, and "smell and see" what a savour of life the Lord is. So St. John turned about to "see a voice." There, hearing was sight. And so our Saviour Christ says, "touch and see" [Luke 24.39], and there feeling is seeing. All things concur to this seeing, and therefore in all the works of your senses, and in all your other faculties, See ye the Lord. Hear him in his word, and so see him. Speak to him in your prayers, and so see him. Touch him in his sacrament, and so see him. Present holy and religious actions unto him, and so see him.[6]

We will consider three of these faculties: hearing, seeing, and sensing.

A. Hearing

By hearing God, we normally (but not exclusively) mean that we hear an inner voice in the form of thoughts, words, and sentences. It is as though someone is talking directly to our minds from within. The inner voice speaks to a "hearing heart" in ways similar to our own inner self-talk. One of the tasks of this book is to train readers how to recognize the Shepherd's voice as distinct from other tapes that are playing in their minds and hearts. According to John 10, the sheep will be able to learn this. For now, let us survey some of the biblical descriptions where people hear God's voice directly.

In 1 Samuel 3, Samuel heard the audible voice of God calling his name. God seemed to be talking to him out loud so that Samuel heard the voice with his natural ears. I'm quite surprised how common this is, even in very conservative churches. I began to survey the people who attend our *Listening Prayer* seminars over the last three months. So far, over fifty participants claim to have heard God's voice audibly.

I have a Mennonite friend whose grandfather was facing a colostomy. It would involve the surgical removal of his intestines such that his bowel movements would be redirected to an external bag attached to his side. In desperation, his grandfather cried out to the Lord in Low German, "Not the bag!" He heard the Lord echo back from heaven *out loud*, "Not the bag." When this dear old saint met with the doctor, they found that the colostomy was not necessary after all.

When Elijah heard God, it was in a gentle whisper,

> The LORD said, "Go out and stand on the mountain in the presence of the LORD, for the LORD is about to pass by." Then a great and powerful wind tore the mountains apart and shattered the rocks before the LORD, but the LORD was not in the wind. After the wind there was an earthquake, but the LORD was not in the earthquake. After the earthquake came a fire, but the LORD was not in the fire. And after the fire came a gentle whisper. When Elijah heard it, he pulled his cloak over his face and went out and stood at the mouth of the cave. Then a voice said to him, "What are you doing here, Elijah?" (1 Kings 19:11–13)

But by no means is God always so soft spoken. In Isaiah 8:11, we read, "The LORD spoke to me with his strong hand upon me, warning me not to follow the way of this people." Wisdom tells us to listen and obey when God addresses us so assertively.

David had high regard for the not-so-quiet voice of the Lord. He says,

> The voice of the LORD is over the waters; the God of glory thunders; the LORD thunders over the mighty waters. The voice of the LORD is powerful; the voice of the LORD is majestic. The voice of the LORD breaks the cedars; the LORD breaks in pieces the cedars of Lebanon. He makes Lebanon skip like a calf, Sirion like a young wild ox. The voice of the LORD strikes with flashes of lightning. The voice of the LORD shakes the desert; the LORD shakes the Desert of Kadesh. The voice of the LORD twists the oaks and strips the forests bare. And in his temple all cry, "Glory!" (Psalm 29:3–9)

Isaiah spoke of a voice behind his head saying, "This is the way" (Isaiah 30:21). Solomon received wisdom when he asked literally for a "hearing heart" (1 Kings 3:9). Jesus heard his Father's voice from heaven at his baptism (Matthew 3:17), at his transfiguration (Matthew 17:5), and while preaching (John 12:28). He also claimed only to say what he heard the Father tell him to say (John 12:49).

As for us, we have already read that Jesus Christ proclaimed his sheep *would hear his voice*. In Revelation 2:7, Christ again repeatedly challenges the churches, "He who has an ear, let him hear what the Spirit says to the churches." To each heart Christ offers, "Here I am! I stand at the door and knock. If anyone hears my voice and opens the door, I will come in and eat with him, and he with me" (Revelation 3:20).

Let us assume for a moment that these passages are possibilities for today's believer. What would it be like to hear God's voice now, to recognize it, to "share a meal together as friends" (Revelation 3:20)? In general, the voice of the Lord is a gentle inner whisper in our hearts, and is often not spectacular or bizarre. Therefore, it is easy to dismiss as one's own thoughts.

On one hand, we tend to despise the weirdness of grandiose prophets. On the other, we tend to devalue God's voice in our own hearts because it isn't accompanied by *enough* hoopla. (This reminds me of Naaman in 2 Kings 5:1–27.) Yet as we begin to respond regularly to what we *might* be hearing from God, we find his living word accompanied by striking confirmations, whether it comes as a shout or a whisper.

By way of illustration, my family was driving through the mountains up to Kelowna, BC. We had just passed the city of Merritt around 10:30 pm when the transmission on the van failed. The moonless night was pitch black.

I left Eden and the children in the van and started to run back down the steep hill towards Merritt. Dozens of trucks and cars passed me, but even if they had seen me in the dark, all were travelling too fast to stop and pick me up. As I ran in silence, a quiet impression brushed past my mind (Oh so quiet—it's scary how quiet it was!): "You might want to get right off the highway for the next vehicle."

I asked aloud, "All the way off?"

Again, the quiet whisper came, "Yes, all the way off." I said, "Okay" and crawled over the white concrete barrier onto the gravel beyond.

Shortly, the headlights of the next vehicle came around the corner behind me. As it passed I shuddered and thanked God for his voice. A semi-trailer pulling half a mobile home flew by, overlapping the white line so far that, had I waited for further confirmation, a house would have hit me in the back at 120 kph! Phew! You can see why I believe it's important to listen whenever we think God may be speaking.

Granted, in my zeal I tend to think I'm hearing God at times when he actually hasn't spoken. Many is the time that I've distinctly "heard him tell me" to go to a particular café where he would have a divine appointment waiting. Upon arrival, I wind up waiting with a puzzled look on my face until—two cappuccinos later—I conclude that I have missed it again. But ever since the truck incident, I've never felt too bad about that. I'm willing to look silly quite often if it's going to save a life or a soul once in a while, particularly my own!

This does raise one question, however: Why is it so difficult to discern God's voice from my own thoughts? We will revisit this question throughout the book. But for now, let's return to John 10. Listen to the confidence of Jesus in our ability to discern. "When he has brought out all his own, he goes on ahead of them, and his sheep follow him because they *know his voice*. But they will *never follow a stranger*; in fact, they will run away from him because they do not *recognize* a stranger's voice" (John 10:4–5).

The operative word here is "recognize." Our recognition of the Shepherd's voice grows in the same way that we come to know any other friend's voice. Phone-voices become familiar over time. The tone and the content of our friends' voices help us easily pinpoint the source even with a single greeting. When I pick up the phone and hear "Scradley!" I know that my friend Kim has called. When I hear, "Zzzzzzerzak!" I know that it's Paul. When I hear "Guess who!" I know that it's Jody. Many of my friends simply greet me with a "Hey!" but by frequent contact I usually recognize the voice. So too with Jesus: as our relationship with him grows in intimacy, so does our ability to recognize his voice. One hint: God's voice is often the one you hear right after you've asked him a question and right before you've begun to rationalize the answer away. Prayerful first impressions are at least worth checking into.

One day I was at a friend's house meditating quietly on the recognition verses contained in this chapter. I challenged God, "You *say* that we'll recognize your voice. You *say* we'll recognize deception. Yet I don't see this quality of discernment in the church. Please show me your heart on this." At that moment, my friend's canary began to sing. Just then, an ugly black fly also began to buzz around against the window. The first sound was beautiful. The second was irritating. Then I believe Jesus whispered this question, "Are you having any trouble at all distinguishing the bird's song from the fly's buzz?"

"No," I answered.

He continued, "Even when you hear them at the same time?"

"No."

"Then here is your answer. My character—my DNA—is *far* more dissimilar to that of the stranger than is the difference between a canary and a fly. My heart for the church is that she would know my voice so well that *all* of the sheep could distinguish between my voice and any others, *even when we're talking at the same time.* In fact, I want you to know my voice even if I am telling you something very strange (remember Abraham and Isaac). And I want you to know when the enemy is speaking *even when he's quoting Scripture* (remember the temptations of Jesus)."

◀)) *Tuning In* • • • • • • • • • •

In the next chapter, you will develop a confidence in your ability to test, confirm, and recognize God's voice. For now, consider this question:

Have you ever had an experience where you thought you heard God's voice, similar to my experience on the highway outside Merritt? Did you listen to the voice or not? What happened as a result?

B. Seeing

The Bible brims with the language of "spiritual sight." Men and women of God received messages from the Lord in a variety of visual ways. They saw visions, dreams, mental images and physical object lessons that conveyed the word of the Lord. With the eyes of the heart, the saints of old even claim that they "saw" God (Isaiah 6, Ezekiel 1, and Daniel 7).

"No One Has Ever Seen God"

Whenever I talk about spiritual sight, invariably the objection is raised, "But the Bible says no one has ever seen God" (John 1:18; 1 John. 4:12). It is true: no one has ever seen God *as he is* with his or her *natural eyes.* Even mediated visions of the Lord's glory left the witnesses ill (Daniel 8:27), blind (Acts 9:9), and fearing death (Judges 3:22; Isaiah 6:5). Their first inclination was to dive for cover (Revelation 1:17). How is it then that something we are told *never* happened is elsewhere taught as the norm?

David wrote concerning his daily prayer life, "As for me, *I shall behold your face* in righteousness; I will be satisfied with *your likeness* when I awake" (Psalm 17:15). On the day of Pentecost, Peter preached David's words about Jesus: "*I saw [beheld] the Lord always before me* [my face]. Because he is at my right hand, I will not be shaken" (Acts 2:25).

Some of these encounters with God were even described as "face-to-face." Jacob saw God face-to-face when he wrestled with him (Genesis 32:30). Moses spoke with him face-to-face in the tent of meeting (Exodus 33:11; Numbers 12:8). *All* the children of Israel saw God face-to-face when he thundered down from Mount Sinai (Numbers 14: 14; Deuteronomy 5:4). The judgments of God are executed face-to-face (Ezekiel 20:35).

When we read these testimonies, each meeting is still mediated in some way, i.e., they saw God via the Angel of the Lord, they saw God in a vision, they saw God in the fire or in the cloud or in the judgment. No one has ever seen God directly as he is with the naked eye. Yet he can and should be seen with the eyes of the heart. Paul explains this tension in his famed "love chapter": "Now we see but a poor reflection as in a mirror; then we shall see face to face. Now I know in part; then I shall know fully, even as I am fully known" (1 Corinthians 13:12).

Using the reflection analogy, imagine looking at the image of the sun as it reflects off the surface of water. Are you looking at the sun? Yes and no. Is that really the sun that you see there? Yes and no. No one should look directly at the sun in the sky with the naked eye. Even the sun's reflection in the water can be blinding. Although we are only looking at a reflected image of the sun, it is fair to say that we are seeing it in the water. Now, when we "see" the Lord in action or in a vision or a dream, are we seeing him? Is that really God? Yes and no. It is not God "as he is," but it is a true image of the Lord and his glory, revealed to us by God's Son (John 1:18) and God's Spirit (2 Corinthians 3:18).

The Eyes That Do See God

Mystics like St. Bonaventure and Hugh of St. Victor spoke of three sets of eyes: 1) the eyes of the body (physical eyes); 2) the eyes of the mind (reason); and 3) the eyes of the heart (spiritual sight). This third kind of sight is of major concern to the biblical writers, for it is with these eyes that we "see" wisdom and revelation.

Paul prayed for the believers in Ephesus (and everywhere),

> I keep asking that the God of our Lord Jesus Christ, the glorious Father, may give you *the Spirit of wisdom and revelation,* so that you may know him better. I pray also that the eyes of your heart may be enlightened in order that you may know the hope to which he has called you, the riches of his glorious inheritance in the saints, and his incomparably great power for us who believe. (Ephesians 1:17–19)

Spiritual sight enables us to "fix our eyes on Jesus" (Hebrews 12:2) and to see "the light of the knowledge of the glory of God in the face of Christ" (2 Corinthians 4:6). Paul testifies that "we, who with unveiled faces all behold [see] the Lord's glory, are being transformed into his likeness with ever-increasing glory, which comes from the Lord, who is the Spirit" (2 Corinthians 3:18). The glorified Christ gives this counsel to the churches in Revelation: "get salve to put on your eyes, so you can see" (Revelation 3:18). Which eyes? He is speaking of the eyes of our heart, the eyes of our spirit, the eyes of faith. With these alone do we see truth, wisdom, and revelation. With these alone do we behold him. Spiritual sight is not merely important—it is absolutely critical to knowing Christ and walking in his kingdom!

In the Scriptures, the word "behold" or "beheld" is used nearly 1,400 times. It simply means "look." At other times, we might reword it to say, "pay attention." On occasion, "behold" refers to physical sight. But most often, the word "behold" in its context means, "open the eyes of your heart." The authors and speakers call us to "see" by faith some spiritual truth or picture (vision) that is known by the heart and seen in the mind. In addition, we can add another 200 occurrences of the word "Lo." It means (surprise!) "Behold." Lo and behold. Look and see. Picture this by faith. See it with your "heart-eyes."

Of course, none of this is really new to us. Who hasn't sung:

> Turn your eyes upon Jesus,
> Look full in his wonderful face,
> And the things of this earth will grow strangely dim,
> In the light of his glory and grace.[7]

Many of our churches also sing:

> Open the eyes of my heart, Lord
> Open the eyes of my heart
> I want to see you
>
> See you high and lifted up
> Shining in the Light of your glory
> Pour out your power and love
> As we sing Holy, Holy, Holy.[8]

The problem is not that we don't know the words; it is often that we don't take them seriously. Modernism has diluted spiritual sight into an abstract concept rather than a spiritual reality. Cessationism has taught us that visions and dreams were for special people in another era. Alarmists have so over-reacted in fear that they have labelled virtually *all* spiritual imagery as "New Age." In all three cases, the fruit is the same: a condition of spiritual "eyes tight shut."

Guided Imagery?

When I teach on seeing Christ, I often bump into fears that this is a version of guided imagery or visualization—a psychological or New Age technique that can be spiritually hazardous. Indeed, when visualization is activated independently of a relationship with God or guided by any spirit other than the Spirit of Christ, the Bible warns us to beware (1 John 4:1–4). How does that sort of visualization differ from meeting Jesus in some sort of internal picture? By teaching on this subject, have we crossed a line into enemy territory? Or, by rejecting all forms of visualization techniques outright, have we surrendered ground that was created for us and belongs to us?

In my opinion, guided imagery has become an evangelical bogeyman, used by some Christians to induce fear of all imagery, imagination, and spiritual visions. Those who have repented of occult practices sometimes swing into a paranoia of picturing anything. Some even teach that if we picture Jesus in our minds and he begins to speak, we are probably meeting a demon.[9] Driven by fear of deception and excessive zeal for objective truth, they seek safety from spiritual seduction in spiritual blindness rather than in Christ. Please be warned: Shutting the eyes of your heart does *not* protect you from deception. Rather, it opens you to getting spiritually "blind-sided."

By contrast, consider how Christ himself exhorts us to the true and righteous use of spiritual sight.

> "The knowledge of the secrets of the kingdom of heaven has been given to you [the disciples], but not to them [the conservative religious teachers]. Whoever has will be given more, and he will have an abundance. Whoever does not have, even what he has will be taken from him. This is why I speak to them in parables: *"Though seeing, they do not see; though hearing, they do not hear or understand."* In them is fulfilled the prophecy of Isaiah: 'You will be ever hearing but never understanding; you will be ever seeing but never perceiving. For this *people's heart has become calloused; they hardly hear with their ears, and they have closed their eyes.* Otherwise they might see with their eyes, hear with their ears, understand with their hearts and turn, and I would heal them.' *But blessed are your eyes because they see, and your ears because they hear.* For I tell you the truth, many prophets and righteous men longed to see what you

see but did not see it, and to hear what you hear but did not hear it." (Matthew 13:11–17)

Jesus certainly warned us to be alert to false christs and deceiving spirits (Matthew 24:23–26). But he never recommends fear as a refuge nor alarmism as a mission. Yet such fear is often compounded when we are asked by someone else to picture something in our minds. This is generally an overreaction to the real tragedies of spiritual control and abuse. We ought not to surrender control of our minds to others in blind faith. But in reality, if such fears were justified *carte blanche*, what would we make of reading a novel, listening to a story, or hearing someone report a vision? Should we try our best not to picture what they are describing? Are we in spiritual danger when they paint a vivid scene in our imaginations? In each case, a third party is "guiding us" into a world of "imagery." Must we truly blindfold our spiritual eyes for fear that seeing anything at all is dangerous? Surely the fear itself is an even greater door to deception and bondage. Surely those who sow this paranoia in our minds are exerting their own form of dangerous mind control.

Historically, whenever the church has repented of spiritual blindness, the Lord has enlightened the eyes of the heart and restored the promise of the Spirit for an outpouring of vision. And in these cases, the religious spirit has raised its head to cry idolatry, witchcraft, heresy or New Age. One might well ask: "If the fruit of these warnings is spiritual blindness, which is truly the false teaching?" Should we not be far more alarmed that we don't see at all than by what we may see and test by God's Spirit, his Word, and his church?

In perusing Scripture, here is what I see: Jesus promises a Holy Spirit who will guide us into all truth. He offers us protection from deception, illusion, and vain imagination. This same Guide uses imagery as he communicates. His inspired authors lead us into the imaginary world through dreams, visions, symbols, and stories. They provide us with images, colours, textures, and sounds. The prophets received a vision and then commanded us to "behold" it for ourselves: "I saw this—now you look at it too." This is not merely the guided imagery of men; it is the prophetic ministry of the Spirit.

When Hebrews says, "Fix your eyes on Jesus" (Hebrews 12:2) or Paul says, "I pray that the eyes of your heart would be enlightened" (Ephesians 1:18) or Jesus counsels us to acquire eye-salve (Revelation 3:18), they are exhorting us to activate faith-filled vision. When Paul says that with "open face" we *behold* the glory of the Lord and are changed from glory to glory by the Spirit" (2 Corinthians 3:18), he is commending us to that internal gaze wherein we behold a vision of the true Lord Jesus.

57

◀)) *Tuning In* • • • • • • • • • •

If you have wrestled with fear and resorted to shutting the eyes of your heart, I encourage you to pray for a restoration of your spiritual sight:

> Lord Jesus, open my spiritual eyes and heal them from blindness. Holy Spirit, guide me into the holy imagery of what David calls "the Hiding Place," where prayer is a literal meeting with Jesus. Good Shepherd, show and tell this sheep what I need to see and hear. Grant me discernment and recognition of truth from error in that place. Deliver me from evil *and* the fear of evil as I follow your word that says, "look up, and lift up my head; for my Redeemer draws near" (Luke 21:28). Redeemer God, I invite you to draw near even now.

Removing the Earmuffs

After I taught this material at a local church, one of the students came up afterwards in tears. She shared that she had not heard from the Lord for about fifteen years. She remembered hearing his voice and seeing his face before that, but everything since then had gone blank. She desperately wanted to know why.

So we asked the Lord to show her what was blocking her from hearing and seeing in the Spirit. Instantly, she saw a picture in her mind of a set of earmuffs over her own ears. We asked the Lord if the earmuffs had a label that we needed to know. The word "fear" came to mind right away. We had to point out to her that she was *already* beginning to see and hear again! We asked the Lord, "From where did these earmuffs of fear come?" He showed her the cover of a book that she had read in the 1980's. This Christian author had taught that if you close your eyes in prayer and see an image of Jesus, and he begins to speak to you, you could not know who or what spirit that is, but it is certainly not the Lord Jesus. He warned that it is probably an evil spirit masquerading as an angel of light trying to deceive you. What a contrast to what we read in John 10 about our ability and authority to discern! Nonetheless, the Lord showed this student that when she read that book and embraced the fear that it preached, the eyes and ears of her heart were shut off from seeing and hearing the Lord for a full decade and a half!

When she renounced the fears and the lies that she had received, we asked the Lord what he wanted to do about the earmuffs. The student said,

"He's taking them off!"

"Who is?" We asked.

"Jesus!" She said.

"How do you know that?"

Bursting with joy, she announced, "I can see him! I can see him!"

Evoking Visions

The truth is that the authors of Scripture knew no such fear. They painted vivid pictures for us—they describe visions with colours and textures and sounds. They testify to what they saw and draw us into their experiences firsthand. They say to us—no, they command us—"Behold!"

As we obey—as we open the eyes of our heart to behold God—we see, for example, the temple of God in Revelation 4 and 5. John says, "Behold!" And so we see (with our hearts) the throne, the emerald rainbow, the angels, the cherubim, the elders, the crystal sea, the flashes of lightning, and the roll of thunder. As we fix our heart's gaze into the centre, we hear a voice say, "Behold, the Lion" and with John, we turn to see—to behold—a Lamb. Then, with the throngs of heaven, we join in worship of the Lord Jesus, singing: "Worthy is the Lamb, who was slain, to receive power and wealth and wisdom and strength and honour and glory and praise!"

The Bible calls such prayerful and visual reading of God's Word "meditation." We must not diminish this practice to mere thoughtful pondering. As one focuses the eyes of the heart on spiritual picture-truths of the biblical prophets, a miracle awaits. As Evelyn Underhill says,

> The subject of meditation begins to take on a new significance; to glow with life and light. The contemplative suddenly feels that he knows it; in the complete, vital, but indescribable way in which one knows a friend. More, through it hints are coming to him of mightier, nameless things. *It ceases to be a picture, and becomes a window* through which the mystic peers out into the spiritual universe, and apprehends to some extent—though how he does not know—the veritable presence of God.[10]

So John is not just telling us about his vision of God. He is *evoking* a vision of God in us. We are not reading about his spiritual experience. We are having a deep and personal encounter with the Lord ourselves![11] When one crosses this threshold, prayer becomes much more than an exchange of information. With the eyes of our heart, we *step into* prayer as an encounter, a meeting with the living Christ. The ultimate beholding occurs when we gaze into his face with worshipful attentiveness. The great revivalist Andrew Murray placed enormous emphasis on this type of spiritual gazing, not someday in heaven, but today in our hearts.

> *To gaze upon the heavenly Christ* in the Father's presence, to whom all things are subject, will transform us into heavenly Christians, dwelling all the day in God's presence, overcoming every enemy... Blessed is the man who knows, then, in living faith to say: "But *we see Jesus* crowned with glory and honour." Blessed is the man who knows to look away from all that he finds in himself of imperfection and failure, to *look up and behold* all the perfection and glory he finds in Jesus. "Consider Jesus!" is indeed the keynote of the Epistle. The word "consider", from the root of the Latin word for Star, originally means to contemplate the stars. It suggests the idea of the astronomer, and *the quiet, patient, persevering, concentrated gaze* with which he seeks to discover all that can be possibly known of the stars which the object of his study is... Consider Jesus. *Gaze upon him,* contemplate him![12]

Do This.

To those with eyes to see, Jesus responds with this awesome promise, "Lo [Look!], I'm with you always" (Matthew 18:20).

"I'm Just Not Visual"

People often say to me, "I'm just not visual. Is that okay?" If that is your experience, let me begin by answering, *"You* are okay." The ability to see is not a measure of personal worth or spiritual maturity. That's not the issue. However, I would challenge the notion that God created and intended anyone to be non-visual. My experience with non-visual people is that they can normally trace their inability to see to a moment when they chose to shut their spiritual eyes. It may have been through a fearful experience or a fear-filled teaching. It may have been their way of repenting of occult practice or coping with an overwhelming tragedy. But the common thread is fear. You might compare it with a child shutting it's natural eyes to hide from a scary reality. Now imagine never reopening your eyes for fear of what you might see. Imagine learning to live with your other senses until you assumed that this is normal. That is the state of much of humanity. And *that* is *not* okay. To that condition, Jesus says, "Get eye-salve."

Others experience the opposite extreme: They close their eyes and are faced with a barage of images. It feels like opening the door to a closet that's been stuffed to the ceiling with gobbledygook and it all falls out at once. Or turning on a radio and having all the stations blasting at you simultaneously. Be encouraged: You *can* sort through it. The Lord will teach you the discipline of tuning in to one "station" at a time and hearing one voice on each station. Be patient with yourself—learning to focus is a normal part of learning to see.

◀)) *Tuning In* • • • • • • • • • •

Have you ever "seen" God with the eyes of your heart? Take time to meditate on the experience.

* As you picture him now, how does he appear to you?
* What form does he take?
* What expression is on his face?
* What does his expression communicate to you?

C. Sensing

Sensing is a third type of perception when listening for the Lord. Common terms for sensing include discernment, intuition, impressions, burdens, vibes, and gut feelings. Some describe it as, "I just know that I know that I know." In the classic book, *The Cloud of Unknowing,* the author refers to "sensing" as "an awareness of God, known and loved at the core of your being."[13] Our senses can be awakened to a conscious awareness of God's presence—his "felt presence."[14] In that felt presence, we may not admit that we hear a voice or see an image, but we can sense that if the Lord were to speak, he would be saying or doing such-and-such. The difficulty here is not that he is far away, but that he is so incredibly close.

> Now what I am commanding you today is not too difficult for you or beyond your reach. It is not up in heaven, so that you have to ask, "Who will ascend into heaven to get it and proclaim it to us so we may obey it?" Nor is it beyond the sea, so that you have to ask, "Who will cross the sea to get it and proclaim it to us so we may obey it?" No, *the word is very near you; it is in your mouth and in your heart* so you may obey it. (Deuteronomy 30:11–14)

Sometimes when we engage in listening prayer ministry, those who are wired best for sensing God's presence will struggle to see or hear. Yet they sense the nearness of the Lord and "just know" what he is saying or doing.

One participant recalled a painful classroom memory from child-hood. When we asked him if he was able to find Jesus in that memory at first he didn't see or hear anything. After checking for other hin-drances, we asked what he sensed. His reply was so detailed as to be humorous.

"Well, I don't see or hear Jesus, but I sense that he's over by the chalk board, leaning with his back against it, arms folded in front of him, with one leg up kind of like this …"

Such people are struggling to move from mental-sight to faith-sight. They seem to get their break-through when they realize that God has given them the gift of sensing what is in his Father's heart for them.

PRACTICE TIME

Jesus is your friend. In John 15:15 he said, "I no longer call you ser-vants, because a servant does not know his master's business. Instead, I have called you friends, for everything that I learned from my Father I have made known to you." In Psalm 25:14, we read that the Lord confides in those who fear him. (In this context, the word "fear" carries the sense of "obey.") "Confides" is a beautiful term that implies the inti-mate sharing of personal secrets. The Lord Jesus is looking for friends with whom he can share his secrets, confidantes who can be trusted with the sensitivities of his heart.

My friend Kim Unrau and I once did a road trip from Thunder Bay, Ontario to Vancouver, British Columbia. On that trip, he taught me by example how to become good friends: it includes time spent together, asking many questions and listening carefully. Then Kim suggested that if I wanted to grow from knowing God as Father to also knowing him as a Divine Friend, I should try asking friendship questions with him, too. He offered me the following list of friendship questions. As I asked them, I was not to analyze or worry about getting it right. He suggested simply presenting the question and then taking note of what came to mind. We could always weigh the content afterwards.

◀)) *Tuning In* • • • • • • • • •

I believe Jesus is saying to you today, "I am your friend. I am not your psychic hotline. I'm not interested in impressing you or making you seem impressive to others. I want intimacy. So before you rush ahead and ask me to lay out the future of the world for you, would you be will-ing to be my friend for a while? Would you like to hear my feelings and sorrows, joys and hopes?"

Friendship Questions for God

Try asking God a number of friendship questions. Perhaps you can develop some of your own as well. Before you start, take time to "dial down" and invite the peace of God to enter into your heart and mind.

- What's grieving you these days? Why?
- What's exciting you these days? Why?
- What do you like about me? Why?
- What do you see when you look at me?
- When was the last time you wept over me? Why?
- When was the last time you laughed over me? Why?
- If you could meet me anywhere face-to-face, where would it be?
- If my heart is your home, what does that home look like?
- If you could play a game with me, what would it be? Why?

Do this

God *loves* this final question because it shows us the power of symbols. God uses them to sneak past our defence grids when we are reluctant or unable to hear a direct message (2 Samuel 12). By the time the meaning of a symbol dawns upon us, we have already "taken the bait" and received a message we might otherwise have avoided.

Did you also notice how quickly God was willing to answer each question? Did you discard his voice just as quickly by rationalizing it away as "just my imagination"? Why do you suppose we're so prone to reacting that way?

Further, God was not at all offended by the "why" questions, was he? Through much of my faith journey, I was counselled not to ask God "Why?" It was as though the moral of the book of Job was "Don't ask why!" But I figured that if Job's endless questions incited God to show up in power, I would rather risk the deafening divine storm than endure the empty silence. I now believe we concluded that God doesn't answer "why questions" because we didn't honestly believe he answers *any* questions! However, once those answers started coming, I noticed how often he would explain his reasons to a hearing heart. This should not be surprising, given that he's a loving and patient Father. The fruit of this experience is a growing trust when he *won't* tell me why. I know he wouldn't withhold information from me without a good reason.

Hearing God for Others

As you begin to hear God more clearly for yourself, it follows that you might also hear him for others. Whenever we teach on this subject, we begin by asking our congregants to restrict their prophetic experiments to blessings and encouragement.

YES! DO THIS.

When you prophesy to someone (defined simply as sharing something that you believe God has shown you), you don't need to be his or her personal psychic. Just be an instrument of God's friendship and blessing. 1 Corinthians 14:3 says, "But everyone who prophesies speaks to men for their strengthening, encouragement and comfort." Because we value truth and love over sounding impressive, our church restricts itself to prophesying within these parameters: no direction, no correction; no dates, no mates; no births, no deaths.

I once heard this formula: If your motive is love, your purpose is encouragement, and your content is Scriptural, then you cannot miss.

Love + Encouragement + Scripture = Bull's-eye!

◀)) *Tuning In* • • • • • • • • •

We'll leave this chapter with a final encouragement exercise. Ask God the following questions and then write the answers in the form of an encouragement letter to whomever God directs.

- Who do you want me to encourage today? Why?
- What do you see when you look at them? Why?
- How do you feel about them? Why?
- What's one reason why you are pleased with them?
- What word of promise or Scripture verse could I share? Why do you want them to know this?
- What symbolic gift could I give them from you? What does it represent?

..... 3 .....

God, Is That Really You?

*Dear friends, do not believe every spirit, but test the spirits to
see whether they are from God, because many false prophets
have gone out into the world. This is how you can recognize
the Spirit of God: Every spirit that acknowledges that Jesus
Christ has come in the flesh is from God, but every spirit that
does not acknowledge Jesus is not from God.*

- 1 John 4:1–3

"AM I JUST MAKING THIS UP?"

If you've been doing the listening prayer exercises along the way, by
now you will no doubt have some questions about where the answers
are coming from:

- Is this the voice of God's Spirit or simply an active imagination?
  Am I just hearing what I want to hear?
- How do I know whether I'm hearing God and not some counterfeit?
- How can I avoid being deluded or deceived?
- Is it possible to verify whether what I heard was truly the voice of
  God?
- What about those times when I seem to get it completely wrong?

Such questions are an important and helpful part of our learning
curve. However, they will only equip us insofar as we sincerely seek
and expect to find their answers. Far too often they are asked as rhe-
torical statements with no hope of a solution. The silent conclusion
is that we cannot know and can never say with confidence, "God has
spoken." When we stumble on the path by "hearing wrong," it is tempting to lapse into a deafening agnosticism. When we hear wrongly for
ourselves, it may be discouraging. When we hear wrongly for others,
it can also be embarrassing or even hurtful. The fear of failure has
caused many to give up on listening prayer altogether. There is a risk
attached when we open our ears to listen. It's called faith, and faith
often involves a wrestling match with the Creator.

Risky Business

One morning I sensed God was directing me to a coffee shop/bookstore that I normally avoid because of the crowds. But when I arrived, I saw that God had apparently reserved the final seat in the place for me. I sat down, opened my journal, and asked the Lord, "What do you want to say to me today?"

Almost immediately, I noticed a young woman across the room with her back to me. She appeared to be engrossed in a book. I tried to ignore this as a distraction, but the Holy Spirit seemed to keep pointing her out. I finally asked, "Lord, are you trying to tell me something about that woman?" An impression came: "She's chronically ill." That didn't seem very probable. From my angle, I guessed that she was less than thirty years old and in good shape. I suspected that the word was likely a product of wandering eyes and I returned to my journal.

Again an invasive thought interrupted me: "Invite her to the healing conference." The conference in question was a series of meetings with Bob Brasset at the Langley Vineyard. I began to wrestle with God. As if I was going to approach a perfectly healthy stranger, explain to her that "God told me" she was chronically ill, and then invite her to see a faith healer. Yeah, right!

Being a man of such great faith, I rose up boldly, closed my books, and walked directly out the door and got into my car! As I turned the ignition key to make my escape, the voice came a third time, "If you leave now, don't bother teaching others about listening prayer. You can't teach what you don't believe in." Glumly, I turned the car off and trudged back into the coffee shop.

Inside I wove my way up and down the aisles of the bookstore, buying time for the woman to leave before I could reach her. No such luck. When I got back to the coffee area, there she sat, still absorbed in her book, looking even younger and healthier than she had five minutes ago.

I decided to approach her: "This might sound really strange to you, but ..." It sounded like a cheap pick-up line. Then I looked down— the book she was reading was a Bible! I began to gather courage: "I was praying and felt that you [*my courage waned again*] or maybe someone close to you [*hedging my bets—bad idea!*] struggles with a chronic illness. And I'm supposed to invite you [*now nearly mumbling*] to a healing conference that's coming up." [*There God, I did it! I hope you're happy!*]

She looked at me like I had two heads. I wondered why I wasn't wearing a paper bag over both of them. Then she spoke.

"As a matter of fact, I *have* been ill for *five years*. I was feeling angry and bitter towards God this morning. He told me to come here to do my devotions this morning, which is odd, because I *never* come here. So I've just been sitting, reading about Job's sufferings, and asking God why he hasn't healed me yet. Where is this healing conference?"

As a result, she attended the conference and signed up for a series of inner-healing prayer sessions, which I trust will lead to her complete healing. Still, I was troubled. Why hadn't she been immediately and miraculously healed? When I asked the Lord about this, I sensed his voice saying, "The type of faith required for that healing was available. But your hesitancy and the way you hedged your bets stole it from her. That's not an accusation—it's just the truth."

The lesson I learned was that listening to God and believing what he says can be risky and costly to others. But so can NOT listening to him and *not* believing him. Does this sound a tad harsh to you? Could my lack of faith and disobedience defer the healing of a needy and willing soul? It hardly seems fair! But surely I am not the first disciple who both attempted a healing and botched it up simultaneously. Consider Jesus' disciples:

> When they came to the crowd, a man approached Jesus and knelt before him.
>
> "Lord, have mercy on my son," he said. "He has seizures and is suffering greatly. He often falls into the fire or into the water. I brought him to your disciples, but they could not heal him."
>
> "O unbelieving and perverse generation," Jesus replied, "how long shall I stay with you? How long shall I put up with you? Bring the boy here to me."
>
> Jesus rebuked the demon, and it came out of the boy, and he was healed from that moment.
>
> Then the disciples came to Jesus in private and asked, "Why couldn't we drive it out?"
>
> He replied, "Because you have so little faith. I tell you the truth, if you have faith as small as a mustard seed, you can say to this mountain, 'Move from here to there' and it will move. Nothing will be impossible for you." (Matthew 17:14–20)

God does not condemn our lurching efforts in learning to listen. He *does* correct, and sometimes he rebukes, but then he always returns with a bold promise. Foibles will come either way, and a learning curve is okay. So let's get on with the learning!

TESTING THE VOICE OF GOD

Scripture requires even the most confident listeners to faithfully weigh what they are hearing and to allow others to do the same. 1 John 4 tells us plainly to test the voices we hear, to see whether they come from God, because there are many competing voices in the world and in our minds. 1 Corinthians 14:29 teaches us that when someone claims to speak in the name of God, the others should "weigh carefully" what is being said. Until a "word from the Lord" has been tested, we should hold it loosely as an *alleged* message from God. If it is true, it will surely stand up to open-minded scrutiny. This may sound difficult, but rest assured, when you follow the testing-principles laid out in this chapter, we will find that Jesus' confidence in our ability to identify his voice was neither naïve, nor misplaced.

Those Other Voices

Historically, Christians have distinguished the voice of God from three other voice-types—the world, the flesh, and the devil.

The "world" includes the barrage of ungodly messages that we hear through the media, educational and political systems, advertizing campaigns, and so on. St. Paul said, "Do not conform any longer to the pattern of this world, but be transformed by the renewing of your mind. Then you will be able to test and approve what God's will is—his good, pleasing and perfect will" (Romans 12:1–2). He holds "the world" and "the will of God" in direct contrast and calls us to distinguish them clearly in our minds.

The "flesh" (also known as the "sinful nature") generally refers to the dark side of our own mind, will, and emotions. The thoughts, desires, and feelings of the flesh are those that oppose the voice of God's Spirit. Again, Paul encourages us,

> So I say, live by [the voice of] the Spirit, and you will not gratify the desires of the sinful nature. For the sinful nature desires what is contrary to the Spirit, and the Spirit what is contrary to the sinful nature. They are in conflict with each other, so that you do not do what you want. (Galatians 5: 16–17)

The voice of the world is external in origin and relates to the corporate dysfunction of mankind. The voice of the flesh is internal and arises from our own fallen human nature.

The "devil" refers to either oppressive or seductive messages that originate in what the Bible calls the kingdom of darkness. Jesus himself wrestled with the tempting voice of the devil. He was victorious when God's voice reminded him of the written Word of God.

> Then Jesus was led by the Spirit into the desert to be tempted by the devil. After fasting forty days and forty nights, he was hungry. The tempter came to him and said, "If you are the Son of God, tell these stones to become bread."
>
> Jesus answered, "It is written: 'Man does not live on bread alone, but on every word that comes from the mouth of God.'"
>
> Then the devil took him to the holy city and had him stand on the highest point of the temple.
>
> "If you are the Son of God," he said, "throw yourself down. For it is written: 'He will command his angels concerning you, and they will lift you up in their hands, so that you will not strike your foot against a stone.'"
>
> Jesus answered him, "It is also written: 'Do not put the Lord your God to the test.'"
>
> Again, the devil took him to a very high mountain and showed him all the kingdoms of the world and their splendour.
>
> "All this I will give you," he said, "if you will bow down and worship me."
>
> Jesus said to him, "Away from me, Satan! For it is written: 'Worship the Lord your God, and serve him only.'"
>
> Then the devil left him, and angels came and attended him. (Matthew 4:1–11)

In addition to these three voices, I would add a fourth category called "the voices of mental illness." The voices that come through depression, anxiety disorders, O.C.D.,[1] schizophrenia,[2] and dissociative disorders [3] are very real and compelling. They often send negative or self-destructive messages (e.g., "They're better off without me"). In extremes, they come as high-pressure directions masquerading as instructions from God with a threat attached (e.g., "Do this or else!"). God can and does speak to people who struggle with mental illness, but when he does, the message comes as a loving word of invitation to life and love in caring community.

With so many voices clamouring for a listening ear, should we despair of distinguishing God's voice from amongst them all? Wouldn't it be safer to just ignore all of them and figure things out logically for ourselves? Absolutely not.

First, ignoring all voices is impossible. Like it or not, we're hard-wired to hear them. We constantly listen to and sift through volumes of input. Take a moment right now and see what your "antenna" is picking up. It's bound to be quite a cacophony.

Second, retreating to the supposed safety of "figuring things out for ourselves" is just another version of the fleshly mind trying to think independently of God. That is neither safe nor wise. Solomon's words to us turn that plan on its head.

> Trust in the LORD [i.e., his voice] with all your heart and lean not on your own understanding; in all your ways acknowledge him [his voice], and he will make your paths straight. Do not be wise in your own eyes; fear the LORD and shun evil. This will bring health to your body and nourishment to your bones. (Proverbs 3:5–8)

The good news is we need not always know the precise source of the *other* voices. The genuine voice of the Good Shepherd rises distinctively above all of them to speak words of life and hope that can be verified and embraced with great confidence.

Count on His Promises

Clarity of hearing is directly proportional to faith. If we begin with a foundation of trust in the promises of a perfectly faithful God, our spiritual ears will be tuned to hear him. God assures us of this throughout Scripture.

- *I am with you always.* "I am with you always, to the very end of the age" (Matthew 28:20). "I will never leave you nor forsake you" (Joshua 1:5).
- *My sheep hear my voice.* "I am the good shepherd; I know my sheep and my sheep know me ... My sheep listen to my voice; I know them and they follow me" (John 10:14, 27).
- *Call on me and I will answer you.* "Call to me and I will answer you and tell you great and unsearchable things you do not know" (Jeremiah 33:3).
- *When you ask for bread, you won't get a stone.* "Ask and it will be given to you; seek and you will find; knock and the door will be opened to you. For everyone who asks receives, he who seeks finds, and to him who knocks, the door will be opened. "Which of you, if his son asks for bread, will give him a stone? Or if he asks for a fish, will give him a snake? If you, then, though you are evil, know how

to give good gifts to your children, how much more will your Father in heaven give good gifts to those who ask him!" (Matthew 7:8–11)

When we truly believe these words as God's pledge to us—when we come to assume their reliability—the inner static that muddles our hearing is quickly cleared away. Doubt and fear give way to confidence and clarity.

Speaking of Static...

I observed a prayer ministry session with a lady who would pray aloud and then speak the answers from God back to herself, out loud in continuous dialogue. I took notes during this awesome conversation and weighed carefully what was being shared. At times her grief and panic came through in the questions. "Oh dear, oh dear! What shall I ever do?" she would cry. Then the calm voice of the Lord would respond with gentleness and comfort: "My daughter, there is no need for fear. I am with you. Hold my hand, and I will lead the way." This would continue for hours as God did his own marvellous therapy of the soul.

What struck me as important was that whenever doubt would assail this amazing woman, she would hear it as static in her mind's ear. When she would return to the premise and promises of God's ever-present voice, the static would give way to a clear channel once again. Eventually, she learned to identify the static verbally and then return to the conversation with God. She would say, "My daughter, I want you to know ... static ... I want you to know that I love you." As her faith grew in the voice of the Lord, the static was virtually eliminated. The key was using the static to remind her of God's promises rather than merely triggering frustration. If you struggle with static when trying to listen, you might give her simple method a try.

No Doubt About It!

Having rehearsed four of God's promises, let's consider the requirement that we must believe them whole-heartedly in order to hear God clearly:

> If any of you lacks wisdom, he should ask God, who gives generously to all without finding fault, and it will be given to him. But when he asks, he must believe and not doubt, because he who doubts is like a wave of the sea, blown and tossed by the wind. That man should not think he will receive anything from the Lord; he is a double-minded man, unstable in all he does. (James 1:5–8)

Taking my cue from this verse, I used to pray for wisdom, thank God, and then set to work trying to reason my way through life. I hoped that my prayers for wisdom would sanctify my reasoning without my having to actually wait for God's voice. I am sure he did grant me greater decision-making skills, even when I didn't take time to listen for his answers. I suppose he could make us wiser people by spiritual osmosis. But is that what James is talking about here? Reading the passage again, it seems more like he is saying that when we need answers for living, we should ask God, fully expecting to hear his counsel. If we don't expect to hear him, we won't hear him, and we will end up dazed and confused in this world, tossed around by life's problems. The more we expect to hear his voice, the more his answers will become specific, clear, and easy to discern. It's a matter of counting on the truth of his promise to speak.

THE POSTURE OF A LISTENER

God's promise to speak to us is such a generous gesture that it is only fitting that we should listen well. Our posture before God's throne is a key ingredient in becoming good listeners. I am not talking about the physical position in which we pray (although physical posture may serve or hinder our purposes). Rather, I refer to the heart attitude with which we respond to God's voice.

A. Focused Attention

Being focused may be too obvious to stress, but in this fast-food, multi-mediated world with its flood of images assaulting our senses, we must relearn the discipline of concentrated prayer. While God is able to speak "on the fly," we don't always hear him very well that way. Meditative prayer demands a degree of focused concentration. The monastic and/or mystic streams value and practice solitude, stillness, and silence precisely because the disciplines direct the listener's complete attention God-ward. Even the busiest of the great saints, such as Francis of Assisi or Teresa of Calcutta, knew the importance of retreating into attentive, centring prayer. They called it "recollection." I call it "dialing down." The listener progressively eliminates surrounding distractions in favour of a clear, single-eyed attention on God (Matthew 6:22). Seventeenth century mystic Jacob Boehme describes this posture well:

> Cease but from thine own activity, steadfastly fixing thine Eye upon one point... For this end, gather in all thy thoughts, and by faith press into the Centre, laying hold

upon the Word of God, which is infallible and which hath
called thee. Be thou obedient to this call, and be silent
before the Lord, sitting alone with him in thy inmost and
most hidden cell, thy mind being centrally united in itself,
and attending his Will in the patience of hope. So shall thy
Light break forth as the morning, and after the redness
thereof is passed, the Sun himself, which thou waitest for,
shall arise unto thee, and under his most healing wings
thou shalt greatly rejoice: ascending and descending in his
bright and health-giving beams.[4]

The Carmelites compared recollection to the gathering of bees back
to their hives. Like busy bees, our thoughts are often scattered
across the fields of our frantic lives. Each of us must beckon them
back to the hive of one's mind or heart. We quiet ourselves to listen.
Thus, listening prayer is the process by which these thoughts are
transformed into honey.[5]

Similarly, I like picturing the cares and concerns of the day as
leaves swirling in the gusty thoughts of my mind. When I quiet myself
before God and ask for his gift of peace, the leaves begin to fall gently
to the ground in the new stillness of my heart. The riot of thoughts and
swarm of images recede in favour of the One whom my heart desires.

If you are like me, you may find your mind prone to getting
sidetracked, wandering away like a puppy off its leash. Teresa of
Avila has some good advice for us when we find ourselves in this
situation:

If the mind, or to speak more clearly, the imagination, wan-
ders about after the greatest nonsense in the world, laugh
at it, treat it as a lunatic, and maintain your own peace.
Thoughts will come and go, but here the will is mistress
and recalls them without your troubling yourselves in the
matter. If you try to control them by force you will lose your
power over them which comes from the divine nourishment
within you, and neither the one nor the other will gain but
both will be losers. As the proverb says: 'Grasp at too much
and you will catch nothing.'[6]

The Lord invites us to "be still and know that I am God" (Psalm 46:10).
The trick is in learning to become relaxed and attentive without falling
asleep or anxiously striving for a word. This is not so difficult when we
expect to encounter a living and passionate God who shows his face
and pours his love into our hearts.

B. Love-longing

God's voice rings clearest to a heart-posture of devotion, what saints through the ages called the "divine romance." If we treat God as an impersonal force to be manipulated (magic) or merely as a deeper part of our "self" to be discovered (enlightenment), we might access some level of psychic power or information, but we will not attain *him*. The heart that knows God intimately is the one that loves him deeply and thirsts for his presence. Listen to David's desperate, life-and-death love, for example:

> As the deer pants for streams of water, so my soul pants for you, O God. My soul thirsts for God, for the living God. When can I go and meet with God? My tears have been my food day and night, while men say to me all day long, "Where is your God?" ... Deep calls to deep in the roar of your waterfalls; all your waves and breakers have swept over me. By day the LORD directs his love, at night his song is with me—a prayer to the God of my life. (Psalm 42:1–3, 7–8)

The only adequate and necessary force that can penetrate the heavens into the very heart of God is love.[7] Jesus' prescription is "Love the Lord your God with all your heart, and with all your soul, and with all your mind" (Matthew 22:37). God also promises, "Then you will call upon me and come and pray to me, and I will listen to you. You will seek me and find me when you seek me with all your heart" (Jeremiah 29: 12–13). Once again, David is our model here:

> O God, you are my God, earnestly I seek you; my soul thirsts for you, my body longs for you, in a dry and weary land where there is no water. I have seen you in the sanctuary and beheld your power and your glory. Because your love is better than life, my lips will glorify you. I will praise you as long as I live, and in your name I will lift up my hands. My soul will be satisfied as with the richest of foods; with singing lips my mouth will praise you. On my bed I remember you; I think of you through the watches of the night. Because you are my help, I sing in the shadow of your wings. My soul clings to you; your right hand upholds me. (Psalm 63:1–8)

Those who would encounter God must pursue him with the devotion of a lovesick bride. In his famous love song, Solomon used vivid symbolism to describe this yearning of the bride for her divine groom:

> All night long on my bed I looked for the one my heart loves; I looked for him but did not find him. I will get up now and go about the city, through its streets and squares; I will search for the one my heart loves. So I looked for him but did not find him. The watchmen found me as they made their rounds in the city. "Have you seen the one my heart loves?" Scarcely had I passed them when I found the one my heart loves. I held him and would not let him go. (Song of Solomon 3:1–4)

A favourite love-prayer of mine comes from that song: "My dove [God] in the clefts of the rock, in the hiding places on the mountainside, show me your face, let me hear your voice; for your voice is sweet, and your face is lovely ... My lover [God] is mine and I am his" (Song of Solomon 2:14, 16).

If you give your heart to God in unreserved devotion, he will not hesitate to rush in and embrace you. This is the heart-posture that not only hears his voice but also wins his heart.

C. Humble Waiting

Having shared on the posture of focused attention and earnest love-longing, a word of caution is now in order: Encounters with God are a work of grace. We don't *make* him come to us by our own efforts, as if he were obliged. Love does not demand or manipulate. God says, "This is the one I esteem: he who is humble and contrite in spirit, and trembles at my word" (Isaiah 66:2). God is not conquered like some mountain peak that we scale through religious self-effort. He descends in his humility to the quiet, receptive heart. The humble heart is marked by self-surrender to the mercy and will of God. It waits at the feet of Jesus as Mary did, wholly attentive, waiting to receive all that he has for us (Luke 10:39). Quietness replaces exertion. Being replaces doing. The ardent, thirsty love for God is satisfied with his presence as he allows— yes, *allows*—us to drink from his well of life. Jesus claimed, "Whoever drinks the water I give him will never thirst. Indeed, the water I give him will become in him a spring of water welling up to eternal life" (John 4:14). Indeed, listening prayer should be more like the infant's enjoyment of nursing than an exercise in spiritual constipation!

Scripture itself likens the humble heart to a nursing baby. Helpless, the baby cries out hungrily, even frantically for its mother. The mother hears and responds out of her tender, maternal love. She quickly draws the baby to her breast, and the baby is mysteriously transformed! It becomes tranquil, gulping deeply until fully satisfied, then drifting off into a blissful sleep. The nursing baby is a perfect picture of the heart that eagerly waits then humbly receives its nourishment from God. [8] This is God's promise to you: "Can a mother forget the baby at her breast and have no compassion on the child she has borne? Though she may forget, I will not forget you! See, I have engraved you on the palms of my hands" (Isaiah 49:15–16). Later on, Isaiah adds,

> For this is what the LORD says: "I will extend peace to her like a river, and the wealth of nations like a flooding stream; you will nurse and be carried on her arm and dandled on her knees. As a mother comforts her child, so will I comfort you; and you will be comforted over Jerusalem." (Isaiah 66: 11–13)

Knowing this, believing it, and counting on God through Christ to fulfill his word is the posture of true humility.

◀)) *Tuning In* • • • • • • • • • •

In this section, we will learn how to test what we hear from God. Let's prepare by beginning with an exercise in fine-tuning.

- Spend some time dialing down: call those thought-bees back to the hive—let those worry-leaves fall to the ground.
- Picture yourself standing beside Jesus in front of a mirror. Imagine that he's just exhaled a big gust of steam onto the mirror. If he were to use his fingertip to write a message on the mirror about your true identity, what would he write? Read it.
- Now ask him to wipe off the steam so that when you look in the mirror, you can see yourself as he sees you. What do you see?

Hang onto these answers as a test case for confirming God's voice. Here, then, are the basic tests.

I. TEST THE SOURCE

When you receive a message that may be from Jesus, you can directly ask who or what the source is. This may sound funny if you've never tried it, but I occasionally ask aloud, "Who said that?" or "Is this really the true Lord Jesus?" You'll be surprised at how well and how often this works. But when in doubt, just ask. This was a rule in the early church for the prophetic voices that spoke:

> Dear friends, do not believe every spirit, but test the spirits to see whether they are from God, because many false prophets have gone out into the world.
>
> This is how you can recognize the Spirit of God: Every spirit that acknowledges that Jesus Christ has come in the flesh is from God, but every spirit that does not acknowledge Jesus is not from God. This is the spirit of the antichrist, which you have heard is coming and even now is already in the world.
>
> You, dear children, are from God and have overcome them, because the one who is in you is greater than the one who is in the world. (1 John 4:1–4)

It is troubling that we don't practice direct testing like this more often. It seems as though many prophetic churches are bashful about it. I'm convinced that this is because we don't have confidence in our authority to do it—or in God's commitment to enforce it. A similar passage reads,

> Now about spiritual gifts, brothers, I do not want you to be ignorant. You know that when you were pagans, somehow or other you were influenced and led astray to mute idols. Therefore I tell you that no one who is speaking by the Spirit of God says, "Jesus be cursed," and no one can say, "Jesus is Lord," except by the Holy Spirit. (1 Corinthians 12:1)

"But I Don't Want to Hurt God's Feelings!"

When the voice *is* from God, trying to verify it with questions doesn't offend God at all. He welcomes testing. In fact, it was his idea. You can use the questions below and/or ask a few of your own.

- Does the spirit giving this revelation confess that Jesus Christ is Lord?
- Does the spirit saying this acknowledge that Jesus came in the flesh?
- Does this spirit delight in the kingship of Christ and submit to it?
- True Lord Jesus, would you show me (give me an internal visual) the true nature of the one who is speaking?
- Or more simply, is that really you Lord Jesus?

This last question throws some folks off because they can't believe it would be that simple. But it is—if you believe it is. Jesus' promises make it that simple.

Jesus in the Pup Tent

My dear friend Glenn Runnalls[9] introduced me to that fifth question based on this simple illustration:

- If your heart and mind were a pup tent and you were camping out, Jesus would be in the tent with you, because he is your friend. He loves you, and he promises to be there all the time.
- Imagine that you are having a sleepover in the pup tent with him, and it is such a dark night that you can't see him. But because he is your friend, and he loves you, he promises to answer you if you talk to him.
- Imagine that when he answers you, for some reason you don't recognize his voice. When you double-check by asking, "Was that really you?" he won't be offended, and he won't ignore you. Because he is your friend, and he really loves you, you can expect him to reply, "Yes, that was me."
- Now imagine that three bullies have surrounded the tent without you realizing it. Maybe one of them has even snuck into the tent. They represent the world, the flesh, and the devil. You ask Jesus a question, and one of the bullies speaks up, trying to imitate your friend. You may think, "That sort of sounded like my friend, but I'm not sure." So you ask, "Jesus, was that you?" What's going to happen? Will he stay silent? Will he let a sincere seeker (one who doesn't want to be deceived—one who hasn't purposely shut out his voice) fall prey to the bullies' deception? If Jesus is your friend, and he really loves you, won't he speak up, saying, "No, that wasn't me"?

The Spirit of Truth

I believe that Glenn's analogy is faith-filled and dead-on accurate. Here's why: Christ promised to come live in us, along with the Spirit of Truth, who leads us into all truth.

> And I will ask the Father, and he will give you another Counsellor to *be with you forever—the Spirit of truth.* The world cannot accept him, because it neither sees him nor knows him. But you know him, for *he lives with you and will be in you.* I will not leave you as orphans; *I will come to you.*

Before long, the world will not see me anymore, but *you will see me*. Because I live, you also will live.

On that day you will realize that I am in my Father, and you are in me, and *I am in you*. Whoever has my commands and obeys them, he is the one who loves me. He who loves me will be loved by my Father, and I too will love him and *show myself to him*. (John 14:16–21)

But when he, the Spirit of truth, comes, he *will guide you into all truth*. He will not speak on his own; he will speak only what he hears, and he will tell you what is yet to come. He will bring glory to me by taking from what is mine and making it known to you. All that belongs to the Father is mine. That is why I said the Spirit will take from what is mine and make it known to you. In a little while you will see me no more, and then after a little while *you will see me*. (John 16:13–16)

These passages assure me that the Spirit of Truth is alive in me right now. He pledges to speak to me and to lead me into all truth. His job is to glorify Jesus Christ as God's only Son and testify about him (John 15:26). He is to be my counsellor and guide. Further, Jesus promises that on "that day," he too will come to me and live in me and I in him. "That day" refers to the Day of Pentecost when Christ gave the Spirit to the Church and when Christ could come and, by the Spirit, make his home in every heart that loves him. Better yet, while the world cannot see him anymore, Jesus promises that we will see him, because he will show himself to us. He is not referring here to his glorious Second Coming but *now*, in this age of the Spirit, when he appears to your spiritual eyes in the pup tent of your heart.

If this is so, then the question of testing the source is truly as simple as it sounds. In order to test the source of a voice or picture, I can ask my indwelling friend, Jesus, and his Spirit of Truth, "Is that the true Lord Jesus?"

Jesus With a Stick?

During a prayer ministry session with Bobbi, a wonderful Christian friend, we asked her what she sees when she pictures Jesus. Even though she had walked with Jesus for over fifty years, co-labouring with her husband in full-time ministry, she was agitated. "Ever since I was a little girl, when I picture Jesus, I always see him with a stick, threatening to hit me. As I've received inner-healing in the last few years, I don't sense that threat to be true, but I still always see him holding the stick." That was odd—odd enough for our friend Kathy to speak up.

"This might sound like a silly question, but I'm going to ask it. Jesus, is that really you?"

Instantly, the false picture of Jesus vanished, and everything went blank. Then Kathy said, "Jesus, would you show Bobbi what you truly look like?" Instantly, a vision came of two enormous open hands welcoming Bobbi to leap into his love. Immediately, her face lit up. Enraptured, she plunged into those awesome, inviting hands. She saw his true heart for her and felt the warmth of his love completely envelop her. All that was required was for someone to directly test the source of her false picture of Jesus.

The Spirit of the World

On another occasion, a young man came to me to voluntarily test whether he was hearing God accurately. He felt that the Lord was telling him to sleep with his girlfriend. The voice had even used Scripture to justify this direction. He asked me how he could know whether or not this was the voice of God. I *felt* like arguing with him, but I have learned the hard way how ineffective this is. So I suggested we test the source directly. I spoke out, "We take up God's invitation and our authority in Christ to directly test the source of this revelation. If it is the Holy Spirit, we welcome you. If it is another spirit, we summon you to present yourself before the Lord Jesus for testing."

The young man answered, "I see a large dark cloud with lightning crackling around it, and the voice is coming from there." In my mind, I thought it might represent the power and glory of God (Ezekiel 1) or else the darkness might be our hint. But before I could ask another question, this fellow jumped in his seat.

"I just heard a voice from behind me say, 'Nice try', and then Jesus stepped up and blew the cloud away. There's just a little gremlin-looking thing where the cloud was."

Busted!

"And who are you?" We asked.

It shrugged in defeat, "The spirit of the world." This was the messenger who had tried to masquerade as the Lord. Again, a basic, direct test that took no more than a minute made the source of the voice obvious.

II. TEST THE CONTENT

Of course, we don't stop at testing the source of an alleged word from God. We also examine the content of the message. This leads us immediately to the question: When do we ever have the right to claim, "God has spoken—thus says the Lord"? From whom or where do we derive that type of authority? Isn't that rather "subjective"?

I doubt that any amount of "proof" is sufficient to make us certain that God has spoken in the legal or scientific sense of those words. However, neither is it necessary. When multiple authorities (even subjective ones) agree together, we may accumulate ample "warrant" (not proof) to be "confident" (not certain) that God has spoken.[10]

Let me explain: Imagine a stool consisting of three legs and a seat. Each leg represents an authority by which we can weigh what we hear from God. They include the written word of God, the gathered people of God, and the indwelling Spirit of God. If all three legs support the content of a revelation, then we are warranted in sitting or abiding on it in faith. Now let's take a closer look at the different components of the stool.

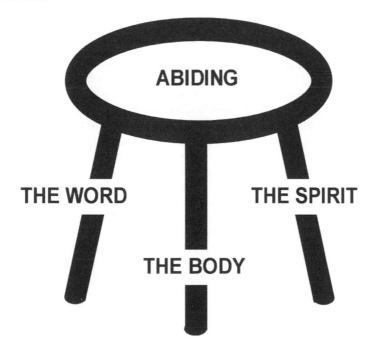

A. The Bible

The first question we should ask about any word from God is whether or not it lines up with the plumb line of Scripture. Note that we do not ask, "Is it *in* the Bible?" The question is both broader and narrower than that. First, we cannot restrict God's living voice to only that which we specifically find between the two covers of the Bible. This would reduce Scripture to just another religious box in which to confine God. The Bible represents a testimony not merely of what God said and did but also of who he is, what he says, and what he does. It is about all that Jesus *began* to do and teach (Acts 1:1). What we see and hear from him now extends from and lines up with that testimony.

I think of Scripture as a powerful telescope, like the Hubble. It is able to scan the heavens far beyond what the naked eye can perceive. Scientists no longer assume the entire universe to be contained within their telescopes' field of vision. So too, even though the Bible provides us with an incomparable revelation of God, no theologian should assume that the sixty-six books of the Bible capture all of who God is, what he does, and what he says. Like scientists, we can expect to keep making surprising new discoveries about the Lord and his ways. Our limitless God will continue to unfold his mysteries, yet these will always harmonize with the immutable truth previously revealed in his Word.

Second, lining up revelation with Scripture is also *narrower* than asking, "Is it in the Bible?" Not all Bible passages apply to all people at all times. Not everything its characters did is fair game for us today (e.g. polygamy). Not everything commanded by Moses is to be obeyed today (e.g. public stonings). We need to test what we hear according to the redemptive direction of God's word—to themes consistent with the gospel of God's grace and Jesus' vision of the kingdom. In that sense it remains our authoritative standard or "measuring stick" for verifying what we see and hear.

Now contra the Protestant Reformation, Scripture is not our *only* authority in confirming God's voice. The Protestant motto, *sola scriptura* (Scripture alone), would have left them with a wobbly, one-legged stool. Ultimately, it does not stand up to sound biblical teaching or actual Protestant practice. Even the staunchest proponent of *sola scriptura* assumes a dependence on more than Scripture. For example, the very fact that the Protestant teachers taught this in their churches assumes that the masses were not left alone with their Bibles. They were encouraged to gather as the Body of Christ to listen as Spirit-filled teachers explained the Word to them. Word, Body, and Spirit—we can't seem to keep them apart. Whenever and wherever two or three believers gather, the three-legged stool spontaneously appears. The question is: will we pause to hear the Word, hear each other out, and listen to the Spirit as the three work together to testify to the Truth?

Thus, after taking seriously the testimony of Scripture, we need to look to a second leg: the community of faith.

B. The Body of Christ

Some people balk at the tradition and institution of the church, and they have good reason. The church has often responded horrifically to its own prophets. As Stephen said to the Sanhedrin, "Was there ever a prophet your fathers did not persecute?" (Acts 7:52). Yet we ignore the family of faith to our own peril. Our spiritual heritage includes the wisdom and revelation of generations among whom the Spirit spoke and acted. Wherever two or three are gathered in Christ's name we have assurance of his presence (Matthew 18:20). Thus, a reliable word from God should meet this criteria: "Does it find confirmation in your community of faith?" And not just any group will do. My perspective is that the true Body of Christ is a community that names Jesus as Lord and Saviour, is in sincere pursuit of truth, and bears the fruit of the Spirit.[11] Our faith family may include our spiritual mentors and confidantes, a home group, a local church or a church tradition.

While people who claim to hear God are often not well-received by "religious" people, we could stand to put a little more confidence in God's Spirit to discern God's voice through God's people. Isolationists who are reluctant to share what they hear for fear that they might be seen as "off their rocker" should consider the possibility that they *are!* This very hesitancy may be a huge red flag. When I think God is teaching me something that seems novel, I normally bounce it off several groups of believers that have a reliable track record in listening prayer and who have the courage to disagree with me. Even if I were to receive unfiltered revelation from heaven, I know that I would still need help with interpreting, applying, and discerning the appropriate time to share it with others. I may dial into God's frequency, but others provide the fine-tuning. This is God's design. It reinforces the value he puts on interdependence and relationships.

Even when we find a Scripture to support a possible word from God, and even if we find a church that agrees with that message, we still only have two legs to our stool. History has repeatedly shown that a third authority is required: the inner, convicting witness of the Holy Spirit.

C. The Holy Spirit

With this leg of the stool, our first question is, "Does the Holy Spirit testify to your own heart that this is truth?" Apart from the conviction of this indwelling guide, the church would still be using the Bible to support slavery. Women would still be silenced in all churches. The military crusades may have continued (perhaps they have). But the Spirit has led us into truth that our Bibles and church traditions alone did not. The reverse is also true: Even if the church and the Bible *seem* to support a prophetic message, if the Holy Spirit does not confirm it in your own heart to be true, please take a second look. Ask the hard questions. Don't be intimidated into thinking that your honest questions will grieve the Holy Spirit, for it is his own testimony that we are seeking.

When individual believers have neglected or been prevented from hearing God's confirming word for themselves, this has caused many to perish in various suicide cults or to be spiritually abused in controlling movements. How opposite this is from God's truth! Within the context of the new covenant community, God promises: "I will put my law in their minds and write it on their hearts. I will be their God, and they will be my people. No longer will a man teach his neighbour, or a man his brother, saying, 'Know the LORD,' because they will all know me, from the least of them to the greatest," declares the LORD (Jeremiah 31:33–34).

The apostle John agrees:

> I am writing these things to you about those who are trying to lead you astray. As for you, the anointing [the Spirit of Truth] you received from him remains in you, and you do not need anyone to teach you. But as his anointing teaches you about all things and as that anointing is real, not counterfeit—just as it has taught you, remain in him. (1 John 2: 26–27)

These men were not advocating extreme individualism. It is advice for those who remain in the community. They are stressing that each member has their own direct line to God and must use it to test what is taught.

The experience of this inner witness varies from person to person. Sometimes we hear, "Yes, that's true," or "No, that's not right." Others just seem to know intuitively. Still others experience an emotional or physical reaction that confirms or denies what is being said. God is not an emotion, but he does experience emotion and he does use it to communicate—more often than we think!

God loves to grant his peace and rest when we are on the right path; and he is willing to withdraw it when we're getting off track (e.g., Psalm 32). He may tune us in to what he feels about a certain word (peace and joy versus grief or even nausea) so that we may embrace or reject it based on a heart connection rather than mere information.

Our culture constantly pits logic and emotion against each other. Many discard emotions in favour of reason, believing that emotions are an unreliable measure of truth. They trust "objective," self-created pro-and-con lists over "gut feelings" or intuition. They fail to see that the flesh can skew and manipulate their supposed objectivity as easily as it can manipulate their emotions. On the other hand, many live by exclusively trusting their emotions, which can range from an erratic roller coaster ride to intuitive expertise that puts reason to shame. Do you feel the reason/emotion conflict at war in your own heart and mind? Perhaps the war can end! Under the influence of God's Spirit, heart, mind, and emotion and reason can co-exist as interdependent channels for his voice. I suggest you recognize the Spirit's confirming work within you as it functions through both your thoughts *and* feelings, reasoning with your mind *and* triggering your emotions. The false dichotomy of head and heart dissolves as God delivers a revelation of experiential knowledge. You can *know* God's truth with all your heart, mind, soul, and strength. This is the inner confirmation of the Holy Spirit.

◀)) *Tuning In* • • • • • • • • • •

- Think of a specific time when you heard a truth and your spirit (or rather, God's Spirit in you) leaped with a positive "Yes!" What was the truth you were agreeing with? What did your inner response sound like? What did it feel like?
- Think of a specific time when you heard something from which your spirit (and God's Spirit in you) recoiled. What was the lie you were disagreeing with? What did your inner response sound like? What did it feel like?

D. The Seat of Abiding

I used to teach that when all three legs of the stool are in place, we are warranted in our belief that God has spoken. However, one day when I returned home from teaching this material, my wife and I decided to go for a walk. We had traveled less than two blocks when we noticed a three-legged stool sitting out in the middle of the road. It was an odd "coincidence," considering that I had just taught on the topic. What caught our eyes was that the seat was broken in two. Was God trying to show us something? I put the question to "Agora," an Internet newsgroup where members post ideas for discussion on an electronic bulletin board. I received a reply from Glenn (the pup tent guy). The Lord showed him that the seat was an essential symbol in the stool analogy. He felt that even if all three legs were assembled, a broken seat would make the stool unsafe. To him the seat represented the "place of abiding."

It is not enough to use the above tests as a technology for testing while neglecting the call to abide. To "abide" is to faithfully remain in a humble and teachable state. Jesus says, "Abide, remain here, sit here" (John 15). To proclaim a God-message with authority, we must abide in the Word, abide in the Body, and abide in the Spirit of the Lord himself. It is always possible to proof-text a passage, find a few gullible yesmen, and develop a warm fuzzy feeling inside. But even with all these things, we might still be completely deceived. However, when we *abide in the Lord* and the three tests are in agreement, we are warranted in proclaiming confidently, "God has spoken."

◀)) *Tuning In* • • • • • • • • • •

Let's review the message God gave you when you asked, "What do you see when you look at me?" What did Jesus show you? Why did he show you that? Hold it up to these three tests:

- Does the *Word* confirm it? Can you find a Scripture verse or verses that teach the same truth?
- Does the *Body* confirm it? Present what you heard to two or three credible people whom you trust to hear from God. Ask them, "Does this sound true to you? Does this sound like something God would say?" What is their response?
- Does the *Spirit* confirm it? Try reading the message aloud to yourself. Ask the Holy Spirit what he thinks. How does your heart respond to it?

III. TEST THE FRUIT

Finally, having tested the source and the content of any given word, we want also to test its fruit. In other words, we want to examine the results of believing and following what we hear. So we ask, "As you lean into this word in faith, does it bear the fruit of the Spirit in your life?"

I had a friend who seemed to hear God very well. He would get these amazing revelations, often accompanied by great euphoria. But he stopped listening to that voice "from heaven," because it consistently left a wake of devastation behind him. Every time he followed that direction, it "felt" right and seemed reasonable. Yet, time after time, listening to that voice resulted in injury to those he loved most. In that sense, the Holy Spirit was not confirming what he heard. When what seems to be God's voice wreaks nothing but havoc for you and those around you, there is a good chance it isn't really him talking. There are two main questions we can ask pertaining to fruit.

Immediate Impact

If that promise were really true, how would I feel?[12] The twentieth century church generally taught that feelings don't matter. The analogy used was that of a fact-faith-feeling train, where feelings were an optional "caboose" that may or may not follow truth, faith, and knowledge. The ultimate removal of the caboose from the literal trains in Canada was a striking picture of what happened to our faith as emotion was dispatched to the side-rails of the soul.

How different this is from Paul's teaching. He describes the expected, immediate fruit of a word from God: "But everyone who prophesies speaks to men for their strengthening, encouragement and comfort" (1 Corinthians 14:3). He speaks of a love poured into the heart (Romans 5:5) and a kingdom of righteousness, joy, and peace in the Holy Spirit (Romans 14:17). He talks about a "peace that passes understanding" (Phil. 4:7). Peter also describes a filling of "inexpressible and glorious joy" (1 Peter 1:8).

Jonathan Edwards, the eighteenth century evangelist through whom God brought about America's "Great Awakening," summarized the importance of our heart's response to God. He said, "true religion, in great measure, consists in the affections,"[13] which include passion and fervency of love for God. So too, the great Methodist preacher John Wesley confessed that at his conversion his heart was "strangely warmed"[14] with a direct, unmediated testimony of his spiritual sonship from the Holy Spirit, as described in the epistle to the Romans. "For you did not receive a spirit that makes you a slave again to fear, but you received the Spirit of sonship. And by him we cry, 'Abba, Father.' The Spirit himself testifies with our spirit that we are God's children" (Romans 8:15–16). He felt the love, acceptance, and forgiveness of God *in his heart.*

By contrast, the voices that weaken, discourage, and distress you are most often not from God. For even his call to repent *usually* carries the tone of kindness (Romans 2:4, Titus 3:4), grace (Titus 2:4), and tender wooing (Hosea 2:14). Isaiah says, "A bruised reed he will not break, and a smouldering wick he will not snuff out" (Isaiah 42:3).

St. Ignatius Loyola, founder of the Jesuits, noted that all emotions boil down to either consolation or desolation.[15] Messages from God bring consolation: they cause us to grow in faith, hope, and charity, and all interior joy. They inflame us with love for the Creator and induce tears of repentance for sin and passion for Christ. Desolation, on the other hand, diminishes faith, hope, and love, and is therefore not the work of God's Spirit. Desolation is marked by apathy, sadness, and separation from the love of God. Rather than gathering us into God's presence, desolation beats us up and sends us out, causing us to shrink back in shame and hopelessness, allowing our love for God to grow cold and callused.

But even when the Lord occasionally speaks sharply to us, the fruit will be positive and constructive. The Lord chastens those he loves, with a view to their salvation or restoration (Hebrews 12).

> But if an unbeliever or someone who does not understand comes in while everybody is prophesying, he will be convinced by all that he is a sinner and will be judged by all, and the secrets of his heart will be laid bare. So he will fall down and worship God, exclaiming, "God is really among you!" (1 Corinthians 14:24–25)

Paul is not advocating the humiliation of visitors through public exposure of their hidden sins. Rather, those who are awakened to God's presence as he speaks through his people will respond to him in repentance and worship.

My friend Ryan is as gentle as a teddy bear. He laughs with those who laugh and weeps with those in pain. He is a beautiful manifestation of the tender heart of God. Encouragement, strength, and comfort flow from him constantly. But on the odd occasion, God will ask him to deliver a hard message to his friends. I notice that when he does, the fruit is consistently positive. One day a friend was complaining to him and spewing out a stream of lies about herself, her life, and God. Suddenly filled with the Spirit, Ryan rebuked her sharply, "Get behind me, Satan!" (Matthew 16:23). The girl paused, burst into tears, and spontaneously repented of her attitude and her lies. Ryan was able to follow through with a message of hope and restoration. Normally such a statement would have been inappropriate and destructive, but the right word at the right time brings good fruit.

Long-term Influence

This speaks to the question of character. As you respond to God's voice, it should have a particular effect on your character. Here is the life-evidence that God is really your source:

> But the fruit of the Spirit is love, joy, peace, patience, kindness, goodness, faithfulness, gentleness and self-control. Against such things there is no law. (Galatians 5:22–23)
>
> My brothers, can a fig tree bear olives, or a grapevine bear figs? Neither can a salt spring produce fresh water. Who is wise and understanding among you? Let him show it by his good life, by deeds done in the humility that comes from wisdom. But if you harbor bitter envy and selfish ambition in your hearts, do not boast about it or deny the truth. *Such "wisdom" does not come down from heaven* but is earthly, unspiritual, of the devil. For where you have envy and selfish ambition, there you find disorder and every evil practice. But *the wisdom that comes from heaven* is first of all pure; then peace-loving, considerate, submissive, full of mercy and good fruit, impartial and sincere. Peacemakers who sow in peace raise a harvest of righteousness. (James 3:12–18)

The point here is that outcome (fruit) matters. A true word from the Lord is an invitation to transformation. Where God's voice is heard and received, expect to see moral reform, changes in character, and an increase in integrity. We mustn't merely hear the Shepherd's voice—we must also follow it. The apostle James presses this point. He knows the blessing of putting feet to the words that our ears hear.

> Anyone who listens to the word but does not do what it says is like a man who looks at his face in a mirror and, after looking at himself, goes away and immediately forgets what he looks like. But the man who looks intently into the perfect law that gives freedom, and continues to do this, not forgetting what he has heard, but doing it—he will be blessed in what he does. (James 1:23–25)

◀)) *Tuning In* • • • • • • • • • •

Let's watch the fruit of knowing how God sees you: For the next month, begin each day by thanking God specifically for this revelation. Take note of how your heart responds to this knowledge. You might want to write down or draw what you saw and heard. Hang it somewhere that you'll see it every day. After one month, see how embracing this message impacts:

- Your character and attitude: I have become more _____.
- Your lifestyle.Think of an example.
- Your self-image. Think of an example.
- Your circumstances: Think of an example where accepting this message even affected your environment.

Crunching It into a Moment

Based on a direct testing of your source, confirming your content, and seeing good spiritual fruit, you can affirm with great confidence, "I heard God!" If this process seems overwhelming and complicated, let me reassure you: such testing often occurs spontaneously and automatically within us. The process I've laid out here becomes second nature when God's voice has already become familiar. The more "in tune" we are to his heart, to his Word, to his people, and to his Spirit, the less we will need to analyze every conversation we have with him. It is all crunched into a brief, listening moment.

When I ask God, "How much do you love me?" and he reminds me, "Enough to die for you," I don't need to walk through the testing process all over again. I recognize that voice and that message. I already know what the Bible, the church, and the Spirit say about that. I am already aware of the fruit of receiving that message. So I just accept it with the receptivity of a child.

If, however, God tells me it's time to resign, pack up my family, and move across the world, I go through the weighing procedure much more thoroughly. In either case, at the end of the day (or the year), I trust that I can know if he has spoken to me. So can you!

4

Was That Just My Imagination?

"No eye has seen, no ear has heard, no mind has conceived what God has prepared for those who love him"—but God has revealed it to us by his Spirit. The Spirit searches all things, even the deep things of God.

- 1 Corinthians 2:9–10

"We cannot have faith [belief in what is unseen] unless we have imagination; imagination is the vehicle through which faith is expressed." Our prayers are often fitful and half-hearted because we cannot "see" the One to whom we pray, and we cannot envision what we are praying about.

- R. Paul Stevens, *Poems for People Under Pressure*, 90.

"WAS THAT JUST MY IMAGINATION?"

Shani sat with my wife, sobbing deeply through a stream of healing tears. She had just witnessed a profound revelation with the eyes of her heart. The Lord had taken her back to a painful memory involving an indecent assault. As she recalled the scene, she saw Christ enter the room and draw next to her, take her hand, and weep for her. As he did, her sorrow became his, and she felt the burden of sadness leave her heart, to be replaced by peace. Suddenly, she gasped.

"I can't believe this! Jesus has just taken my place! I'm sitting beside him, holding his hand! Now he's the one being assaulted!" She resisted the picture. She was horrified that he would be subjected to the trauma and shame that she had felt. But as Jesus lay there, maintaining constant eye contact with her, Shani experienced the deep healing that comes when "the man of sorrows" takes our grief upon himself and releases his own joy to us. Rather than being re-victimized by reliving the memory, God had entered into the pain with her to free her from it forever.

This revelation of Christ left an indelible imprint on Shani's life (and ours). She admits that she never could have nor would she have made up such a startling scenario. She testifies that the fruit of that encounter is a permanent healing of that memory. The event still happened, but it holds no power over her anymore. But what surprised us most was that given all that, immediately afterwards Shani asked, "Was that God... or just my imagination?"

NO SUCH THING AS A BAD QUESTION?

The imagination question is by far the most common question I bump into when leading people into listening prayer. I wish I could say that God's voice is always unmistakable. But that's not usually the case. When the Lord begins to speak to my heart, there is almost always room to wonder if it was "just me, making it up." Even the most profound messages from heaven seem to beg the question, "Was that God... *or just my imagination?*"

Because I was hearing the imagination question so often, I began to present it directly to the Lord, hoping to provoke a response. What I heard, and offer to you for testing, was that *it is an impossible and deceptive question.* I've learned the hard way that certain questions trip us up just by asking them. By considering them, we involuntarily and automatically open the door to one deception or another. For example, when we ask "what if" questions, we unknowingly introduce a flood of fear into our minds. Or when we make "if only" statements, we open ourselves to chains of regret. So it is with the question, "Was that just me?" I believe that even asking the question leads us unwittingly into serious spiritual potholes. Read on... but watch your step!

Conversation-Killer

The Spirit of God is constantly trying to enter into conversations with our soul, the goal of which is to fill us with faith and truth and to enter into relationship with us. Meanwhile, the flesh is bombarding the soul with distractions and trying to resist such conversations with God, shutting them down with doubt and fear and selfishness. The goal of the flesh is independence from God—absolute autonomy from God's fatherly love and influence.

When God begins to speak to us, the flesh and the spirit both present the soul with questions in keeping with their agendas. The flesh asks, "Was that just me?" It's a question subtly designed to reinforce independence, introduce doubt, and end the conversation immediately. When you ask that question, consider what happens to the word God has spoken: It is snatched away before it can become a conversation. Alternatively, the spirit asks, "Is it true?" Because God is

Spirit, and God's Spirit always speaks truth, and God's children have the Spirit within them, whether you hear the Father from above or the Spirit from within, he is the ultimate source of all truth (by which I mean not merely facts, but truth that leads to personal growth). When you ask either question, "Was that just me?" or "Was that truth?" take note of what each question does to your faith level and your ability to receive truth.

Consider the parable of the Sower and the seed:

> "A farmer went out to sow his seed. As he was scattering the seed, some fell along the path, and the birds came and ate it up. Some fell on rocky places, where it did not have much soil. It sprang up quickly, because the soil was shallow. But when the sun came up, the plants were scorched, and they withered because they had no root. Other seed fell among thorns, which grew up and choked the plants. Still other seed fell on good soil, where it produced a crop--a hundred, sixty or thirty times what was sown. He who has ears, let him hear."
>
> "Listen then to what the parable of the sower means: when anyone hears the message about the kingdom and does not understand it, the evil one comes and snatches away what was sown in his heart. This is the seed sown along the path. The one who received the seed that fell on rocky places is the man who hears the word and at once receives it with joy. But since he has no root, he lasts only a short time. When trouble or persecution comes because of the word, he quickly falls away. The one who received the seed that fell among the thorns is the man who hears the word, but the worries of this life and the deceitfulness of wealth choke it, making it unfruitful. But the one who received the seed that fell on good soil is the man who hears the word and understands it. He produces a crop, yielding a hundred, sixty or thirty times what was sown." (Matthew 13:3–9, 18–23)

The seed is the word of God. The soil is your heart. When God speaks a word to your heart, the crux of the parable is: "What happens to the seed?" The parable gives us four scenarios.

First and most often, when I ask, "Is that just me?" the enemy snatches away God's words like the crows snatch away the seed. It's gone before it can even germinate. Such a question is really an accusation: "That was just you. You're just making this up. It's just your imagination. You don't hear God. Other people might, but you can't." The question makes us prone to habitually discarding the Spirit's blessings and promises into the "imagination bin." Doubt! And the word is gone, the conversation is over, the fruit never comes. If I "just made it up," I will never act on it, water it, test it or share it. It's just gone.

The Neutral Zone?

Second, "Was that just me?" is sometimes darker than mere doubt. Like the stony ground, it represents defiance and a demand for autonomy from God. It is really an assertion, "I can do what I like. I am independent of either God or the enemy. I can be good and wise and right aside from either influence."

Thus, we create a false model in which we have three potential sources of input: God, the devil, and a neutral third voice called the imagination or "just me." We wrongly assume that we act independently of either the kingdom of light or the kingdom of darkness. Such a mental neutral zone appears nowhere on the New Testament map. Paul suggests throughout Romans 8 that our mind is always focused on and flowing with either God's Spirit or our fallen nature, aligning its loyalties to one kingdom or the other. Even the Old Testament prophets who were accused of speaking from their "own imaginations" were in direct opposition to God, leading his people astray.

> The word of the LORD came to [Ezekiel]: "Son of man, prophesy against the prophets of Israel who are now prophesying. Say to those who prophesy out of *their own imagination*: 'Hear the word of the LORD! This is what the Sovereign LORD says: Woe to the foolish prophets who *follow their own spirit* and have seen nothing!... Their visions are false and their divinations a lie. They say, "The LORD declares," when the LORD has not sent them; yet they expect their words to be fulfilled. Have you not seen false visions and uttered lying divinations when you say, "The LORD declares," though I have not spoken? Therefore this is what the Sovereign LORD says: "Because of your false words and lying visions, I am against you, declares the Sovereign LORD. (Ezekiel 13:1–3, 6–8)

Note the synonyms in this passage for "their own imagination." They include "their own spirit," "false visions," "lying divinations," "false words," and "lying visions." Rather than being neutral, an imagination that is truly independent of God would be rebellious, deceitful, and wicked—verifiably so.

The irony is that a purely independent heart is the very essence of the flesh. It is the same delusion that Adam and Eve succumbed to in the Garden of Eden. To act independently of God is to fall. Apart from repentance, the seed of the word is burned up when it lands on such a heart.

Third, the cares of this world come and choke out the word. We hear an initial answer, but we're too distracted by the demands of life, too busy to listen or take time to respond. We may rush in for an answer from God, but having received an answer we don't enter into conversation. Or our flesh may supply a standard answer, even from Scripture, just to bring things to a quick close. The word, which was meant as an entry point into relationship, is soon strangled by our schedules.

Finally, the good soil represents the heart that asks a better question, "Is that true?" If I hear a word that might be from God, I begin to engage the word, weigh the word, and start a conversation with God around that word. As I acknowledge the truth of that word, I conclude that it originated in God. I begin to lean on it and act on it. The seed springs to life and grows into a fruitful plant.

If you are asking, "Why don't I hear God?" go to the parable. The Sower is sowing his word in you. The question is, "What's happening to his seed?" When God plants a seed, which question are you asking? The proverb, "There's no such thing as a bad question" is absolutely false, for our questions themselves arise from either the flesh or the Spirit. Our questions are either doubt-filled or faith-filled. They either lead to conversation or they cut it off. Each question is subversive—one subtly lures you away from God, the other subtly woos you to him.

Impossible to Tell?

Another pothole in the "just my imagination" model is that it despairs of distinguishing God's voice from our own thoughts. We become agnostic about hearing the Lord, because the question makes it seem impossible to confirm whether it's him or "just me." How opposite this is to Jesus' promise that his sheep would discern his voice from the others! It leaves us shrugging in indecision, out of step with John's assertion that we can test and know which spirits come from God.

Either/Or?

In asking "Was that God or my imagination," we also inadvertently set God's voice and our imagination at odds, as if we were restricted to an either/or choice of opposing categories. It's a little like pointing to the ocean and asking, "Is that water or is that blue?" In truth, the answer to "was that God or my imagination?" is frequently *yes*—not either/or but *both/and.* Your imagination provides a stage upon which God acts—a venue for the mind of Christ (1 Corinthians 2:16). Your spirit has become one with God's Spirit (1 Corinthians 6:17). Is it any wonder that telling them apart can be tricky?

My point is that it's never *just* you. In the context of imagination, God's Spirit and mine are both engaged, agreeing and conversing. This is not to say that when your spirit becomes one with God's Spirit you no longer have identity. Your personality and humanity do not dissolve into nothingness in the godhead (as in the eastern religions). You don't become God or identical to God. Rather, His Spirit fills your spirit. They unite to share the fundamental qualities of truth and goodness. They enter a beautiful love-union of agreement while remaining individuated so that a personal conversation might continue.

Just God?

Just as I have urged the reader to believe that it's never "just you," so now I remind you as prophets that it's never "just God." We hear that claim a lot. Prophets are occasionally overwhelmed by the weight of the prophetic anointing, or they hear God's voice clearly and urgently, or they find the message accompanied with powerful ecstatic manifestations. When this happens, they might believe that they are receiving pure revelation. They may assume that their own faculties are completely suspended and that the Holy Spirit's word at that point needs no testing--just obeying--and that immediately. They are sometimes even offended if the pastor treats it as any other word that needs testing, or as if it were of no greater importance than the still small voice.

Let's hear the wisdom of A.J. Heschel, in his brilliant work on the prophets:

> The prophet is a person, not a microphone. He is endowed with a mission, with the power of a word not his own that accounts for his greatness—but also with temperament, concern, character, and individuality. As there was no resisting the impact of divine inspiration, so at times there was no resisting the vortex of his own temperament. The word of God reverberated in the voice of man.
>
> The prophet's task is to convey a divine view, yet as a person he *is* a point of view. He speaks from the perspective of God as perceived from the perspective of his own situation.[1]

God not only speaks through the grid of your humanity, he is also quite thrilled to do so. He unashamedly clothes his word with your personality, your limitations, and your subjective nature. We should not esteem any word, however powerfully packaged, as being above Paul's mandate to test all things. Nor should we underestimate the power of a word heard in quietness and spoken gently. We act as prophets some of the time. But we live as people all of the time. Let's respect that.

THE IMAGINATION SCREEN

But if your imagination is *not* simply a third, neutral voice, then what is it? How does it work? How are you to use it? What role does it play? What follows is an alternative model of the imagination that directs us towards an older but far superior question to ask God and ourselves when we're listening.

I offer my model of the imagination as a picture that I believe God progressively gave me during listening prayer. I present it for you to weigh for yourself using the tools provided in the previous chapter.

Your Imagination

1. IMAGINATION IS NOT A VOICE
It is more like a *screen* upon which the mind projects and ponders images.

2. THE SOUL
is like a *projector* that loads and sends images to the screen.

3. THE FLESH & THE SPIRIT
are the *films* that compete to fill the soul with thoughts and images.

4. THE WILL
is like the *projectionist* who chooses what will be showing.

1. The Imagination

The imagination is like a screen upon which the mind projects images.

This model does not see the imagination as a voice at all but rather a screen upon which the soul (or mind) projects and ponders images. My mind "uses my imagination," as a visual venue for observing that which is coming from, through, or to my mind. The question is *not*, "Was that *just* my imagination?" or "*just* my mind?" Instead, we ask, "What is on my imagination right now? From where or who is it coming?" Again, we test the source, the content, and the fruit of what we see and hear. We ask, "Is it true? Is it good? Shall I engage those thoughts or dismiss them?"

2. The Soul

The soul is like a projector that sends images to the screen.

The soul is our essential self—our sense of "I" (the mind, will, and emotions). With my soul, I think, feel, and choose. Like a projector, the soul is filled with thoughts and images which it projects onto the imagination-screen.

As it does, realize also that the soul-projector may have a cracked, dirty, or warped lens that distorts the images we see. The cracks could represent personal wounds or trauma in our lives that affect our inner vision. The dirt represents the defiling effects of the world that cloud our thinking. Warping may signify lies and biases we take for granted. Add to this the cultural, familial, and/or religious filters that we slip over the lens of our minds. The renewal of the mind through the washing of the Word and the ministry of God's Spirit is necessary in the cleansing, repair, or replacement of that lens.

3. The Flesh and the Spirit

The flesh and the spirit are the films or sources of all onscreen images.

Two sources continually compete for control of the projector: Our *spirit* (or heart)—in concert with God's Spirit—struggles against our *flesh* (or ego)—in cahoots with the world and the devil. The spirit and the flesh each want to fill the soul with their messages and so influence the soul in one direction or another.

According to Paul in Romans 8:5–9, there are no neutral films on the market. The "films" we project onto our imagination screen are either "of the spirit" or "of the flesh."

> Those who live according to the sinful nature [flesh] have
> their minds set on what that nature desires; but those who
> live in accordance with the Spirit have their minds set on
> what the Spirit desires. The mind of sinful man is death,
> but the mind controlled by the Spirit is life and peace; the
> sinful mind is hostile to God. It does not submit to God's
> law, nor can it do so. Those controlled by the sinful nature
> cannot please God. You, however, are controlled not by the
> sinful nature but by the Spirit, if the Spirit of God lives in
> you." (Romans 8:5–9)

The terms "flesh" and "spirit" have some modern equivalents. Paul's use
of "spirit" is very similar to psychologist Carl Jung's use of "Self" (with a
capital S) or pop psychology's "authentic self." On the other hand, Paul's
use of "flesh" varies—it can mean our body, our humanity, our selfish
desires, or our fallen nature. In the preceding passage, the "flesh" corresponds roughly with modern terms like "ego" or "self" (with a small s),
as in "selfish."

The films of the spirit are in sync with the voice of the Heavenly
Father, the Good Shepherd, and the Spirit of God. The films of the flesh
will always conform to and promote the lying messages of the world,
the fallen nature, and the devil. While the Spirit rolls out the autho-
rized truth, the flesh merely delivers a poorly pirated copy, a deceptive
but identifiable counterfeit.

4. The Will

The will is the projectionist that chooses what will be showing.

Please don't mistake my description of the imagination for passivity. It
is not as though we are automatons that sit idly and helplessly watching internal movies. The projectionist in this scenario is our will. Our
will is the God-given ability of our hearts to choose. We can choose
whether or not to use our imaginations: "Shall I turn on the projector?"
We can choose what to set our minds on: "What film should I load and
watch?" We choose how we maintain our minds: "Does the lens need
work?" We choose whether or not our desires become actions: "Having
seen what's on the screen, shall I act on it?" We choose whether to
accept or decline God's invitations to trust and obey. Ultimately, the
will-projectionist chooses whether to use the imagination in the service
of the flesh or in submission to the Spirit. We choose which influence to
attend and engage, and with which source we will forge an alliance.

THE BETTER QUESTION:
IS THAT THE SPIRIT OR THE FLESH?

In the above model, the question, "Is that God or just my imagination?" becomes irrelevant, even nonsensical. As I gaze at the imagination screen, I am now equipped with a question that can be answered with a greater degree of confidence: "Is this the voice of the flesh or the voice of the Spirit?"[2] Even where there is mixture of messages (and there usually is), I can begin an informed, deliberate sifting process that leads me to an understanding of the truth: Spirit or flesh? Shepherd or stranger? Christ assures us: you *can* and *will* know (John 10:1–10). He never even considers a neutral third option; there *isn't* one. So much simpler!

By way of example, consider asking Jesus for a promise and hearing the answer, "I love you and will never leave you nor forsake you." Using the former question, "Was that God or my imagination?" you might conclude that it is impossible to know. Perhaps you just thought it up yourself in order to pat yourself on the back. Or perhaps it really was a message of comfort from the Lord specific to your situation. You just don't know for sure. And if you aren't sure, it's difficult to receive that truth wholeheartedly. But by asking our latter question, "Did that sound like the flesh or the Spirit?" the answer is easy. The message becomes easy to test and confirm, and you are inclined to receive it into your heart with faith.

So when you hear what you think is God's voice, is it *in* your imagination? Of course! Is it *in* your mind? Absolutely! You can determine with confidence whether the source is the Spirit or the flesh by simply testing what you see or hear on the screen.

Checking the Scriptures

Confirming this model, Paul teaches that neither the imagination nor the mind can produce a single independent, spiritual thought or insight. All revelation is produced by God's Spirit in our spirits—downloaded from the mind of Christ into our minds.

> "No eye has seen, no ear has heard, no mind has *conceived* [*imagined*-NASB] what God has prepared for those who love him"—but *God has revealed it to us by his Spirit*. The Spirit searches all things, even the deep things of God. For who among men knows the thoughts of a man except the man's spirit within him? In the same way no one knows the thoughts of God except the Spirit of God. *We have not*

received the spirit of the world but the Spirit who is from God, that we may understand what God has freely given us.

This is what we speak, not in words taught us by human wisdom but in words *taught by the Spirit,* expressing spiritual truths in spiritual words. The man without the Spirit does not accept the things that come from the Spirit of God, for they are foolishness to him, and he cannot understand them, because they are *spiritually discerned.* The spiritual man makes judgments about all things, but he himself is not subject to any man's judgment: "For who has known *the mind of the Lord* that he may instruct him?" *But we have the mind of Christ.* (1 Corinthians 2:9–16)

USING YOUR IMAGINATION: FOR FLESH OR SPIRIT?

Based on the imagination-screen model and the flesh/spirit question, let's unpack the uses of the imagination. In this sense, the imagination is the God-given ability of our hearts to:

*   Paint inner pictures
*   See through inner windows
*   Enter through inner doorways

I. PAINTING INNER PICTURES

We call the heart's ability to paint inner pictures "active" imagination. We use our active imagination to create mental images on the canvas of our heart. We picture things, such as visions or images.

A. Spiritual Pictures

When we walk in the Spirit, we use our active imagination creatively and recreatively, for meditation, and for intercession.

1. Creation

Creativity is a mark of the Creator's image in us. Artists, musicians, writers, dancers, discoverers, and inventors tap into and extend God's ongoing work of creation, whether they recognize him in it or not. While the creative talents can be distorted and misused, their root source is the Divine Artist and Inventor. Far from being a neutral function, human creativity is the imitation of God. Generally the creative process grows and flows rather naturally. But at other times, the "inspiration"—the breath of God—is infused much more conspicuously. This can range all the way from prophetic dance to having a vision that solves a scientific puzzle.

Case in Point: Nicola Tesla

Nicola Tesla (1856–1943) was Yugoslavia's counterpart to the inventors Bell, Edison, and Westinghouse. The son of an Orthodox priest, Tesla was a great industrial scientist and inventor who was the first to patent the "wireless telegraph" (radio) and to discover the principle of the rotating magnetic field. From this foundation, he created many alternating-current devices as well as the Tesla coil.[3] Needless to say, his life had a global impact. The utilization of AC (alternating current) power was his "baby." One biographer recounts one of Tesla's moments of creative inspiration.

> In 1882, while walking with a companion and reciting poetry in a Budapest park at sunset, Tesla suddenly froze into a rigid trance-like state. To his friend's dismay, Tesla soon began to speak of an inner vision: "Watch me. Watch me reverse it," he said, over and over again, in a voice bubbling with enthusiasm. The friend thought he was ill; but the great inventor later explained that he was actually "seeing" an alternating-current motor in operation: "I have solved the problem. Can't you see it right here in front of me, running almost silently?"... Over the next few months, he continued to elaborate upon the detailed blueprints in his mind, where they remained stored for six years until he was able to put them into practical application.[4]

If I had to make an educated guess, I would say that Tesla was seeing a vision from God and repeating the voice of God. Others might write it off as a flash of creative, albeit eccentric, genius. My point is that the two explanations are not at all in conflict. Spiritual epiphanies and human creativity are both examples of an imagination tuned in to the Creator's wavelength. Spirituality is creative; creativity is spiritual. Imagination provides the venue for both.

2. Recreation

Recreation is often seen as unspiritual or sub-spiritual. I suppose we picked this notion up from any of a number of movements that confused "the flesh" as fallen nature with "the flesh" as physical constitution. Assuming both versions of the flesh are evil, the Gnostics, ascetics, and puritans exemplify groups that debased human physicality in various ways. From there, we developed a sacred/secular split whereby all things not directly "spiritual" in the church, worship or ministry sense were relegated to secondary importance. Physical and mental recreation, including imaginative exercises, lost their place in nurturing the soul. Or rather, we dismissed God from his place in those activities, as if he were somehow unconcerned and uninvolved in our recreational life.

However, if we believe that the presence of God is to be experienced in all things, why not in recreation as well? I would argue that the renewal of body, mind, and spirit is literally re-creative. When we use the imagination "recreatively" we mimic God's restorative processes. Just as God uses the rain to wash pollution and dust from the atmosphere, he uses recreation to cleanse our minds from accumulated emotional and mental smog. Just as God restores the fertility of farmland when we give the soil an occasional "time out," he uses our recreational recesses to restore our productivity and efficiency. The imagination is a great help in this process. From seeing "checkmate in six moves" to picturing Tolkien's epic battles, the Spirit can use our imagination as a vehicle with which to refresh us.

3. Meditation

Meditation is an active use of the imagination wherein we picture and ponder spiritual truth. When we purposely use our minds to dwell on some aspect of God, Christ, or his Word, we are meditating. When I picture the Lord during meditation, I am not necessarily *beholding* him in the strict sense of God revealing himself (though it is meant to transition into that). My mind is painting the picture and thinking the thoughts, but this is still a spiritual and Spirit-filled activity. It is not merely a neutral "just me" activity. God is involved.

Isaiah 26:3 counsels us that God will keep in perfect peace those whose minds are fixed on him, because they trust in him. Oswald Chambers encourages this use of the mind in meditation: "Is your imagination stayed on him or is it starved? It is no use waiting for God to come; you must put your imagination away from the face of idols and deliberately turn your imagination to God... look unto him and be saved."[5]

As we meditate on God, he is watching and listening, inspiring and responding. His Spirit prods my spirit to initiate the picture painting that sows faith-seeds, which do indeed sprout.

◀)) *Tuning In* • • • • • • • • •

A classic meditation exercise used by mystics of all creeds is to picture God's light giving you a shower. In the evening, I like to imagine the light of God shining on me, penetrating and cleansing my heart. I actively receive his healing light into my soul. As I picture this, I thank God for washing away shadows of stress or sin. I invite you to use this exercise as a means to embracing this Scriptural truth.

> God is light; in him there is no darkness at all. If we claim to have fellowship with him yet walk in the darkness, we lie and do not live by the truth. But if we walk in the light, as he is in the light, we have fellowship with one another, and the blood of Jesus, his Son, purifies us from all sin. (1 John 1:5–7)

As you practice this, realize that real cleansing light is permeating your soul. Thank God that real peace is displacing the shadows. Expect real transformation in your heart and mind as you submit to his light-showers.

4. Intercession

Intercession takes active meditation a step further by picturing the person we are praying for and presenting that picture to God.

When I use my imagination to intercede for friends, I picture myself walking them to Jesus and asking him for mercy. If I see Jesus begin to act upon them in some way, I have again moved from intercession into revelation. I have presented my request in picture form. Then I also see God's answer in picture form. The point is that this method of prayer begins by using the active imagination as a launching pad, and then God brings about the lift off.

Marriage Altar Intercession

I consider myself to be a very weak marriage counsellor. But as a pastor, I am occasionally required to meet with struggling couples. Usually those meetings go well, but I'm often disappointed by the lack of bliss that will follow. Frankly, I see more "success" through a simple imaginative-intercession exercise that I do in my marriage-coaching sessions.

For example, a wonderful Christian couple that I love very much was struggling with their relationship. Though they both love God, after over twenty years, their marital life had crumbled into a separation. To tell the truth, it looked hopeless to me. The only truly helpful role I played was in prayer. I imagined bringing them each by the hand to a marriage altar where Christ was waiting for them. I pictured them kneeling before him and asking for mercy. I told the Lord that only a miracle would save the marriage now. In that picture, I watched as Jesus reached out and laid a hand on each of their bowed heads. I recall him saying, "What God has joined together, let no one separate." Perhaps this was his answer! Or perhaps it was my request? In either case, I believe his Spirit and mine were in agreement about God's heart for the situation.

The couple attended our church the following Sunday, where they received a powerful confirmation of God's intentions. We did a high-risk corporate listening exercise in which everyone asked the Lord for a promise or blessing and then wrote it on a piece of paper. We gathered up the promises in baskets and laid hands on them, asking God to deliver the messages to their appropriate recipients. After the messages were handed out, the congregation testified to the stunning ways that God matched specific promises to deep needs. Specifically, the husband I had been praying for picked up the promise, "I will heal your marriage. Love, God."

Within a week, the couple was living together again. Although it was a bumpy road and took a few more miracles, by their next anniversary, God had restored their marriage. Yes, their own choices were involved, but those choices were informed by God's voice and strengthened by the many that prayed.

◀)) *Tuning In* • • • • • • • • •

- Ask the Lord whom you should picture before him today. Ask him where he would like to meet that person.
- Picture yourself taking that person to meet God there. Present that person to the Lord. Tell the Lord why you are burdened for that person and ask for his help.
- Watch what Jesus does. Bless what he is doing and ask for more. Stand in agreement with him in it. Pray that he will fulfill that picture in that person's life. In the days that follow, watch for confirmations that God is at work.

B. Fleshly Pictures

When we walk in the flesh, we can also abuse our active imagination.

Lusting or Coveting

The Scriptures explain the trouble with these uses of the imagination:

> Do not love the world or anything in the world. If anyone loves the world, the love of the Father is not in him. For everything in the world—the cravings of sinful man, the lust of his eyes and the boasting of what he has and does—comes not from the Father but from the world. The world and its desires pass away, but the man who does the will of God lives forever. (1 John 2:15–17)

While John contends that using the active imagination to wish for what you cannot or should not have is *worthless,* Jesus makes it clear that it is also far from *harmless.*

> "You have heard that it was said, 'Do not commit adultery.' But I tell you that anyone who looks at a woman lustfully has already committed adultery with her *in his heart.* If your right eye causes you to sin, gouge it out and throw it away. It is better for you to lose one part of your body than for your whole body to be thrown into hell." (Matthew 5: 27–29)

Apparently, God's opinion is that deeds done in the heart (with the imagination) are real, spiritually significant actions. The idea that nobody gets hurt when I fantasize murderous or adulterous thoughts is a lie. I suspect that just as the thoughts of prayerful imagination can heal a marriage or cleanse a heart, so too the thoughts of a renegade imagination have the power to curse or defile a third party. At the very least, Jesus reveals that the fleshly imagination can curse or defile the one using it.

The scariest prophetic word I ever received was a serious warning from a godly friend. He said, "You will receive the desires of your heart—good or evil." his point was that I must deal with fleshly desires, because they have a way of growing into schemes and schemes tend to find fulfillment as acts. We do well to reserve our active imaginations for the work of the Spirit rather than the flesh.

II. SEEING THROUGH INNER WINDOWS

We call the heart's ability to see through inner windows "passive" or "higher" imagination. At this level, we use the imagination to *see, hear* and *sense* invisible realities through the windows of our heart.

We move beyond active picturing (visualizing) into watchfully perceiving unseen things. In passive imagination, our meditation ceases to be a picture and becomes an open window through which we peer out into the spiritual realms. Our heart-eyes are opened: what was a picture frame is now a window frame. What we see through that window is not our creation at all but a peek into the invisible world of the Spirit.

A. Spiritual Windows

When we walk in the Spirit, we use passive imagination to behold Christ, receive revelation, and discern spiritual reality.

1. Beholding Jesus

There is a subtle difference between picturing Jesus and beholding him. When I picture him with my active imagination, I have no doubt that this is a Spirit-filled, Spirit-empowered ability. It is an effective act of meditation whereby I see with the eyes of faith what I believe God has called me to imagine. While it is not "just me," neither is it "just him." I am looking for a deeper experience in which my meditation transitions to his revelation: my image of him is replaced by his image of himself. He is showing himself, or some aspect of himself, to me, just like he promised (John 14:21).

2. Receiving Revelation

Through the passive imagination, we also receive messages in the form of dreams and visions. With the active imagination, the Spirit helps us paint pictures for God to which he responds. The passive imagination now sees and receives his response.

Leanne Payne calls this the "true imagination" by which "we creaturely receivers 'see' and 'hear' the inaudible, the invisible. It involves our loving and receiving from God, and from all that he has made and calls good."[6] Like Tesla, we may hear God say, "Now watch! Watch me reverse it!" The current of spiritual images now flow back to us, informing us of God's heart and inviting us to receive his life. What may have previously been benign information to the mind now comes as life-changing, spiritual power for the heart.

3. Discerning the Spiritual Reality

Through this window, we not only behold the Lord; we are also awakened to spiritual activity around us. God allows us to see, hear, and sense the invisible planes that exist behind this world. He may tune us in to others' thoughts, emotions or spiritual states. Or he may make us aware of the presence of angels, demons or his own Spirit in our world, whether intuitively or through our physical eyes.

B. Fleshly Windows

When we walk in the flesh, we may use passive imagination to behold fantasies, delusions, and deceptions. Or we may actually discern genuine spiritual reality, albeit through the filtered lenses of psychic or demonic means.

1. Fantasies, Illusions, and Deceptions

By this I mean that the flesh will allow us to escape into dangerous dream worlds. Rather than refreshment or recreation, these fantasies capture us in delusion and lure us away from reality. It's good to test the effects of the romance or fantasy genres on our minds. It's one thing if they stir our imaginations to face life, marriage, and spirituality in a creative and constructive way. But if they cause dissatisfaction, discontent, fear, paranoia, escapism or distraction from life in this world and in God's kingdom, you're likely gazing through the wrong spiritual window.

2. Psychic or Demonic Discernment

Just because something is real or it works does not guarantee that it's also good. Many occult and New Age methods work: they *do* open our eyes to spiritual reality. Whether by psychic or demonic power, the windows of our imagination can reveal the invisible world. Yet God has forbidden many of them: divination, sorcery, use of mediums (Leviticus 19), interpreting omens, witchcraft, casting spells, necromancy (Deuteronomy 18). When we really need revelation, the Lord promises to deliver it to us himself or through his prophets (Deuteronomy 18:15). But using the "wrong windows," even to see the very same things that God will show us, is spiritually illegal. Why is that?

First, God's windows are pure. Occult and psychic windows may include distorted panes that make lies seem true and evil seem good. Furthermore, they are not always accurate (Deuteronomy 18:22), because they aren't committed to the author of truth.

Second, using God's window of revelation leads to greater spiritual freedom. Using alternative windows comes with a price; fear, control, and bondage are normally part of the package. It has a defiling effect on us (Leviticus 19:31), leaving us "slimed" through their use.

Third, there is a loyalty issue. Even if the first two reasons were set aside—if you were guaranteed truth and power by using a spiritual window other than God's—the master of that window (whether the self or a spirit) ultimately demands and gets your loyalty. God is not into sharing his Lordship. He knows that no one can serve two masters. Even if your psychic or astrologer "got it right," God neither appreciates nor tolerates his gospel truth being confirmed by demons (Mark 3: 11–12) or psychics (Acts 16:16–17).

Perils of the Psychic Window

Lois incurred all three of these costs that come from peering through the wrong window. Although she was a Christian, she visited a psychic about ten years ago because of fear of the future and the unknown. The psychic accurately reported some details of Lois's personal history and correctly perceived that she had two children. The psychic foresaw that Lois would have a third child and then be divorced by her husband. Both of these predictions were eventually fulfilled. She also added that one of her three children would die as a child.

Terrified, Lois made some gruesome decisions. When she became pregnant, she decided that if one of her children were to die, she hoped it would be the youngest, because she had not yet bonded to it. She also chose to deliberately *not* form a mother-child bond with this new baby. She thought that if she lost it, it might not be as painful. The child was born without a hitch, and eventually won his mother's heart. So instead of coping with her fears by pushing the little boy away, now she vowed to protect it from the death she feared was coming. Rather than picking up the shield of faith, she became paranoid of every possible mishap and extremely controlling of the little fellow's every move. He became both clingy and abusive to his mother. The psychic's prediction functioned as a curse—first over the child's alleged death, but now also every day of his young life.

After a decade of this, Lois is asking Jesus to break every curse, nullify the psychic's prediction, and deliver her from all fear of evil. She is choosing faith over fear, trusting the Lord rather than her psychic.

Sidebar to Christian Prophets

I have observed too many "prophets" who act as psychics. They are in the habit of attempting to access others' minds or other realms independently of God's leadership. The Christian prophet who tries to scan other people and "read their mail" rather than hearing God's diagnosis is out of line. The Christian use of psychic power is *not* prophetic. It is a horizontal version of discernment, complete with the distorted lenses that come from reading man's heart rather than God's. These ways are fleshly. If God won't tell you what you need to know, moving on to Plan B and discerning it for yourself is folly. A simple test that keeps me honest is the question, "Right now, am I reading this person's heart or am I reading God's heart?" This helps me point my spiritual satellite dish in the right direction.

III. ENTERING INNER DOORWAYS

The third use of our imagination moves another step past painting internal pictures or peering through spiritual windows. At this level, we actually step through the internal doorway of our hearts into spiritual meeting places with God. I call the heart's ability to enter inner doorways "interactive imagination." We "penetrate" unseen places to commune with the living God.

A. Spiritual Doorways

When we walk in the Spirit, we use our interactive imagination to open only one door and to follow only one Shepherd, to follow him wherever he goes!

Only One Gate, Only One Shepherd

We need to review John 10 when it comes to entering spiritual doors. Christ said,

> "I tell you the truth, *the man who does not enter the sheep pen by the gate, but climbs in by some other way, is a thief and a robber. The man who enters by the gate is the shepherd of his sheep.* The watchman opens the gate for him, and the sheep listen to his voice. He calls his own sheep by name and leads them out. When he has brought out all his own, he goes on ahead of them, and his sheep follow him because they know his voice. But they will never follow a

stranger; in fact, they will run away from him because they do not recognize a stranger's voice." Jesus used this figure of speech, but they did not understand what he was telling them. Therefore Jesus said again, "I tell you the truth, *I am the gate for the sheep.* All who ever came before me were thieves and robbers, but the sheep did not listen to them. *I am the gate; whoever enters through me will be saved. He will come in and go out, and find pasture.*" (John 10:1–9)

This passage speaks about our doorway into spiritual pastures. There is only one legitimate entryway and the sign over that door reads "Jesus Christ." Accessing spiritual realms through other means is considered break-and-entry. People who do so are labelled as thieves. Jesus is making a very exclusive claim here. He's not making room for "many paths" or other gurus. He presents himself as the only Christ and the only way to God (John 14:6; Acts 4:12). Many are not happy about such a narrow door (Luke 13:24). Sometimes I'm not happy about it either. It sounds offensive and fundamentalist (shudder!).

But Jesus was compelled to tell the truth, and with it, the good news: *his* door is unlocked. When you knock, it opens. His door doesn't require us to go through religious rituals or attain a certain level of spiritual sophistication before we can enter. His door is unlocked to the disabled, the children, the prodigals, and the poor. The very reason that Jesus takes his stand as the only true door is precisely so that you will *not* be locked out or need to jump through endless hoops. If you find another door to the spiritual world, read the fine print! There is always a cover charge. Jesus' door stands wide open between our hearts and the throne room of God (Revelation 3:20—4:2). His door grants our hearts permanent access to heavenly meeting places where God reigns and rules (Ephesians 2:6; Hebrews 10:20). My chapter on "the Meeting Place" will clarify how we use our interactive imaginations to step over the spiritual threshold into these meetings with him.

Follow Him Wherever He Goes

Revelation 14:4 describes a heavenly company that follow the Lamb wherever he goes. What an adventure! The spiritual journeys he takes his disciples on totally ruin the false image of God as a "party-pooper." Imagine Ezekiel's wild ride in the Spirit:

In the sixth year, in the sixth month on the fifth day, while I was sitting in my house and the elders of Judah were sitting before me, the hand of the Sovereign LORD came upon me there.

I looked, and I saw a figure like that of a man. From what appeared to be his waist down he was like fire, and from there up his appearance was as bright as glowing metal. He stretched out what looked like a hand and took me by the hair of my head. The Spirit lifted me up between earth and heaven and in visions of God he took me to Jerusalem, to the entrance to the north gate of the inner court, where the idol that provokes to jealousy stood.

And there before me was the glory of the God of Israel, as in the vision I had seen in the plain. (Ezekiel 8:1–4)

Philip the evangelist was also transported, body and all, when the Holy Spirit opted to save him bus fare from Gaza to Azotus (Acts 8:38–39). Distance is irrelevant when one passes through spiritual portals in prayer. Of course, such phenomena were restricted to the characters and events of Scripture. Or were they?

Mary of Agreda

Mary of Agreda was a Spanish nun whose passion was intercession.[7] Each day she entered her prayer cell, where she would plead for the souls of the Native people of the American southwest. So great was her burden for the aboriginal people that God took note. In her spirit she would "go" to what are now Texas and New Mexico. She would meet various tribes there, talking about Jesus to those who had never heard of him before. Reports began to come to Fray Alonzo de Benavides, father-custodian of New Mexico, of a "woman in blue" who would miraculously appear to the First Nations people, proclaiming the kingdom of God. He decided to get to the bottom of this. Corresponding with priests in Spain, he tracked down Maria de Jesus, now mother superior of St. Clare in Agreda. She admitted that she was indeed the woman in blue, sharing her faith among the Natives. He crossed the Atlantic to investigate. She was able to describe the clothing and customs of specific tribes by name and identify specific individuals among them. When he asked her where she learned to speak all the Indian languages, she replied, "I didn't. I simply spoke to them—and God let us understand one another." Mary of Agreda allegedly experienced over five hundred of these prayer trips over the course of a decade while never once physically leaving the four walls of her convent in Spain.

Stephen of the Wheelchair

I first met Stephen at the end of a renewal service. His care-worker, Anita, brought him forward for prayer. When Stephen was a boy, a drunk driver had hit him and his mother. His mother was killed instantly, and Stephen wound up in a wheelchair with very little use of his body. His speech is very difficult to decipher, proceeding at about five to ten words per minute. When he was presented before me, his halting speech revealed a depth of pain I cannot imagine. He asked, "I believe that God has a purpose for my life. But I am confined to this wheelchair. How shall I then live?" I was at a loss for words. No human wisdom can satisfy such a question. I looked to heaven for an answer. It came in the form of a question: "You've been in India in prayer, haven't you?" I asked. Stephen's eyes widened. A smile began to form. Another question came, "And in Africa—you've seen Africa in prayer, haven't you?" Now he was becoming radiant. He nodded, "Yes. I have roamed the earth in prayer. That is my purpose." Later, one of his care-workers shared with me that Stephen owns a copy of *Operation World*, a prayer manual that outlines in great detail the prayer needs of every nation on earth. He meticulously works his way through that book each day in his prayer time. While his body confines him, the Lord has released Stephen's spirit to roam the globe.

The invitation to follow Christ through his spiritual door is an awesome prospect to those who will jump through with both feet. But those who attempt to straddle the threshold will find his way lifeless.

B. Fleshly Doorways

When we walk in the flesh, we either leave the door shut completely or we open and enter forbidden doors. In the former case, modernism tells us there is no door and conservatism tells us to be afraid of every door. In the latter, a host of voices tell us that any door will do. Counterfeits to Ezekiel's experience beckon us, such as soul-travel or astral-projection. Many opt for the leadership of a spirit-guide who can escort them into those spiritual regions. I've seen too many things to be a skeptic and I've wasted too many years to remain tentative. On the other hand, I'm also not so foolish as to merrily waltz through just *any* door with *any* guide.

L.A. and the Big, Black Loogie

L.A. is a friend who used to practice New Age meditation and was able to set others up with a spirit guide. She would take people into an imaginary elevator, slowly descend ten spiritual levels using breathing techniques, and then open the doors to another plane. Once there, she would introduce her "clients" to their new spirit guide. She didn't tell me what happened after that, except that it was "trippy." This practice was an escape for her from the unpleasantness of the rest of her life.

When L.A. became a Christian, she received prayer from a fellow who knew God's voice. The man didn't know her at all, but the Lord showed him that she was held in spiritual slavery to a spirit guide that was systematically destroying her life. While it professed to give her reprieve from her troubles, it was in fact stirring them up. The minister led her in a prayer of renunciation and repentance. He commanded the spirit guide to release her and to go to the place that Jesus Christ had assigned it. L.A. began to cough, then choke, and then with a violent heave, spat out a large, tarry glob of reddish-black ... something. Disgusting! Whatever it was hit the wall and stuck there, apparently the sole physical manifestation of her now defunct spirit guide. Real doors, real spirits, real bondage, and real goo—messy proof that not just any door will do.

Another Trans-Atlantic Trip

I must follow up with a more uplifting story of prayer and the imagination. Kate is a godly intercessor who frequently steps through spiritual portals in prayer. One day as she sat in her favourite prayer chair, her thoughts were directed to a worship leader friend in Great Britain. She asked the Lord how to pray for him, and she was immediately taken in her spirit to see this friend. Her testimony is that she observed him pacing back and forth, preparing to lead worship but seemingly hesitant. She felt led to lay her hand on his chest and speak to his heart. In this vision-place, her hand sank right through his chest and heart, and came to rest on his spine. (Hey, I just got it: "backbone" is courage!) Then she said to him, "Go for it. Go for it. Go for it."

The following day, she e-mailed a general inquiry to her friend. She asked what God had been doing in his life but was careful to give no hint of her experience. He replied that on the previous day, he was preparing to lead worship in a conservative church, and he wasn't sure whether the Lord was giving him liberty to really "go for it." As he listened to the Lord, he felt an intense burning in his chest and heard an inner voice repeat the phrase "Go for it!" three times. Responding to that message, he led the congregation in a glorious night of freedom in worship.

In Moments of Doubt

Even knowing and experiencing these types of testimonies has not made me immune to doubts or misunderstandings. In those times, the words of George MacDonald strengthen my faith:

> In moments of doubt I cry,
> "Could God himself create such lovely things as I dreamed?"
> "Whence then came thy dream?" answers Hope.
> "Out of my dark self, into the light of my consciousness."
> "But whence first into thy dark self?" rejoins Hope.
> "My brain was its mother, and the fever in my blood its father."
> "Say rather," suggests Hope, "thy brain was the violin whence it issued, and the fever in thy blood the bow that drew it forth. But who made the violin? And who guided the bow across its strings?... Man dreams and desires; God broods and wills and quickens."[8]

The Dance

On that note, I invite you now to "the dance." Meeting Jesus is more than picturing him on a canvas or seeing him through a window. It is a fully interactive meeting, like a dance where he leads and we follow, where he acts and we respond. The Lord of the Dance says, "Come; step with me through my door. Join me in the Meeting Place of your heart."

Part II

Encountering God: The Meeting Place of Your Heart

· · · · · 5 · · · · ·

The Meeting Place

"Where have you been, my son? Where have you tarried so long? Where have you traveled? What have you been seeking in the world? Happiness? And where should you have sought it but in God? And where should you have sought God but in his temple? And what is the temple of the living God but the living temple that he has prepared for himself, your own heart? I have watched, my son, while you wandered, but I did not want to see you stray any longer. I have led you to myself by leading you into yourself, for here I have chosen a palace for my dwelling."[1]

- John Amos Comenius, *The Labyrinth*

THE CAVE

I sat in the cave, exhausted. Nothing left to give. Nothing left to pray. The little campfire continued to crackle, as always. Shadows danced on the walls where the bard had scrawled a few paintings. I stared over the flames and out into the night, thankful for shelter from the wind-driven drizzle. Sometimes Jesus would come and sit close by. At times, his invisible presence would fill the cavern. Now something was different. The Ark of the Covenant had materialized. No one had carried it in—it just appeared one day without explanation. Weird. No matter, I was so tired that I just lay down beside it, drifting in and out of sleep. This was my place of reprieve from the pressures of people, ministry, and the whole external world.

This continued for weeks. All verbal prayer had given way to this internal, quiet vision. Prayer consisted of this silent resting by the Ark—worship, confession, and intercession had ceased. I began to wonder if this was fruitful, if it was even prayer at all. Perhaps I should have started writing prayer lists again. But I had no heart for that. Even my forays into reading Psalms ended with my forehead pasted to the pages of my Bible. All I knew was that weary dread would surrender to peace whenever I retreated to the cave in my heart where Christ and the Ark would manifest.

One afternoon, I was meeting with a handful of other pastors. One of them, a faith-healing evangelist full of faith and power, came bustling in. He was energized, if not ecstatic. Given my state, this was terrible news. He began ranting about their latest revival meeting where the "fire of God had fallen" on the service. He raved about how *everyone* in the meeting with a disease or illness had been healed and how *all* the demons had been driven out. His little testimony was fast escalating into a raging revival sermon. I thought I might die. I began to plead to the Lord silently, "Jesus, please help me not to judge this man. I really do want you to bless him. And I want the fire of God in our meetings too. I long to see people get saved, delivered, and healed. But Lord, when this guy describes it, he just tires me out. His package is so totally different than mine. Are we to be passed by because of that? I can't even pray anymore. *All I do is lie by the Ark in that stupid cave day after day*. I don't even know if it's real any more."

At that very moment, the raving prophet turned to me and spoke,

> I believe the Lord would say to you, "There has been a famine of hearing God in the land. But like Samuel in 1 Samuel chapter 3, you have been willing *to remain lying beside the Ark of my covenant*. You've made it your *resting place*. Therefore, you will witness me restore the voice of the Lord to my people."[2]

How does one respond to a word like that? It didn't suddenly recharge me. But it did send me back to the cave to rest by the ark. On my next prayer visit to that place in my heart, the ark somehow opened and out spilled thousands of pearls all over the floor. I asked the Lord, "What are those?"

"Pearls of understanding," he said.

"What shall I do with them," I wondered.

He replied, "Begin stringing them together."

In some way, this is what I'm hoping to accomplish in this chapter.

THE MEETING PLACE

The story of the cave is a personal example of how my prayer life has evolved. It has morphed from a one-way verbal communiqué to the "God-out-there" into a visual, internal meeting with the indwelling Spirit of Christ. In this chapter, we will examine prayer as an intimate meeting place with Jesus in the hope that you will understand what that means and how you can *and probably have* experienced it for yourself already.

By way of definition, we will describe a "place" as "somewhere— whether physical, historical, or spiritual—where we meet with Jesus to behold and be held." The bulk of this chapter is dedicated to unpacking that definition. You will probably find that, just as with listening prayer in chapter one, "the Meeting Place" is something you've already experienced. I hope to awaken a meeting place in you once again and call you to nurture this precious gift from the Lord.

I. A PLACE

I find it helpful as we begin our journey to think of prayer as a context, a venue or a place where we wait on God's presence and his voice. It doesn't get much more vivid than this:

> I come to the garden alone,
> while the dew is still on the roses,
> and the voice I hear, falling on my ear,
> the Son of God discloses.
>
> And he walks with me, and he talks with me,
> and he tells me I am his own,
> and the Joy we share, as we tarry there,
> none other has ever known.
>
> He speaks, and the sound of his voice
> is so sweet the birds hush their singing,
> and the melody that he gave to me
> within my heart is ringing,
>
> And he walks with me, and he talks with me,
> and he tells me I am his own,
> and the Joy we share as we tarry there,
> none other has ever known.

C. Austin Miles, 1912

Miles shares the meeting place vision that inspired this hymn. As he sat holding his Bible in a darkened room, he testifies,

> My hands were resting on the Bible while I stared at the light blue wall. As the light faded, I seemed to be standing at the entrance of a garden, looking down a gently winding

path, shaded by olive branches. A woman in white, with head bowed, hand clasping her throat, as if to choke back her sobs, walked slowly into the shadows. It was Mary. As she came to the tomb, upon which she placed her hand, she bent over to look in, and hurried away ... Mary reappeared; leaning her head upon her arm at the tomb, she wept. Turning herself, she saw Jesus standing, so did I.[3]

If such visions seem "out there" and ethereal to you, it will help if we anchor ourselves firmly to the Scriptures and to historical Christianity. But beware: if sages like Ezekiel, Isaiah, and John the Revelator seem safe, you may need to dust off your Bible.

A. Biblical Meeting Places

Those with an inherent trust in the Bible usually gain easiest access to a meeting place through biblical images, locations, and events.

1. Biblical Images

In practice, encountering God in biblical images is probably not new or unusual to you. Most Christians already have been to three common meeting places: Psalm 23, the Cross, and the throne. When you hear the reading of Psalm 23, do you ever find yourself in the green pastures, by the still waters, in the valley of the shadow of death, or at the table spread for you? Do you see the Good Shepherd with you, along with his rod or his staff?

Have you ever been at the Cross while singing, "At the Cross, at the Cross, where I first saw the light, and the burdens of my heart rolled away. *It was there* by faith *I received my sight* ..."? Perhaps you go there during the Lord's Supper as the Passion account is read. Do you see the soldiers, the women, the mockers, the thieves, and the crucified Christ? Where are you standing in that picture?

Or what of the Throne Room of God? It is virtually impossible to read the fourth and fifth chapters of Revelation without stepping into the scene. When singing "Holy, Holy, Holy," do you sense that you are present in the courts of the Lord, alongside the seraphim, the angels, the elders, and all the saints?

For those who struggle to find a meeting place with the Lord, you need to know that these common images count. I return to them repeatedly to receive peace from the Good Shepherd, to receive grace from the crucified Saviour or to worship the King on his throne.

2. Biblical Locations

Can you recall ten biblical places where our heroes in the faith met God—whether once or with regularity? Take a moment to jot them down. Pick one of those stories and try to remember as many details about it as you can. Where were they? Who was there? What action occurred? How did God appear? What reaction did he provoke? Did you picture the location? Did you behold the Lord in that place? If so, you've just taken another step into the Meeting Place.

The biblical locations you remember may have included any number of mountains (Moria, Sinai, Zion, the Mount of Transfiguration, etc.). There is also a series of meetings under a tree, from Abraham to Gideon to Nathanael. God also showed up frequently at worship centres including altars, tabernacles, and temples. At other times, wherever he happened to descend became "holy ground" requiring the removal of shoes. My favourite biblical meeting place is the "tent of meeting" because it shows us something of the deep desire of God to meet personally with his people.

Originally, God's plan for Israel was to meet with them around a simple earth or stone altar, just as he had with Abraham.

> Then the LORD said to Moses, "Tell the Israelites this: 'You have seen for yourselves that I have spoken to you from heaven: Do not make any gods to be alongside me; do not make for yourselves gods of silver or gods of gold. Make an altar of earth for me and sacrifice on it your burnt offerings and fellowship offerings, your sheep and goats and your cattle. *Wherever I cause my name to be honoured, I will come to you and bless you.'"* (Exodus 20:22–24)

The presence and the voice of the Lord were available to every covenant son and daughter. There were no elaborate rituals, no hierarchy of priests, no exclusions of women, children, or disabled people. Access to God was direct and unrestricted.[4] But the Israelites were afraid and unbelieving: "When the people saw the thunder and lightning and heard the trumpet and saw the mountain in smoke, they trembled with fear. They stayed at a distance and said to Moses, 'Speak to us yourself and we will listen. But do not have God speak to us or we will die'" (Exodus 20:18–19). It was only after this that the countless details and ornate ceremonies for Old Testament Judaism were delivered. Approaching God was mediated through priests with precise formulas and an elaborate spiritual security system. The presence of God was locked away in the vault of the Holy of Holies.

Now here is the good news: God created a back door to the system. While the tabernacle became the official "Tent of Meeting" (Exodus 27: 21), Moses provided an alternative meeting place where anyone could meet with God.

> Now Moses used to take a tent and pitch it outside the camp some distance away, calling it the *"tent of meeting." Anyone inquiring of the LORD would go to the tent of meeting* outside the camp. And whenever Moses went out to the tent, all the people rose and stood at the entrances to their tents, watching Moses until he entered the tent. As Moses went into the tent, the pillar of cloud would come down and stay at the entrance, while the LORD spoke with Moses. Whenever the people saw the pillar of cloud standing at the entrance to the tent, they all stood and worshiped, each at the entrance to his tent. *The LORD would speak to Moses face to face, as a man speaks with his friend. Then Moses would return to the camp, but his young aide Joshua son of Nun did not leave the tent.* (Exodus 33:7–11)

I am so touched that even then God provided a way that "whosoever will may come."[5] Unlike the tabernacle, the rules that marginalized women, children, Gentiles, and people with disabilities did not apply. It was never God's heart to exclude anyone. Provision for spiritual intimacy was made for *all* that would call on the name of the Lord.

3. Biblical Events

Moving from locations to events, we ask the Lord to bring a Bible story to mind for meditation. As an event comes into focus, review the author's description of the story. Then go to prayer with it. Closing your eyes, ask the Lord to help you picture it. Look for colours, shapes, and textures. Take note of the various characters and their actions. Where are you in the story? Where is Christ? Walk through the plot with him, interacting as if you were there—because in some sense, you are!

One day, as I listened to a Chuck Swindoll radio sermon from the gospel of Mark, he suggested that as he recounted the narrative, we might "use our imaginations to step into the story." (How's that for "guided imagery"!) When we step into a biblical narrative we look around us, our chief concern being to find the Lord in the story. What is he doing? What is he saying? Then we can draw near to him. And James says that if we do, then Jesus will draw near to us (James 4:8). We can talk to him there, behold him there, and even be held by him there.

Stepping In

This devotional practice is nothing novel. It has been a tried and true approach to God throughout the Christian era. The Stations of the Cross, a devotional discipline practised for centuries by Catholics, Protestants, and Orthodox alike, is one example of stepping into the biblical narrative. Jesus invites us as disciples to follow him as he walks us through fourteen scenes from the Passion narrative. Using pictures or statues depicting these scenes provides a focal point where we "enter the story." We prayerfully consider the final week of Christ's earthly ministry, meeting him in the story with open eyes and open ears. We ask where we fit into the story, what part we played in his death, and where Jesus meets us in his resurrection. Like it or not, we were there. The Lord prophesied to Zechariah of us, "They will look on me, the one they have pierced, and they will mourn for him as one mourns for an only child, and grieve bitterly for him as one grieves for a firstborn son" (Zechariah 12:10).

As we step into the story, we meet the Lord and he reveals our complicity so that he can also reveal his grace. Some of our modern poets and musicians have captured our personal involvement in Christ's passion beautifully. Bono of U2 sings,

I was there when they crucified my Lord
I held the scabbard when the soldier drew his sword
I threw the dice when they pierced his side...[6]

Canadian Bruce Cockburn concurs,

It could have been me put the thorns in your crown
Rooted as I am in a violent ground
How many times have I turned your promise down...[7]

The Rosary is another example of stepping into the biblical stories. Many have the impression that the Rosary is nothing more than a series of beads representing some extremely repetitive prayers, most of which are directed to Mary the mother of Jesus. The Protestant mind recoils from this, especially as a means of penance. But with a little more light on the topic, I believe there would be a lot less heat.

First, fingering through the Rosary beads and repeating memorized prayers like "Hail Mary" makes much more sense when we understand that the Rosary is basically a timing device. While outwardly the devotees pray vocally, inwardly they are called to ponder (visually behold; enter) fifteen gospel stories. These include five joyous mysteries (surrounding Christ's birth), five sorrowful mysteries (from his passion), and five glorious mysteries (from his resurrection and ascension). Without benefit of an alarm clock or timer, how long should we dwell on each of those mysteries? While meditating inwardly on each mystery, the prayer moves through the beads one prayer at a time, reciting aloud an "Our Father" (the Lord's Prayer), ten "Hail Marys," [8] one "Glory be to the Father," [9] and one "O My Jesus." [10] Each bead represents one prayer: when the finger bumps into the larger "Our Father" bead, the time has come to meditate on the next gospel story

Far from being mindless rote, St. Bernhard, the great Doctor of the Church, prescribes the correct use of the Rosary:

> While your lips pronounce the words *let your mind 'picture'* the Mystery—not as an event which took place centuries ago, but as events taking place *now* in your presence. In each mental picture thus formed, *see also yourself* there *in* the scene, *studying* the scene. [11]

You need not accept or engage in the use of Rosary beads, but I hope you will now see what they are intended to be: a devotional aid to the discipline of stepping into the Gospels at the heart level.

The Jesuit priests also made a discipline of stepping into biblical stories. Ignatius Loyola, their founder, recommends entering each story and activating each of the five senses in meditation.

> Prayer: After the Preparatory Prayer and the three Preludes, it is helpful to pass the five senses of the imagination through the first and second Contemplation, in the following way:
> First Point: The first Point is to *see the persons with the sight of the imagination*, meditating and contemplating in particular the details about them and drawing some profit from the sight.
> Second Point: The second, to *hear with the hearing* what they are, or might be, talking about and, reflecting on oneself, to draw some profit from it.
> Third Point: The third, to *smell and to taste with the smell and the taste* the infinite fragrance and sweetness of the Divinity, of the soul, and of its virtues, and of all, according to the person who is being contemplated; reflecting on oneself and drawing profit from it.
> Fourth Point: The fourth, *to touch with the touch*, as for instance, to embrace and kiss the places where such per-

sons put their feet and sit, always seeing to my drawing profit from it.[12]

When we hear that the Jesuits were to read all four gospels once per week, then we're not so surprised that their official name was "the Society of Jesus" and that they became Roman Catholicism's most powerful missionary movement.

In Practice

Teresa of Avila also beautifully models the process of stepping in, finding herself connecting visually, emotionally, and intimately with the Lord in a variety of gospel scenes. Note how vividly she describes and experiences each detail.

> If you feel happy, *think of him* at his Resurrection, for the very thought of how he rose from the tomb will delight you. How he shone with splendour! How beautiful and majestic, how victorious, how joyful he was! What spoils he brought back from the battle, where he won a glorious kingdom that he wishes to make all your own! Is it much for you *to look* but once on him who gives you such riches? If you have trials to bear, if you are sorrowful, *watch him* on his way to the garden. What grief must have arisen in his soul to cause him, Who was patience itself, to manifest it and to complain of it! *See him* bound to the column, full of suffering, his flesh all torn to pieces because of his tender love for you—persecuted by some, spat upon by others, denied and deserted by his friends, with none to plead for him. He is stiff with the cold, and in such utter loneliness that you may well console one another. *Or look on him* again—laden with the Cross, and not allowed to stay to take a breath. He will gaze at you with those beautiful compassionate eyes, brimming with tears, and will forget his own grief to solace yours, only because you went to comfort him and turned towards him.[13]

To say "it is as if" she is there would diminish her experience. In some non-literal, but very real spiritual sense, Teresa *is* there. She bursts into heart-felt prayer as she shares this holy moment with the Lord. His sufferings have become her meeting place:

> O Prince of all the earth, Thou Who art indeed my Spouse! Art Thou reduced to such sore straits, my Lord, my only Good, that Thou art willing to consort with such a miserable

comrade as myself? Yet Thy looks tell me that Thou find-
est some comfort even in me. How can it be that Thou art
forsaken by the angels, and that Thy Father consoles Thee
not? If it be Thy will to suffer thus for me, what do I suffer
for Thee in return; Of what have I to complain? Shame *at
seeing Thee* in such plight shall make me endure all the
trials that may come to me: I will count them gain that I
may imitate Thee in something. Let us go together, Lord:
"whither Thou goest, I will go" and I will follow where Thou
has passed.[14]

Danielle in the lion's den

Despite the above examples, we need not plunder only centuries of
church history in order to observe stepping-in phenomena. Meeting
the Lord in biblical narrative is as near as your Sunday school. Just as
we must enter the kingdom like children, so too, we find children easily
sliding into Bible stories for a meeting with Jesus.

My favourite stepping-in story involves my friend Danielle. I
was to speak at a seminar in Drayton Valley, Alberta and would be
provided with billeting. I secretly asked the Lord if I could stay with
a family that included someone with a disability. To my delight, the
family had a daughter named Danielle who happens to have Prader
Willi Syndrome.[15] When I told her about meeting Jesus in Bible stories,
she consented to giving it a try. We went to her favourite story, Daniel
(Danielle) in the lion's den. She closed her eyes and entered the lion's
den. Suddenly she began to tremble. "What's wrong?" I asked.

> Danielle: "I'm scared!"
> Brad: "Why?"
> Danielle: "Those lions sure look hungry!"
> Brad: "Maybe we should find Jesus. Is he anywhere around?"
> Danielle: "I see him up at the door to the lion's den."
> Brad: "Hmmm. What do you think we should do?"
> Danielle: "I think we should call him down!"
> Brad: "Go ahead."
> Danielle: "Jesus, please come down."

What happened next was beautiful. Jesus immediately came down to
sit right beside Danielle. She relaxed and felt the peace of his nearness.
Once the lions became a non-issue, Christ took her on his lap and then
laid his wounded hands on her back (her syndrome includes a spinal
problem). He began to bless her and pray to his Father for her healing.

I think her parents and I were more touched through this than she was. It inspired great faith in us to continue praying for her.

◀)) *Tuning In* • • • • • • • • •

- Ask God to remind you of a Bible story that has meant a lot to you. Can you picture the details of that story?
- Can you see the characters? What are they doing?
- Are you able to exercise all five senses within the story?
- Where is Jesus in the picture? What is he doing? Can you draw near to him? Ask him what he wants you to know about this story.
- Where does the story's truth meet your life?

B. Personal Meeting Places

We continue our survey with some personal meeting places, including physical locations as well as internal venues where you can cultivate encounters with the Divine. Those with less background in Scripture or church often find these meeting places more easily accessible at the outset.

1. Physical Locations as Meeting Places

Do you have a familiar physical place where you enjoy meeting with God? Some have a favourite room set aside for prayer. Others have a preferred chair or desk where they like to sit or kneel. Particular walks or outdoor settings can become special meeting places. When many people use the same location to pray or worship there can be a sense of accumulated glory—it becomes holy ground.

I once signed up for a day of caving while speaking at a Christian youth retreat. The caving guides led us into a vast network of little caverns that were formed by a rockslide several centuries ago. We squeezed our way under boulders, over rat nests, and past aboriginal cave art. Upon entering one large room with a low ceiling, my sister-in-law Didi whispered to me "God likes this room." To me it was just another space between the stones. She was fairly new to the world of discernment, but I didn't want to dampen her faith so I let it slide. An hour later the guides gathered us back to the same spot and announced that this is the room where they took all their caving groups for a talk about Christ and a time of prayer. Apparently those with open hearts could feel an atmosphere of light and glory in this favourite meeting place.

At one particular park gazebo in Abbotsford, so many people pray there privately that there is a sense of accumulated glory—it has become holy ground. My friend Joe loves to meet with God there. After an extended period where he could not get to the gazebo, Joe finally returned. Approaching the bench, the ears of his heart were opened to hear the excited voices of angels rustling through the surrounding shrubs; he audibly heard them saying to one another, "Joe's back! Joe's back!"

My belief is that you, like Joe, can count on the truth that God anticipates your arrival for those familiar meetings. You can either literally go to those spots or you can return to them internally wherever you happen to be praying.

Psalm 23 describes one of David's familiar meeting places. As a shepherd, he would wander the quiet green pastures, arm in arm with the Lord. He would enjoy God's peace beside nearby streams and invoke it in dark, dangerous crevices. Inspired worship would bubble up from David's heart, as God would restore his soul. A banqueting table of spiritual delights would fill his inner man whenever he met with his own Good Shepherd. Years later, David would be able to step back into those fields in prayer because deep within his heart, they had become a familiar meeting place.

Perhaps more than anyone else, Brother Lawrence of the Resurrection has taught the church how to "practice the presence of God" in the familiar places of our daily lives. He engaged in constant communion with God throughout fifteen years of culinary chores in a Carmelite monastery. He learned that God's presence was just as sweet and near when washing pots and pans as it was in his prayer cell. It made no difference to him because even the sink became a meeting place.

When I come home to find Eden kneeling in her flowerbeds, I know that she is never just gardening. She is immersed in her favourite familiar meeting place, conversing with God about things of the heart that need planting, watering, weeding, and pruning.

◀)) *Tuning In* • • • • • • • • •

- Do you have some favourite spots where you enjoy walking or sitting with the Lord? Take time to recall some of those meeting locations.
- Are you able to "go there" in your mind? Are you able to sense where Jesus is in that place when you are there with him? Give it a try right now!

2. *Personal Memories as Meeting Places*

My own introduction to "Meeting Place Prayers" came through personal prayer ministry. As a youth pastor, I often found myself wondering how to shepherd youth in crisis without overselling myself as a counsellor. Some of their issues required more help than they were getting from the professionals. They needed miracles of inner healing that only Jesus could provide. Then we heard a rumour that Jesus was willing to "show up" in painful memories. At the time I couldn't find any training materials, so we just held our breath and asked for him to come. He did—powerfully! He came every time we asked for all those who wanted to be free. In fact, the more traumatic the memory, the more dramatic his appearance, especially in the beginning. He was building our faith in his power and goodness.

We soon asked God for a biblical explanation of this phenomenon. The simplest scriptural foundation we could find for the healing of memories was "Lo [look, see, behold], I am with you always" and "I will never leave you nor forsake you" (Deuteronomy 31:6). This begs the painful question, "Oh yeah, well where was Jesus when *that* happened?" Then we would hear some sickening story from the darkest hour of that person's life. I am happy to say that we never have to answer that question—we always defer it to Jesus. It never daunts him—he loves to show us that he is with us, even in our darkest times. When he reveals where and how he was there, the miracle happens: He begins to heal us of the pain that was stored in that memory and has subsequently bent our lives.

The Closet

My friend Heather and I were praying for Terri, a young Christian who struggled deeply with depression, loneliness, and abandonment. When we asked the Lord to track this back to a seminal moment, Terri recalled her early childhood memories of being a kindergarten "latch-key kid." Even when she was five and six years old, she would come home to an empty house or be left to baby-sit her toddler sister. They lived in a house trailer in a rough area of town. It was not uncommon for her to have to pick her way past discarded syringes as she made her way home. She recalled the deep-seated fear and loneliness of those years. She would lock all the doors and hide inside until her parents returned from work.

As we prayed, Terri exploded in a fit of tears, "Where was Jesus then?" It was more of an accusation than a question. She jumped up and ran out of the office, out of the church, and down the street. I sat a little stunned, thinking deep thoughts about lawsuits, and so forth. Heather turned and offered, "I just saw a picture of Terri, hiding in a closet. Do you think I should follow her and tell her?" It sounded good to me, so off she went. As Heather ran down the street, she met Terri running back towards the church. Actually, she was skipping and laughing. Before Heather could say a word, Terri shouted at her, "He was in the closet; he was in the closet!"

Terri recounted how in those scary days at home alone, she would often go to her bedroom and curl up in her closet. She would experience a sense of security and peace there. Now she had seen why. She saw that Christ was there with her—she saw his form and she saw his light, warming the little closet with the comfort of God. His loving presence in that memory transformed it into a precious meeting place for Terri and Jesus.

◀)) *Tuning In* • • • • • • • • •

- Ask God to remind you of a memory that represents a "first" for you. Perhaps it was a first day at school or work. It may be a first performance or a first date. As you step back into that memory, do you remember how you felt that day?
- Now ask Jesus to show you where he was then. If indeed he is always with you and has never left you or abandoned you, you can ask him, "Where were you that day? What were you doing?"
- As you sense his presence in that memory, draw close to him and tell him how you felt. What does he say or do about that?

3. Visions and Dreams as Meeting Places

Scripture is replete with visions and dreams where the visionary or dreamer met the Lord. A meeting-place vision or dream is not so much like watching a movie screen as it is stepping into another realm. Crossing over into other imaginary lands is familiar to readers of Christian authors, such as George MacDonald or C. S. Lewis. But it should be just as familiar to students of the biblical writers and prophets, Daniel and John. Sometimes visions and dreams (or a combination of the two) were something the prophets "saw." At other times, they were more like spiritual places where they were taken to meet God.

The prophet Ezekiel was a captive in Babylon, but his experience of visions was a virtual reality. In Ezekiel 40, he testifies that Jerusalem was captured and...

On the very same day the hand of the LORD was upon me; *and he took me there. In the visions of God he took me* into the land of Israel and set me on a very high mountain; on it toward the south was something like the structure of a city. *He took me there, and behold,* there was a man whose appearance was like the appearance of bronze. He had a line of flax and a measuring rod in his hand, and he stood in the gateway. And the man said to me, "Son of man, *look with your eyes and hear with your ears, and fix your mind* [lit. *"set your heart"*] *on everything I show you;* for you were brought here that I might show them to you. Declare to the house of Israel everything you see. (Ezekiel 40:1–2)

The modern mind concludes that the physical realm alone is the "real world" in contrast to visions and dreams that are "not real." This kind of materialistic worldview infects much of the church. It allows that God exists, but he must be silent and distant. This is often referred to as practical deism. It believes in angels and demons but is ignorant of their activity today. It nods politely to a spiritual realm but judges it as sub-real. Ezekiel would beg to differ!

Afterward *he brought me to the gate,* the gate that faces toward the east. *And behold, the glory of the God of Israel came* from the way of the east. His voice was like the sound of many waters; and the earth shone with his glory. It was like the appearance of the *vision* which I saw—like the *vision* which I saw when I came to destroy the city. The visions were like the *vision* which I saw by the River Chebar; and I fell on my face. And the glory of the LORD came into the temple by way of the gate which faces toward the east. *The Spirit lifted me up and brought me into the inner court; and behold, the glory of the LORD filled the temple.* (Ezekiel 43:1–5)

The biblical worldview knows that truth and spirit are not bound to this world of the five senses. Heavenly and spiritual dimensions are found in the non-fiction shelves of the biblical reality. Visions and dreams are windows or doorways into that domain. As such, visions and dreams create gateways into a spiritual (and real) meeting place with the God of glory.

Certainly not all dreams and imaginings are of this nature. We do experience dreams where the emotional "stuff" of the day is just being processed. And our minds do soar on "simulation flights" of fantasy that are of little spiritual import. But Scripture teaches us not to relegate the entire spirit dimension into those categories just because they can't be examined in a science lab. Layers of reality stand behind, within, and beyond the physical one we live in now. In visions, dreams, and meditation, they sometimes overlap.

Dreams

Dreams in the Bible functioned as meeting places with the unique feature that the subject is asleep when the spiritual door opens. Daniel's night-visions best illustrate this. "In the first year of Belshazzar king of Babylon, Daniel had a dream, and visions passed through his mind as he was lying on his bed. He wrote down the substance of his dream" (Daniel 7:1). He records a series of dream visions climaxing again with a throne-room meeting.

> In my vision at night I looked, and there before me was one like a son of man, coming with the clouds of heaven. He approached the Ancient of Days and was led into his presence. He was given authority, glory and sovereign power; all peoples, nations and men of every language worshiped him. His dominion is an everlasting dominion that will not pass away, and his kingdom is one that will never be destroyed. (Daniel 7:13–14)

Daniel describes himself as being "in" this vision within the dream. As he continued to sleep, Daniel was troubled, so he approached one of the dream characters for an interpretation. Apparently he was having a lucid dream in which he could consciously interact with others. For Daniel, the dream world was not this world but it was a real world nonetheless. In that place, he transcended time and space to see the Lord and to perceive the future.

◀)) *Tuning In* • • • • • • • • •

- Ask God to remind you of a vivid dream, whether you dreamed it recently or long ago. It may be a pleasant dream or a frightful nightmare.
- In any case, step back into the dream and find Christ there. Ask him to tell you what each dream-person and symbol represents. Ask him how he would like to resolve the dream and then watch what he does.

Visions

We find a perfect example of a "vision meeting place" in the first few
sections of Revelation. It begins with John's Sunday morning prayer
time. We find him "in the Spirit" (Revelation 1:10) when he *hears* a
voice like a trumpet and turns to *see* the glorified Christ before him.
Is this a vision or a visitation? Did John turn in his spirit or with his
physical body? Did he literally fall at literal feet (v. 17) or did this occur
internally and spiritually in prayer? Such distinctions are unclear and
unnecessary to John. For him, one realm is as real as the other.

Jesus gives John a series of messages for the churches, conclud-
ing each with, "hear what the Spirit says." When we reach Revelation
3:20 Jesus says, "Behold, I stand at the door and knock. If anyone hears
my voice and opens the door, I will come in." Sadly, John's response has
been severed from the command by a chapter break in our Bibles and
our minds. Jesus has put an offer on the table for *anyone* who wills to
open the door where Jesus is *now* waiting. Watch how John responds
to Jesus' offer line by line:

Jesus' offer	John's response
"Behold" (3:20)	"I looked" (4:1)
"I stand at the door and knock"	"There was a door standing open"
"If anyone hears my voice"	"And the voice I had first heard speaking to me"
"I will come in"	"Come up here! At once I was in the Spirit" (4:1–2)
"I give the right to sit with me on my throne" (3:21)	"Behold, a throne in heaven with someone sitting on it" (4:2)

135

The contrasts are striking. There is a doorway. On one side is my heart where Jesus longs to fellowship. On the other side is the throne room of heaven. For Jesus to come to my side, I must open the door and invite him in. For me to cross over to his side, there is an open door and a standing invitation (cf. Heb. 4:16; 10:19–22). It is amazing too that the throne scene is full of awe, worship, and glory. Crowds of saints, angels, and creatures are ecstatic with praise. Yet to those who overcome, their rightful place in the scene is at the very centre on the throne with King Jesus and his Father.

All this to say that John *went* somewhere: He entered a vision of the throne room. In his spirit, John was *really* there. The message to him and to *anyone* with ears to hear is "*Come up here!* Come through the open door to the always-available throne of grace. Draw near with confidence and meet with me."

I would argue that any vision or dream might become a meeting place with the Lord just by inviting him there. If (a) you are *in* a dream or vision (even the memory of a dream) and (b) if he is with you *always*, then (c) finding him there is the obvious next step.

4. Your Heart as the Meeting Place

Ultimately, whether through meditation, memories, or dreams, all these personal meeting places occur within the temple of our hearts (or souls or spirits, depending on the passage). We have become the dwelling place of Christ. Paul says, "I pray that out of his glorious riches he may strengthen you with power *through his Spirit in your inner being*, so that Christ may *dwell in your hearts* through faith" (Ephesians 3: 16–17). The great mystics of the Christian church explored this concept to oceanic depths.

St. John of the Cross exhorted his own soul,

> O thou soul, most beautiful of creatures, who so earnestly longest to know the place where thy Beloved is, that thou mayest seek him and be united to him! Thou art thyself that very tabernacle where he dwells, the secret chamber of his retreat where he is hidden. Rejoice, therefore, and exult, because all thy good and all thy hope is so near thee as to be within thee; yea, rather rejoice that thou canst not be without it, for lo, "the kingdom of God is within you." [16]

His dear friend Teresa of Avila concurs,

> Let us realize that we have within us a most splendid palace built entirely of gold and precious stones... there is no struc-

ture so beautiful as a soul filled with virtues, and the more perfect these virtues are the more brilliantly do the jewels shine. Within this palace dwells the mighty King Who has deigned to become your Father, and Who is seated on a throne of priceless value—by which I mean your heart.[17]

The English mystic and theologian Julian of Norwich had a similar vision. Here was a fourteenth century woman of such passion and devotion for Christ that she begged him to put her flesh to death so that a priest would need to deliver last rights. Sure enough, at the age of thirty, she fell deathly ill and was so near death that a priest came to preside over her passing. As he held up a crucifix before her face, Julian became transfixed and went into a series of sixteen "showings" (visions that included seeing, hearing, and sensing) that came throughout the next few days. On the third day of these showings Julian miraculously recovered and was able to record these raw visions for us (published as *The Short Text*). She then dedicated the next *thirty years* of her life to meditating on what she saw and heard. She then finally wrote a commentary on each of the visions (*The Long Text*), which earned such respect that some held her as the foremost theologian of her day. We leave off our discussion of "place" with what she saw:

> And I was still awake, and then our Lord *opened my spiritual eyes* and showed me my soul in the middle of my heart. I saw my soul as large as if it were a kingdom; and from the properties that I saw in it, it seemed to me to be a glorious city. In the centre of that city sits our Lord Jesus, true God and true man, glorious, highest Lord; and I saw him dressed imposingly in glory. He sits in the soul, in the very centre, in peace and rest, and he rules and protects heaven and earth and all that is. The Manhood and the Godhead sit at rest... and my soul was blissfully filled with the Godhead, which is supreme power, supreme wisdom, supreme goodness. In all eternity Jesus will never leave the position which he takes in our soul; for *in us is his most familiar home and his favourite dwelling.*[18]

> Our good Lord showed himself in various ways, both in heaven and on earth, but the only *place I saw him occupy was man's soul...* At different times he showed himself reigning, as I have said before, but principally he showed himself in man's soul. He has made *that his resting-place and his glorious city, a glorious throne* out of which he will

never rise or remove for all eternity. *The place where the Lord dwells* is marvellous and noble.[19]

Both the Catholic and Orthodox traditions tell the same story. In his book on "Living Prayer," Orthodox Archbishop Anthony Bloom cites some of his heroes in faith. As they sought after God, the Eastern Church looked inward.

> St. John Chrysostom said: 'Find the door of the inner chamber of your soul and you will discover that this is the door into the kingdom of Heaven.' St. Ephraim of Syria says that God, when he created man, put in the deepest part of him all the kingdom... to find God we must dig in search of this inner chamber, of this *place* where the whole kingdom of God is present at the very core of us, *where God and we can meet.*[20]

◀)) *Tuning In* • • • • • • • • • •

- Ask God to lead you into the meeting place of your heart. If your heart is his home or temple or castle, what does it look like? What are its features?
- Find Jesus there and ask him to give you a guided tour.

C. God Himself as the Meeting Place

The Psalms present an array of metaphors for God himself as a meeting place. We find various psalmists running "into" God for safe-haven. As they think of God, they compare him to familiar places of shelter. Spiritually speaking, they hide in him.

> In the shelter of your presence you hide them from the intrigues of men. (Psalm 31:20)

> For you have been my refuge, a strong tower against the foe. I long to dwell in your tent forever and take refuge in the shelter of your wing. (Psalm 61:3–4)

> But let all who take refuge in you be glad; let them ever sing for joy. Spread your protection over them, that those who love your name may rejoice in you. (Psalm 5:11)

> The LORD is a refuge for the oppressed, a stronghold in times of trouble. (Psalm 9:9)

The LORD is my rock, my fortress and my deliverer; my God is my rock, in whom I take refuge. He is my shield and the horn of my salvation, my stronghold. (Psalm 18:2)

Turn your ear to me, come quickly to my rescue; be my rock of refuge, a strong fortress to save me. (Psalm 31:2)

If you make the Most High your dwelling—even the LORD, who is my refuge. (Psalm 91:9)

You are my hiding place; you will protect me from trouble and surround me with songs of deliverance. (Psalm 32:7)

When David had fled from Saul into a cave. Have mercy on me, O God, have mercy on me, for in you my soul takes refuge. I will take refuge in the shadow of your wings until the disaster has passed. (Psalm 57:1)

When we ask the Lord for a "safe place" and he shows us a fortress or shield or any type of protective refuge, he is really offering himself. The dynamic is mutual. Jesus said, "On that day you will realize that I am in my Father, and you are in me, and I am in you" (John 14:20). God is in you (his house—John 14:23) and you are in him (your Refuge). We find perfect peace when we dwell with the One who dwells within us.

II. A MEETING

At the end of the day, the point of this chapter and this book is *not* a place but a person. The place is simply a spiritual venue in which we can meet with Jesus for communion, fellowship, and interaction. The goal is to behold him and to be held by him.

A. Behold: Gazing Prayer

We have discussed at length what it means to behold. The primary purpose for spiritual sight is to look into the face of Christ. The experience of seeing Jesus' face ranges from impression to vision to visitation. Whether you vaguely picture him or can count vividly detailed eyelashes on his face, these "beholdings" are fruitful. You cannot sow in the Spirit without reaping in the Spirit (Galatians 6:7–8). You cannot behold his glory (even dimly) without also being touched by his glory. The expression of his face can soften a hard heart, heal a broken spirit, or free a soul in bondage. His eyes alone penetrate any darkness, deliver us from any evil, and forgive us from any sin. Truly, the glory of God *is* found and experienced in the face of Christ (2 Corinthians 4: 6). There is power and love released in his gaze.

Teresa of Avila taught her nuns to gaze on Jesus that he might gaze on them.

> I am not now asking you to meditate on him, nor to produce great thoughts, nor to feel deep devotion: I *only ask you to look at him.* Who can prevent your turning *the eyes of your soul* (but for an instant if you can do no more) on our Lord? You are able to look on many ugly and vulgar things: then *can you not gaze upon the fairest sight imaginable?* If He does not appear beautiful to you, I give you leave never to think of him, although, daughters, he never takes his eyes off you! He has borne with many offences and much unworthiness in you, yet these have not sufficed to make him turn away: is it much to ask that you should *sometimes lift your gaze from earth to fix it on him?* See: He is only waiting for us to look on him, as the bride says.[21]

The expressions on Jesus' face are full of meaning. Every look, every smile, every wink is packed with significance. He knows what to say and how to say it with a single glance. Julian of Norwich took careful note of his expressions. What did she note?

> *Jesus wants our souls to look at him with gladness, for the face he shows us is happy and loving; and how he shows us three kinds of face-a suffering, a compassionate and a blessed face.*

> Glad and cheerful and sweet is the blessed, loving face with which our Lord looks at our souls; for he is constantly in love-longing towards us while we live, and he wants our souls to look gladly on him so as to give him his reward.

> When we sorrow and suffer, he shows us the face of his Passion and his cross, helping us to endure through his own blessed strength. And when we sin he shows us his face of pity and grief, strongly protecting and defending us from all our enemies. And these two are the faces which he most often shows us in this life; and mixed with them is the third, which is his blessed face, shown in part as it will be in heaven. And that comes to us through gracious touching and sweet illumination of the spiritual life by which we are kept in the certain faith, hope and charity, with contrition and devotion and also with contemplation and every kind of true pleasure

and sweet comfort. The blessed face of our Lord God works this in us through grace. (italics original) [22]

When Comenius' "Pilgrim" beheld the Lord in the sanctuary of his heart, he too took care to describe Christ's expression and the effects it had on him.

I pondered these things within myself and awaited what was to follow. Then behold, a bright light burst forth from above. Raising my eyes toward it, I saw the upper window full of brilliance, out of which a man came down to me. In form, indeed, he was similar to us people, but in his splendour he was truly God. Although his face shone greatly, yet it could be looked upon with human eyes; nor did it inspire terror, but radiated a loveliness such as I have never seen anywhere in the world. Then he, the epitome of kindness and good will, addressed me in these most gracious words... [23]

I am hesitant to share stories of the effects of gazing on Christ, because I believe that our gaze should be his reward for saving us. I believe we ought to fix our eyes on him for his own sake as an offering of worship and gratitude. Friendship with Christ is to want him for who he is and not merely as another avenue to getting what we want. As Archbishop Bloom recounts, "Once the Cure d'Ars, a French saint of the eighteenth century, asked an old peasant what he was doing sitting for hours in the church, seemingly not even praying; the peasant replied: 'I look at him, he looks at me and we are happy together.'" [24]

The power of Jesus' gaze seems to be released into our lives most effectively when we are thinking about him rather than ourselves. Just when we finally forget ourselves and truly focus on him, the Lord Jesus moves in to minister to us.

At a recent seminar where I was helping to deliver this teaching, we led the people to behold Jesus as King on his throne—to forget about ourselves and to offer him unconditional worship as a pure gift. The throne room itself dropped away until at last our only vision was the glorious face of the Lord. The presence of God filled the place, and when we came back to this world, we heard testimonies of unsolicited physical healing.

Healed By One Glance

One woman had a night-vision problem that made it impossible for her to drive after sunset. Headlights from oncoming cars would give her awful pain in her eyes and she described them as going "wonky."

As she gazed into Jesus' face that evening, she felt her own eyes were being healed. The trip home after the meeting confirmed this to her.

The following day, another dear lady in her early seventies shared that as she looked into Christ's face; he took her own face in his hands and just smiled at her. They stayed still and silent for a time. Then without further ado, he withdrew his hands and the vision ended. Her heart was touched by the gentleness of his face and hands, but then she realized that her neck had also been touched. She had a long-term case of severe arthritis in her neck that created immobility and chronic pain. During their brief face-to-face gaze she was instantly and totally healed.

◀)) *Tuning In* • • • • • • • • • •

- Begin to spend a regular and significant time in daily, gazing prayer. I suggest setting a timer to remind you of when it's over so that you can ignore the time completely while you're praying.
- As you retreat into your heart, gaze into God's face. Be still and quiet. Be assured that as you envision his glorious face, this has a transforming effect on your heart and character. As you practice this in your daily prayers, take note of the growing fruit in your life.

B. Be Held: Nurturing Prayer

Of course Christ's agenda is not limited to healing bodies. To behold the face of our Saviour opens a channel of grace into our hearts. We have found by seeing him in action time after time that he loves to take his people in his arms and hold them. As we experience his divine hugs in the Meeting Place, his love and affection are poured into us. As he holds his children, they often feel comforting warmth envelop them, and they may even physically feel the sensation of his arms embracing them.

Isaiah describes this embrace: "He tends his flock like a shepherd: He gathers the lambs *in his arms and carries them close to his heart*" (Isaiah 40:11). In prayer ministry, the Lord will often quiet a wounded child in his arms and then prompt us to read this promise, "The LORD your God is with you, he is mighty to save. He will take great delight in you, he will quiet you with his love, he will rejoice over you with singing" (Zephaniah 3:17). We commonly hear a huge sigh as they sink deeply into his loving arms.

Far from being innovative, this picture of the arms of the Lord is ancient. Perhaps you've been there when singing this hymn:

What a fellowship, what a joy divine,
leaning on the everlasting arms;
what a blessedness, what a peace is mine,
leaning on the everlasting arms.

(Refrain)
Leaning (leaning on Jesus), leaning (leaning on Jesus),
safe and secure from all alarms;
leaning, leaning, leaning on the everlasting arms.

O how sweet to walk in this pilgrim way,
leaning on the everlasting arms;
O how bright the path grows from day to day,
leaning on the everlasting arms.

What have I to dread, what have I to fear,
leaning on the everlasting arms?
I have blessed peace with my Lord so near,
leaning on the everlasting arms.[25]

This isn't meant to be an abstract idea or an empty metaphor. The hymnist is describing a real experience in a real relationship with a real person. As we invite the Lord to hold us in our spiritual meeting places, he imparts real peace, real love, real security, real guidance, and real healing.

Some of our modern worship leaders have remembered this same message:

I sing a simple song of love to my Saviour, to my Jesus
I'm grateful for the things You've done
My loving Saviour, oh precious Jesus
My heart is glad that You've called me Your own
There's no place I'd rather be, than...

In Your arms of love, In Your arms of love
Holding me still, holding me near in Your arms of love.[26]

The healing effects of spending time in God's arms are phenomenal. On many occasions when I have worked with people who are extremely angry with God, they have approached him in prayer and begun to beat on his chest. Instead of spurning them, he scoops them up even as they would continue this inner tantrum. Eventually—sometimes minutes, sometimes weeks—the love and peace of God finally prevails. The anger drains away, replaced by a deep intimacy between God and his child.

◄)) *Tuning In* • • • • • • • • • •

- As an extension of your experience in gazing prayer, allow yourself to experience the nurture of being held in God's arms. In quietness and trust, let his strength and security pour into you.
- Press your ear to his heart. Such nearness and tenderness softens the heart and enlarges our capacity to receive love. Note: Don't feel ashamed to fall asleep in his arms.

Meeting Must Become Dwelling

I am convinced that *behold and be held* is a "now-Word" for the church. If ever we've needed our hearts softened and healed, it's now. But thank God! If you have a heart, then you *do* have a meeting place within you. If you have invited God into your life, there is a precious Person waiting there for you even now. Even if you have wandered from him, he has never left his home in your heart. He invites all those who are tired of wandering to return to him there.[27] He calls those with eyes to see and ears to hear to draw near—to behold and be held.

   With the saints of the church I urge you: Do not merely run to the meeting place in times of emergency. Do not use it only for occasional visits or retreats. The Most High has made your heart his home. Let's make it our home as well. Make his presence in you your own permanent residence. The meeting place must become our dwelling place (Psalm 27:5; 90:1; 91:9). We can learn what it is to "dwell in the house of the Lord forever" (Psalm 23:6).

   Ask Jesus, "You have created within my heart a dwelling place for your presence. Would you now show me that place? Would you now meet with me there?" As he begins to reveal such a meeting place to your heart, step into it by faith. Find the Lord there and welcome him. Draw near to him and he *will* draw near to you. Gaze on him, listen to him, invite him to hold you. Resist every distraction and remove every block that would hinder such communion. Seek this pearl of the kingdom with all your heart. You *will* find it. Ask for it and you *will* receive it. Then move in for good. Live with him and in him forever. This is the promise of the Meeting Place.

Meeting God To Intercede

Carry each other's burdens, and in this way you will fulfill the law of Christ.

- Galatians 6:2

ENCOUNTERING OTHERS
IN A MEETING PLACE

My first encounter with *other people* in a meeting place with God was a rude awakening! Until that day, I had never used the meeting place for "intercession" (a fancy word for praying on behalf of others). It was strictly reserved for retreat, refreshment, and solitude. I had never seen anyone other than Jesus and I in my favourite little cavern of the heart. Little did I know that by introducing third parties into my meeting place, God would launch me into the spiritual arena of visual intercession and burden bearing—the topics we will cover in this chapter.

Feet to the Fire!

On this particular day, I really needed to quiet my heart, because two members in our church were feuding over a petty misunderstanding. They were arguing past each other with no intention of compromise. Resentment was gaining ground, and, frankly, it was giving me a royal headache. I fled in prayer to the cave for some peace. I found Jesus there and was about to recline with him when, suddenly, these two squabblers were standing in our presence. I was outraged! "Get them out of here!" I cried to the Lord. I supposed that somehow I was having difficulty leaving my troubles at the door. I guessed that my lack of peace was polluting the meeting place.

"No, I've brought them here. I want you to put their feet to the fire," The Lord said. Taking this cue, I grabbed each of my uninvited guests by the hand and, using my imagination, I sat them down and made sure that their bare feet were actually extended into the flames so God could really "turn up the heat" of conviction. Then I noticed something: my own feet were in the fire too!

"I'm putting your feet to the fire too, because we are going to talk about some resentment you've been carrying," he said.

Then Jesus began to confront me about my anger to an old friend who had left the faith after years of battling side by side in the spiritual trenches. He showed me that my resentment was rooted in the belief that all the time and energy that we had invested into one another and into kingdom ministry was now wasted. The Lord spoke the truth that unmasked the lies I believed. He said, "Do not be deceived. You *cannot* sow in the Spirit without also reaping in the Spirit. You think that what you've invested has been wasted because you cannot see the harvest in your friend. Remember the parable of the talents (Luke 19). When I took the blessing away from the one who had squandered it, I gave it to someone else who would be faithful with it."

> "Then he said to those standing by, 'Take his mina away from him and give it to the one who has ten minas.'
>
> "'Sir,' they said, 'he already has ten!'
>
> "He replied, 'I tell you that to everyone who has, more will be given, but as for the one who has nothing, even what he has will be taken away.'" (Luke 19:24–26)

Jesus went on, "You do not need to know where I replanted those seeds. You only need to trust that your labour is never in vain. Now you can release your friend in forgiveness and repent of your resentment." With this new truth in my heart, I found the release rather easy (repenting to my friend in person for my many judgments was more difficult).

At that moment, I came back to the cave scene. "What about these two?" I asked.

"Oh, they're done," God replied. And with that, they vanished.

The next morning at our Sunday service, one of the two parties involved in the conflict ran up to me. "I can't understand what happened," she blurted, "but the whole issue with P— is totally resolved. I can hardly believe it!"

The dreaded confrontations and mediation meetings that threatened to fill my schedule and grate on my nerves were gone in a flash. Since then, I've learned to meet with others in the cave *before* I meet them in a counselling office or a boardroom. The pastoral yoke became *much* lighter as a result and intercession became much more interesting and effective.

Healing Others in the Meeting Place

Once I realized that I could intercede for others in the meeting place, I thought I should share the good news with our intercessors. However, I was way behind the curve on this one. When I talked to them, each smiled and said, "That's what I've always done. Didn't you know about that?" One elderly Mennonite lady was greatly relieved, admitting, "I've prayed like that since I was a little girl. I didn't know if it was okay. I thought maybe I was the only one, and I didn't dare tell anyone before! I was afraid they might have thought I was weird. But it just seemed right." Indeed it is *right* and *effective*.

My cousin Mel gave me an example. Her nephew Jesse, in kindergarten at the time, had a large screen TV fall on him. It shattered his jaw and cheekbones, his nose, and split his pallet. We were concerned that he might even lose his life. Mel took him in her arms of prayer before the Lord where he directed her to a "healing river" meeting place. Jesus took the child from her and carried him into the river. He soaked him in the river, carefully washing away the blood and wetting the broken bones. She could see him get dipped into the water, then walk out on his own, perfectly normal, without any scars.

Mel phoned the hospital to share this with Merilee, the boy's mother. The nurses called her from Jesse's hospital bedside, where he lay totally unresponsive. As Merilee listened to Mel's vision, her heart ignited with faith for healing. When she returned to the hospital room, she found Jesse, utterly weak moments before, now sitting upright and announcing forcefully, "I'm hungry!"

As Mel continued to witness Jesus and her nephew in this meeting place, peace would fill her heart, and miracles continued to occur back at the hospital. Each stage of Jesse's recovery was dramatically accelerated as God's strength and healing love filled his little body. His bones mended beautifully and today, he has recovered completely with no trace of disfigurement. Now the healing river has become a common meeting place where Mel takes the sick for mercy.

Burden Bearing Others in the Meeting Place

Have you ever felt the pain in someone else's heart? When you hear what others have experienced, do you ever sense the weight of their burden come upon you? Are you sensitive to the emotional or spiritual climate when in the company of others? Do you experience that as a blessing or does it overwhelm you at times?

"Burden bearing" is the God-given ability *to feel and carry someone else's burdens.* As we empathize with others in their pain, we may feel what they feel and bear what they bear. Paul stresses, "Carry each other's burdens, and in this way you will fulfil the law of Christ" (Galatians 6:2). He taught us that as we share in each other's suffering, we are also able to share in each other's comfort (2 Corinthians 1:7). In fact, burden bearing was a major aspect of Paul's ministry: "Besides everything else, I face daily the pressure of my concern for all the churches. Who is weak, and I do not feel weak? Who is led into sin, and I do not inwardly burn?" (2 Corinthians 11:28–29).

But burden bearing was never meant to be accomplished on our own as simple empathy. God's design is that we would *bear those burdens to him and before him in prayer.* Except for Christ himself in Gethsemane, Jeremiah is second to none as our model for burden bearing. Listen as he fully bears both the sins and sorrows of his people before the Lord.

> See, O LORD, how distressed I am! I am in torment within, and in my heart I am disturbed, for I have been most rebellious. Outside, the sword bereaves; inside, there is only death. People have heard my groaning, but there is no one to comfort me. All my enemies have heard of my distress; they rejoice at what you have done. May you bring the day you have announced so they may become like me. Let all their wickedness come before you; deal with them as you have dealt with me because of all my sins. My groans are many and my heart is faint. (Lamentations 1:20–21)

> The elders of the Daughter of Zion sit on the ground in silence; they have sprinkled dust on their heads and put on sackcloth. The young women of Jerusalem have bowed their heads to the ground.
> My eyes fail from weeping, I am in torment within, my heart is poured out on the ground because my people are destroyed, because children and infants faint in the streets of the city. (Lamentations 2:10–11)

Groups like Elijah House have really helped us to recognize the phenomenon of burden bearing.[1] They have taught burden-bearers how to identify burdens and then carry them, but *only as far as the Cross* of Christ, where they can lay them down at Jesus' feet. For not only are we to bear other's burdens, and then bear them to the Lord in prayer, but we are also to *release them to Christ,* the ultimate burden-bearer, *who takes them upon himself.* This was the essence of his mission:

> Surely he *took up our infirmities and carried our sorrows,* yet we considered him stricken by God, smitten by him, and afflicted.

But he was pierced for our transgressions, he was crushed for our iniquities; the punishment that brought us peace was upon him, and by his wounds we are healed.

After the suffering of his soul, he will see the light of life and be satisfied; by his knowledge my righteous servant will justify many, and he will bear their iniquities. (Isaiah 53: 4–5)

The cycle of burden bearing is that the Lord will make us aware of someone's burdens and call us to share their emotional and spiritual load. He calls us to bring that load to the Cross, where we deliver it over to him as an act of intercession. As he lifts that yoke from our souls, bearing its weight himself, he releases comfort and healing to the one for whom we are praying.

B. J. Palfreyman

Throughout the 1990s, I enjoyed the intimacy of a mentor named Barrie Palfreyman. He was a spiritual father who continually challenged me to push the envelope. He would comment with a wink and a smirk that my material was "a little *avant-garde* for our broader constituency." He hoped I would say of him after he passed away, "Barrie never suffered from a hardening of the categories." Indeed, he did not.

When Barrie fought his final battle with cancer, his schedule and energy levels made it impossible for us to have a visit. He said his good-byes to me via e-mail with deep regrets, but the circumstances seemed to dictate it. Mel (of healing river fame) phoned one day and said, "The Lord is showing me that Barrie is carrying some heavy burdens and can't release them on his own. I believe you need to go visit him and offer to take them for him to the Cross." This was a dilemma. After all Barrie had done for me, how could I now not come to his side? On the other hand, he had respectfully asked to be left to his immediate family in his last days. I swallowed hard and returned the burden to the Lord. If I were to go, God would have to make a way.

On the Friday before he passed away, I got a "back door" phone call from close friends of the Palfreymans. They hinted that there might be a fifteen-minute window of time in which I could steal a last visit with Barrie in the hospital. I arrived at the designated time. I didn't know how long Barrie's energy or clarity would last, so I quickly laid out my concern. Did he have any burdens to unload that I could bear to the Cross on his behalf? He did. For about forty minutes, Barrie shared the burdens of his heart without interruption from hospital staff or other visitors. Then I knelt by his bed and he laid hands on me to bestow a father's blessing.

By the time I returned to my car, I felt a churning in the pit of my gut and a heavy sensation on my forearms and hands, as if I was wearing lead sleeves and gloves. I drove to a safe place and lay down to offer up this burden to the Lord. I sank into a vision in which I was carrying Barrie, full-sized, in my arms. I thought, I need to hand him to Jesus, but couldn't find him immediately. Ahead of me, I saw a river and on the far side, I saw the Lord standing on the bank waiting to receive Barrie into the kingdom of heaven. He said to me, "I want you to carry him for a while."

"I'm not strong enough," I answered.

"Enter the water. The river will help you lift him," was his reply.

As I obeyed, I found that if I stood belly-deep in the river with my arms extended, I could hold Barrie afloat without tiring. I was aware somehow that this was Mel's healing river and that those who bathed in it would return from it whole. Others, like Barrie, would be cleansed of the dust of this world as they crossed it in death. I "felt" the lightened burden of holding Barrie afloat in the river for three days, and then on Monday, it lifted. The next day, I received word that he had crossed over into eternity right around the time that my burden was lifted. This event was one of the great privileges of my life, yet somehow I know that I am just one of many friends and disciples who helped carry Barrie on the final leg of his journey. If *that* is true burden bearing, then it is an awesome blessing.

Getting Stuck

Each of us has the capacity for burden bearing to varying degrees, according to our sensitivity. It appears to me that this sensitivity is much higher in those who have experienced deep emotional wounding themselves. They may pick up burdens from others without knowing it, either by proximity (malls can feel overwhelming!), by witnessing pain (too much *CNN*!), or in relationships (from loved ones, even at a great distance). When they aren't aware of what's happening, burden-bearers can be quite confused as they identify others' pain as their own or project their own pain onto others. If you think of it visually, it's like taking a backpack of pain from someone else and placing it on your own shoulders.

Wounded burden bearers, prone to a type of Messiah complex, often carry around *many* backpacks that they've accumulated from others over the years. The ideal would be to carry each burden to Jesus right away, where you take it off and immediately exchange it for his peace. Unfortunately, sometimes we seem to get stuck along the way and suffer under the weight of unreleased burdens, so we often try to turn off our discernment of other people's pain. Easier said than done. Shutting yourself down rarely works and can create some harmful side effects as well. For example, we may build protective walls that serve only to shield us from love while the weight of the world continues to press in. As a result we become either melancholic or hypersensitive. Wounded burden bearers rarely even realize what is happening to them. But if we can spot them and minister healing to them, they can learn to unload on the Lord rather than internalizing the pain of others.

Breakthrough: The Burden of the Lord

Eric McCooeye of Fresh Wind Ministries has made what I see as a major breakthrough in discipling burden bearers. Rather than using the traditional "backpack model," what he has discovered vastly simplifies *and* deepens the process—it makes burden bearing an act of communion with the Lord and reverses the felt need to shut off.

It boils down to this: when we sense a burden coming upon us, we ask, "Jesus, what is this about?" Then, instead of empathising directly with the one carrying the burden (or turning our discernment *off*), we focus immediately on the Lord and turn our discernment *on* to *his* heart: "Jesus, how do *you* feel about this?" We enter into the fellowship of *his* suffering, sensing his ache for the one who carries this heavy burden. We recognize that he validates their sorrow or anger, but in absolute purity. Then we draw near to him (even in a visual way if you like) and pray, "Lord, let your heart be comforted" and wait for his peace to come.

As we pray in this simple way, specific benefits result.

1. First, our eyes become fixed on Jesus rather than fixated on the pain of the world. Those who have been allowed to share in Jesus' grief say that this is the most sacred experience of fellowship they've had with him.
2. We learn that Christ's perspective on the burden may be quite different from those of the person we are praying for. Sometimes his sadness matches theirs or his anger reflects theirs. But just as often, the burden of Christ is quite different. When they are hurt he may be angry (at their offender, for example), or when they are anxious he might seem quite at peace (he never worries). Then the discerners' task is to align their hearts with the Lord's. It is also generally a much lighter yoke (Matt. 11:30).
3. We are able to offer comfort directly to Jesus. Jesus is perfectly able to receive comfort from us where his heart is grieved. In contrast to the hurting people we try to reach, Jesus has not erected

any self-protective walls. He humbly chooses to receive the comfort of his children, though they have very little understanding of this holy act. It reminds me of the grandfather I met at his own mother's funeral. He held his grandson in a tight embrace, drawing deep comfort from the cuddles of the loving (though rather oblivious) child. The grandpa looked at me through tearful eyes and just kept repeating, "The balm of Gilead" (Jeremiah 8:22), referring to the spiritual salve of Jesus that soothed his heart through this little servant.

4. As Jesus' heart is comforted, a flow of peace issues back from Jesus that comforts our hearts. Experiencing a measure of God's grief can be excruciating, but it inevitably leads to new depths of his comfort and peace as well.

5. Grace is also released to the ones who were originally in need. As the pain in Christ's heart for them is swallowed up in his divine love, his love overflows back to them. We see this confirmed through breakthroughs in their personal healing or in specific answers to previously stalled prayer requests.

6. Discernment ceases to be about sensing all the pain around us and becomes a ministry of awareness of where Jesus is in the situation. So we learn the joy of turning on our discernment meters to God's heart rather than turning them off to the weight of the world.

7. When we bear another's burden, our own wounds may cause us to become stuck in their pain or to pick up their offence. When we pick up Christ's burden instead, he leads us through the sorrow into comfort and then into hope and promise. I find that the words of hope I receive at that point can be shared safely with faith and authority. They don't come off as platitudes. Rather than sounding like Job's amateur therapists, I have a message that rings true.

Is This Biblical, You Ask?

To answer this question, I would like to take special note of Hebrews 12 and Isaiah 53, where we are specifically called to behold the grieving Christ, who is our willing burden-bearer. We are invited to gaze upon him and join in his intercession. When we do, Paul describes the comforting process beautifully:

> For just as the sufferings of Christ flow over into our lives, so also through Christ our comfort overflows. If we are distressed, it is for your comfort and salvation; if we are comforted, it is for your comfort, which produces in you patient endurance of the same sufferings we suffer. (2 Corinthians 1:5–6)

Take note of the process:

- Christ's people suffer, so he suffers with them.
- Christ's suffering flows over into us, so we suffer with him.
- As we fellowship in Christ's sufferings, his sorrow begins to turn to comfort.
- Christ's comfort flows into us, and we are comforted.
- Christ's comfort also overflows to those for whom we intercede, and they are comforted and strengthened.

Kathryn

Kathryn, a prayer minister from Vancouver, Canada, was feeling stuck in her burden bearing. The Lord took her back to a memory when she had attended a funeral as a girl. She did not know the deceased or his widow very well, but when she saw the widow in the foyer, a deep grief came over Kathryn and she began to weep bitterly. She remembered that the widow herself had seemed to be at peace, but she couldn't imagine how. As Kathryn wept, someone attending the funeral had turned to her with a scornful look, as if to say, "What's your problem? You're not the widow. You have no right to mourn like that! Get it together!" In that moment, the burden got "stuck" and Kathryn had carried it ever since.

When Kathryn returned with the Lord to that memory, it was too difficult for her to carry the widow's burden to Jesus, so she tried Eric's new model. She asked Jesus, "Where were you in that memory?" and immediately saw Jesus sitting in the corner on the floor, weeping just as heavily as Kathryn. This was a profound validating message to Kathryn, as if to say, "I know. I wept too. Your tears and your burden were not inappropriate or disproportionate. I felt it too. The widow could not express or endure it, so *we* carried it for her."

"What must I do?" Kathryn asked.

"Turn from the widow's grief and minister to mine. Draw near, daughter."

Kathryn chose to turn from the widow to Christ. She approached him and they wept together. A little hesitantly she offered, "Lord, let your heart be comforted." Holding one another, she *felt* and *followed* Jesus' heart as together their grief turned to deep peace, and their peace turned to joy. Never before had she drawn such a deep draught from the cup of intimacy with him. Yet it was not quite over. The Lord also revealed to Kathryn that he had dislodged this old grief from her heart and would do so for the widow as well. His river of grace would overflow its banks and extend to her lonely heart.

This type of burden bearing can work in at least two directions. As in the illustration above, Jesus is willing to enter our life memories to bear every burden. Or as Teresa of Avila discovered, we can take our burdens into Jesus' life-memories, such as his prayer of sorrow on the Mount of Olives (Luke 22:44).

> If you have trials to bear, if you are sorrowful, watch him on his way to the garden. What grief must have arisen in his soul to cause him, Who was patience itself, to manifest it and to complain of it! See him bound to the column, full of suffering, his flesh all torn to pieces because of his tender love for you—persecuted by some, spat upon by others, denied and deserted by his friends, with none to plead for him. He is stiff with the cold, and in such utter loneliness that you may well console one another. Or look on him again—laden with the Cross, and not allowed to stay to take breath. He will gaze at you with those beautiful, compassionate eyes, brimming with tears, and will forget his own grief to solace yours, only because you went to comfort him and turned towards him.[2]

In either case, our focus is on his heart. Our sorrow is washed into his, where it turns to comfort, love, and renewed joy.

Christ *does* indeed grieve over the sins and sorrows of this world. Moreover, he invites us to feel his burden for the world (share in his sufferings) as an act of prayer. He also allows *his heart* to be touched by our devotion and comfort—a miracle of his humility. Finally, he pours his healing grace back onto his children as his heart is turned to joy.

Summary

These are the major applications of the meeting place in intercession. Whether in intercession or burden bearing, Jesus will come when we invite him. He can appoint any memory, vision, or Bible story of his choosing as a venue from which to hear and answer your requests on behalf of others. When the great Burden Bearer and Chief Intercessor invites you to participate in his prayer life, let his Spirit fill your prayers with his love and power.

> We do not know what we ought to pray for, but the Spirit himself intercedes for us with groans that words cannot express. And he who searches our hearts knows the mind of the Spirit, because the Spirit intercedes for the saints in accordance with God's will. (Romans 8:26–27)

◀)) *Tuning In* • • • • • • • • •

- Do you carry a burden for someone else? Why not take them to Gethsemane and meet Jesus there in prayer?
- Look for him as he's weeping before the Father on their behalf. Kneel beside him and agree together in prayer.
- Ask the Lord what he feels about that burden and connect with his heart. Speak those words, "Lord, let your heart be comforted" and then watch what he says and does. Follow him emotionally until he comes to peace or joy. Let his comfort overflow to you.
- Then ask him, "Why are you at peace concerning this burden?" or "Why are you joyful about this person?" He will usually answer with a word of promise that ignites faith in us to intercede.

····· 7 ·····

Overcoming Blocks to Meeting God

And it will be said: "Build up, build up, prepare the road!
Remove the obstacles out of the way of my people."
                                                    - Isaiah 57:14

STOLEN SEEDS AND CONCRETE WALLS

John Schmidt, a dean at Columbia Bible College, invited me to join him in praying for Josh. This young man of God was seeking help in his quest to hear God's voice. He claimed that he could not and had never been able to hear the Lord. By now, you'll know that I would be quite skeptical about a claim like that. I tried the frontal attack, "You can, you have, and you do hear God. You hear him well and often. You just don't realize it."

"No," he insisted, "I can't. When I listen, I hear total silence. When I look, I see a blank screen. Never any pictures. I'm totally blocked." As in Jesus' parable of the sower and the seed (Matthew 13: 3–9), any truth-seeds that the Sower was casting into Josh's heart were being snatched away faster than he could recognize them. He was frustrated—almost stubborn—about this rut. He felt as if there was an enormous wall between him and God, cutting off all communication between them.

"A wall?" I asked. "If we could see that wall, what would it look like?"

Josh answered immediately, "It's made of concrete blocks. It goes on forever to the left and the right. It's taller than I could ever climb."

"That doesn't *sound* like a blank screen to me. It sounds like you can picture the wall quite clearly. Who do you suppose is showing you that 'vision'?"

Josh was waking up. "God?" he suggested.

John asked, "If that wall had a name, what would it be?"

Josh hesitated, "What comes to mind is 'Pride'."

"You *saw* a wall and you *heard* it called 'Pride'. It sounds like the eyes and ears of your heart are working just fine!"

"Okay, but Jesus is still behind that wall," Josh said. "What should I do?"

"Why not ask him?" John suggested.

A few moments later Josh said, "I sense that he wants me to repent of my academic pride that analyzes everything and dismisses God's messages as soon as they come."

Josh prayed a prayer to that effect, watching the wall, now vivid in his mind, while he prayed. As he surrendered his intellect to the Lordship of Christ, he saw a door appear on the wall. Then Jesus opened the door from the other side and welcomed him through. As he stepped through the door, a new and expansive world—a meeting place—opened up before him. For the two hours that followed, I scrambled in shorthand to record the revelations that the Lord showed to him.

I. REMOVING BLOCKS

Everyone who gives themselves to listening prayer has or will eventually run into what we call "blocks" to hearing and meeting with Jesus. I am talking about those times when we just can't seem to connect with him. There *is* such a phenomenon as "the silence of God," which we'll see at the end of this chapter. But in this age of the Spirit's outpouring with a Saviour who has "so much more he longs to tell us" and a Father who never leaves nor abandons his precious children, we are *waaaaaay* too comfortable with a silent God. I suspect that it is not so much that God is silent but rather that we have acquiesced to any number of blocks that shut him out.

This chapter will discuss a simple approach to overcoming blocks, and then address specifically some of our most common barriers. I trust that God will use it to assist you in removing personal impediments, but also to equip you to support others who need a breakthrough.

Let's begin then, with this indisputable fact: *God is never blocked.* When approaching obstacles to hearing, faith is essential. Not the kind of vague faith that strives to pull itself up by its own bootstraps, but specific confidence in God's character. God makes all the difference in the world. When you bump into a block, it is by design. He loves you, and he is up to something.

A Mazing Grace

Recently, I met with Kate, the intercessor I mentioned in chapter four who steps through spiritual doors in prayer. The way that God uses her imagination in prayer has challenged my western paradigms to the "nth degree." She prays in the spirit across both physical and temporal distances. Yet for months her experience in prayer has *not* been a journey so much as a maze. She began to hit walls and dead ends. Things became quiet and dark. Had God forgotten or abandoned his faithful child? As she cried out to him, the Lord began to label each wall in the maze: fear issues, trust issues, and mind issues. In her heart, Kate began to realize that she feared her spectacular prayer experiences were *not* of God. At the same time, she also feared that they *were* of God and what that implied. She feared where this could lead and the responsibility it gave her. She was afraid that where she was going love could not keep her. She wondered if she could trust God and was tempted with self-protection. She was driven to figure things out and tempted to lean on her own understanding. These were Kate's walls, her blocks to communion with God.

Graciously, the Lord took Kate's hand and began to lead her through the maze. He showed her the need to confront each wall and his willingness to remove them. As Kate's trust grew, she realized that God was up to something: the maze became a labyrinth. It had a centre of rest and communion, and she was given strong assurance that they were traveling there together.

But why the maze/labyrinth at all? Why not just bypass it altogether? The Lord showed Kate that this process was an act of his cleansing grace. He showed her that she wore these issues like one thousand pounds of clothing. At each turn, she was shedding more and more layers. Things were becoming lighter; she was becoming freer. Where he was taking her in the spirit meant ditching the extra luggage, "throwing off everything that hinders" (Hebrews 12:1). From her story, and the stories of countless others, I draw three powerful truths.

A. God is Never Blocked

Whenever we have trouble hearing, do we honestly imagine that God is blocked? That he has somehow thrown up his hands in frustration? Do we believe that the God whose voice can roll like thunder or roar like the ocean surf is unable to drown out and crash through every one of our barriers? God is fully capable of speaking to you at any time he wishes in a way that you cannot mistake. It is no trouble at all for him to bypass any block in our hearts. So why doesn't he?

B. God Led You There

Whenever we feel blocked in our ability to hear, it is because something exists in our heart that God wants us to see. He could speak right past it, but in his kindness, the Lord is dissatisfied with leaving it there. If there is some sort of spiritual tumor in our souls, it is the goodness of God *not* to ignore it. Instead, he leads us directly to it. For this reason, I am not frustrated when I hit blocks, as if they are something standing between God and I that I must somehow circumvent on my own. Rather, I become very attentive, believing that God, who never lets go of my hand, has led me to notice it. He says, "Hey Brad, let's have a look at this boulder over here. It's something I'd like to remove from your heart." If I'm not inclined to follow him into dealing with my issues, he positions himself so that when I run towards him, I end up tripping over my issues. Why? Because he is totally committed to setting me free.

Pruning the Creepers

Kim, a pastor friend in Kelowna, BC, describes this with a neat visual of pruning creeping vines. He gets people who feel blocked to imagine that Jesus is standing at the door of their hearts, knocking. They would love to open the door and let him in to commune with them. But the problem is that a mesh of creeping vines hides the door. Together, Kim and his people ask the Lord to identify the vines. What are they? From where did they come? What kind of shears are required to prune them back? As supposedly blocked as his people are, they always seem to see the vines and the wall. They always know what the vines are and hear what shears are needed. When the vines are cleared away, they open the door to find Jesus every time.

Why this exercise? Why doesn't Jesus just step over the wall or blow the door open? He could do this. The vines don't *really* have any power to restrain him. Those vines represent something that holds his children in bondage, something that is strangling their spirits, something he desires to cut away. And he desires us to play an active role in freeing ourselves from their entanglement so we can grow in faith and maturity during the process.

C. There's Always a Way In

Jesus is never stymied. I once attended a conference in a large building with many doors. During a break, I went out for some fresh air and found myself locked out. I couldn't remember which door was open, but I knew that at least one of them was not dead-bolted. As I walked around the building, checking one locked door after another, it never occurred to me to break any of them down or bang my head against them. I just kept moving on until at last I found an entrance that swung open easily. So it is in communion with God. If Jesus has paid

160

the price to open a new and living way for us into the presence of God (Hebrews 10:20), then I can assume that I am never truly locked out. If a particular door doesn't seem to open, I needn't rage at God or walk away in defeat. I should just proceed to the next door.

When the Voice Stopped

Terri came to me in a panic one day. "The voice has stopped!" She cried. "I can't hear God anymore!"

I said something sensitive like, "Ridiculous. You're telling me you can't hear him in his Word or through his people or sense him in worship?"

"You don't understand," Terri replied. "When I hear him, I actually *hear* him. It used to be so loud and clear that I went to get tested for schizophrenia. The doctors said I was fine. I could hear God all the time, but now it's stopped! What's wrong with me?"

We tried to convince God to reactivate that voice. Instead of working with God's agenda, Terri and I were both intent on forcing our agenda. He wasn't buying it. For a month, the silence continued. Finally, Terri gave in. She told the Lord, "Even if you never speak to me that way again, I will love you and follow you."

He spoke up immediately: "Terri, you have heard my voice so clearly and intimately that you are tempted to ignore my voice in others. I don't want you to be a self-contained and isolated Christian. I am all about building relationships. I will train you to hear me just as clearly through my people as you did in your own heart. For the next while, you will only hear me through others."

And so it was. Terri wasn't truly shut out. She only needed to learn to move on to the next door—the open door—to resume her communion with God.

D. A BASIC TEMPLATE

1. Ask God to show you what the block is.

In so doing, we are surrendering to God's agenda. We are agreeing to look at the issue that is hindering our growth as disciples. We are submitting to his pruning shears. Whenever we take that step, he will provide a word or picture or impression of what that block looks like. Sometimes the block will appear as a wall, a boulder, or similar obstacle. Other times, we may see a dark "something" or slimy little critter. We may even see a person in our lives whom we need to forgive or forsake.

If the nature of the image we see is not specific, we ask God to name it. We may see a label or hear a word that describes the block. Blocks may include emotions, lies, sins, people, demons or many other things. Don't guess. Don't try to figure it out. Just listen. Believe that God has "waved this flag" to get your attention just as he uses physical symptoms to alert us to physical diseases. He is also prepared to resolve the issue.

2. Ask God to show you where the block came from.

Why is the block there? If God identifies a block such as shame, it's important to inquire where it came from. While the Lord is willing to remove shame blocks from our lives, we have a choice. We can allow him to *comfort* us in this moment of shame, or we can ask him to *cure* us at the source of our shame. The former is like picking the bad fruit off of a tree. The latter is like pulling the whole tree out by the roots. While just having him clean away the bad fruit is typically easier at the time, fruit has a way of growing back. Until we've looked at the source of the bad fruit, we may find that it recurs. Dealing with the block at its source often involves walking back into a memory with Jesus momentarily. But having resolved the event(s) that gave rise to the block, you'll find that the block itself is either gone or you can ask Jesus to come remove it.

3. Ask God how it can be removed.

Sometimes the Lord will say, "Just ask." On other occasions, he may ask you to take care of something first. This may involve repentance or forgiveness. He may want you to hear a truth, renounce a lie or break some inner vow you've made. Again, you won't need to sort it all out. Just ask, listen, and obey. When in doubt, I just keep asking the Lord, "What needs to happen next?" until he tells me the block is ready to go.

Most commonly, the Lord will appear in the form of Jesus and perform some creative act of removal. He may stomp on the block, sweep it away, hurl it into an abyss or dropkick it out of existence. Whatever image he chooses, his point is always the same:

> He does not treat us as our sins deserve or repay us according to our iniquities. For as high as the heavens are above the earth, so great is his love for those who fear him; as far as the east is from the west, so far has he removed our transgressions from us. (Psalm 103:11–12)

Taking Out the Trash

Lest this sound complicated, the whole process frequently takes no longer than it took for you to read through the template—or no longer than the time required to take out the trash. One morning when I was running out the door, late for work, Eden called me to take the garbage cans out to the road. Instantly, a seething anger bubbled up from my heart. I knew in advance that this grossly disproportionate emotion was a block just waiting to mess up my day. I asked the Lord what it was and where it came from. By the time I got to the end of my driveway, he told me, "That's some unresolved rage from your high school days. Do you remember fantasizing violent revenge on W— after he threatened you unjustly?"

"Vividly!" I thought, face flushing as I recalled the incident.

The Lord continued, "Do you think we could leave that trash out here too?" By the time I returned to the house to give my wife a good-bye kiss, I was able to repent of this old rage and have the Lord remove it. He restored me to peace and uprooted an old weed in a matter of a minute. I would venture to call that the norm. Even Josh's life-long pride-block was dislodged in less than five minutes. It need not be a big deal. It's just incredibly sad that we put up with them for so long! Blocks are not the mountainous masses we imagine them to be. I picture them as little, wooden children's blocks that our heavenly Father flicks away after discussing them with his children.

II. FACING THE MOST COMMON BLOCKS

The following are some of the most common blocks you may encounter in your journey with Jesus.

A. Mental Blocks

Mental blocks arise when we discard God's voice because of our bondage to rationalism. The trouble is that we lean too heavily on our worldly wisdom and our own understanding. God doesn't require us to shut our brains off when we listen to him, but they do need to get off the throne. The apostle Paul, a man well-educated in both religion and philosophy, warned us of the limitations of our mental assets when it comes to hearing God's message.

> For the message of the Cross is *foolishness* to those who are perishing, but to us who are being saved it is the power of

God. For it is written: "I will destroy *the wisdom of the wise; the intelligence of the intelligent I will frustrate.*"

Where is the wise man? Where is the scholar? Where is the philosopher of this age? *Has not God made foolish the wisdom of the world?* For since in the wisdom of God *the world through its wisdom did not know him,* God was pleased through the foolishness of what was preached to save those who believe.

For the foolishness of God is wiser than man's wisdom, and the weakness of God is stronger than man's strength. Brothers, think of what you were when you were called. Not many of you were wise by human standards; not many were influential; not many were of noble birth. But *God chose the foolish things of the world to shame the wise*; God chose the weak things of the world to shame the strong. He chose the lowly things of this world and the despised things—and the things that are not—to nullify the things that are, so that no one may boast before him. (1 Corinthians 1:18–21; 25–28)

Solomon tells us to trust in the Lord and lean not on our own understanding, to acknowledge him (and his voice) in all our ways so that we can follow as he directs our paths (Proverbs 3:5–6). Yet, so often the little analyst in our minds sends the message, "I'm making this up" or "I need to figure this out." When praying with people, I hear the objection, "I'm getting something, but it makes no sense." What are they really saying? If their rational minds cannot dissect what they are receiving, then they are not receiving it? Or if it makes no sense to the mind, the mind must be making it up? Do you see the faulty logic at work? They actually hear the Lord immediately but then fashion the first objection that comes to mind into a wrecking ball with which to demolish what they heard! We voluntarily relinquish so much of God's gracious encouragement without giving it a thought.

Soozy Q

My friend Susan used to say, "I never hear God anymore." When I challenged her with a few listening exercises, she confessed that nearly every time she asked God a question, she would hear his answer instantly, often in the form of familiar song lyrics. But within about three seconds, her rational mind would contradict what she heard and toss it away by arguing, "That made no sense."

To begin with, the fact that she heard something that seemed to make no sense is likely an indication that she *didn't* concoct the

CA

answer. After all, if she were "making it up," her mi[...] offered up something sensible. Second, if Sue's mind i[...] with the answer she heard, with whom is it arguing? Wh[...] tial answer come from? Perhaps it was from the Lord, pe[...] not. But it is certainly worth weighing. Third, if the answer makes no sense, God is probably baiting us to get us to ask more questions: "Why am I seeing that? What does it mean? I don't get it. Can you tell me more?"

We began to track what Sue was hearing in those first seconds before the inner argument ensued and it turned out that she was *highly* prophetic. When she began to acknowledge the Lord's voice like this, other avenues of revelation opened up, including significant predictive dreams.

To remove mental blocks we need to bring our minds into submission to the Lordship of Christ. We need to have the mind of Christ and believe it. I find that I can fool my overly critical mind into listening by asking it less threatening questions. For example, rather than, "What did God say?" I ask, "While praying, what came to mind? What was my first impression? If Jesus *were* speaking, I sense he would say..." After putting analysis on hold until those questions are answered, I can then put it to work, actively testing whether I was indeed hearing the Lord.

B. Fear Blocks

Fear blocks usually interrupt God's voice because of a bad teaching or a bad experience that we've had concerning the voice of the Lord. We hit a fear block whenever we shrink back through:

- Fear of the unknown
- Fear of deception
- Fear of intimacy
- Fear of repercussions

Behind each of these fears, you will always find a lie. For each lie, Jesus wants to reveal the truth that will set you free from both the lie and from its resulting fear. For example, behind fear of the unknown may be the lie, "If I open my ears to the Lord, I have no idea what he'll say, but it will probably be bad news." Behind fear of deception you may believe the lie, "If I open my heart to listen, I have no way to know whose voice I'll hear. The devil may lead me astray." Behind fear of intimacy is the thought, "If I open up, then God will see what's there. *I* don't even want to see what's there! He may dislike me or even reject me." Behind fear of repercussions we hear, "If I open my ears, I will

Fear that when God does reveal himself & His truth about me, I won't be able to change, I'm too weak & have very little disciplin or self control

hear him, and then I'll have to do something about it. And I don't want to." The hidden lie is that rebellion is better than obedience.

To remove fear blocks, I don't argue with the lies or try to repress them. Instead, I take them like a bull by the horns, speak them aloud to the Lord's face, and wait for his response. When he hears me voicing that lie, his truth comes back like a sword, shredding the lie's power to deceive and deafen me. Sometimes when I tell him my lie, he just laughs. When he does, I never feel mocked or belittled. His laugh is a revelation that frees my heart from taking the lie seriously or fearing its power.

Using our block-removal template, we process fears by:

- Asking Jesus where it came from;
- Asking Jesus to reveal the lie behind the fear;
- Asking Jesus what truth we need to hear.

C. Shame Blocks

Shame causes us to shrink from listening to God's voice by making us feel unworthy to approach him. Shame blocks are nearly identical to fear blocks in that you will always, always find lies behind the shame. Shame tells me lies:

- I'm worthless (just a loser, not worthy to be his child).
- I'm unclean (dirty, too sinful, too far gone).
- I don't measure up (not good enough, not holy enough).

You can see the shame message when Adam and Eve hid from God in Eden (as if leaves could cover their sin!). You can hear the shame message in the prodigal son when he says, "I am no longer worthy to be called your son" (Luke 15:19). You can also hear it in Peter when he realizes who Jesus really is: "Go away from me, Lord; I am a sinful man!" (Luke 5:8). The lie is not that we are unworthy sinners but that there is no forgiveness for us and, therefore, God should leave us to ourselves.

To remove shame blocks we use the same drill as with fear. We speak our feelings directly to Christ's face and wait for his reaction. I am intrigued by his diverse methods with each one that approaches him. Sometimes he says, "Of course you *aren't* worthy! Come, let me wash you and dress you in new white robes." With others, he says, "Of course you *are* worthy. Don't you know that you are my beloved child? Approach me boldly and ask whatever you wish!" Again, sometimes he just settles the whole issue with a hearty laugh.

No End of Tablecloths

When my wife was coming into an understanding of grace, the Lord chose to show her some of the darkness of her own heart. He wanted her to know that her own goodness (and there's lots of it!) would never ever buy her a seat at his banquet table. He was intent on showing her the absolute need for grace, even for the very best of "church kids." She saw that when she came to the banqueting table of God, the shadow in her heart soiled the tablecloth with a sticky, black tar. Horrified and feeling shameful, she told the Lord, "I would rather not eat at your table than ruin it like that." With a smile, he grabbed the corner of the tablecloth and swept it away. "There's more where that came from," he said, and opened a linen cupboard crammed full of fresh white tablecloths. He showed her that it is true that we need mercy and grace every day, because we do violate his holiness with our sin. But his forgiveness is always available and, therefore, we are always welcome to dine with him.

To apply our basic template to this block:

- Ask Jesus where the shame originated.
- Ask Jesus to reveal the lie behind the shame.
- Ask Jesus what truth we need to hear.

D. Sin and Pain Blocks

God's voice can be blocked out because we don't hear well when we're in sin and pain. Pain blocks include any burden that we carry, such as:

- Hurt (because someone actually hurt us)
- Anger (because someone actually offended us)
- Grief (because of some actual loss)
- Guilt (because we have actually sinned)
- Empathy (because someone else we know is struggling)

Later on in chapter thirteen (Listening Prayer for Inner Healing), we will discuss each of these categories in greater detail. We will also look at the amazing way that God lifts the burden of pain from our hearts. For now, let's just focus on dealing with the blinding and deafening effects of our hurt, anger, grief, guilt or empathy. If they are hindering our ability to hear God's voice or see his face, they need to be removed.

Our experience with pain is that *even before* we release our pain to God, and *even before* God heals us, our pain will cease to block out

God's *voice as soon as we honestly confess it to him*. When we hold our pain behind our backs in repression, God may seem strangely silent, even absent! When we risk brutal honesty with the One who sees perfectly into our hearts, the best description I can give to his response is *"Whoosh!"* He rushes in to hear and answer our desperate plea for help.

"I Hate God!"

Judy might just be the ultimate, stereotypical "pastor's wife." In truth, she and her husband work together as a pastoral team, providing discipleship for a fast-growing prairie congregation. Judy's one setback is her migraines—the pain makes it impossible to function at times. We asked the Lord to track these headaches to their source, and he took us into a memory-parable where we hoped to meet with him. Although Judy could vividly recount the setting that she witnessed in her spirit, the Lord was nowhere to be found. This was unusual, given his promises to be with us always and to answer when we call. Yet our invitations went unheeded, and Judy was getting frustrated. Knowing that the standard block at this point was pain, and sensing her rising anger, I suggested that God might be waiting for her to share more (more honestly, I thought to myself).

She began with, "I'm just so disappointed in God about this." No response. "Okay," she added, "I'm actually really quite angry at him." Nothing. Finally, she burst out, "Fine! If you want to know the truth, God, I HATE YOU!"

Whoosh! Instantly, the presence of the Lord Jesus flooded into her heart in full-on "technicolor." He acted, he spoke, he embraced, and he loved her! It was kindness not cruelty that caused him to hesitate. He was not willing to heal a headache but leave the hidden hatred behind. The block was there to expose her feelings so she could be healed in her body, soul, and spirit.

We remove pain blocks through honest confession of how we feel. Sometimes God also waits to hear *why* we feel it. In both cases, he already knows the answer, but he is waiting for our denial to crumble such that we can verbalize how we truly feel. Some prayer ministers also expect to see an emotional expression of the pain and, while I've found that to be helpful, I've observed that it is not a prerequisite to healing if the verbal confession is thorough.

Occasionally, the Lord chooses to remain silent even up until we ask Jesus to bear the burden for us. The reason for this appears to be a faith-building exercise. Those who have never acknowledged hearing his voice may be very skeptical as he starts speaking about their pain.

However, if they begin to physically and emotionally feel the hurt or anger or whatever burden leaving them, the experience of God's voice is much more authentic and believable.

E. Confusion blocks

During the course of listening prayer, we periodically find our heads swimming in confusion, unable to hear because our thoughts start flooding, swirling, or spinning or everything inside suddenly goes blank or black.

Confusion blocks come from either the turmoil of our own racing minds or by the interference of blocking spirits. In the latter case, a sudden and specific body pain may also intrude on our prayers (e.g., a sharp head-pain appears from nowhere). In the case of confusion blocks, I counsel against making a big deal out of it. I simply pray, "Jesus, would you please bind that spirit to the Cross until later? Thank you." Treat it as a distracting fly to be swatted aside ("Shoo!") and return quickly to the business at hand: listening to God.

To remove confusion blocks:

- Dial down: be still before God.
- Let go of worries.
- Take hold of peace.
- Bind away blocking spirits.

F. Demonic, False Christs (Deception)

A demonic, false Jesus is an unclean spirit that attempts to masquerade as Jesus. Their agenda is to either misrepresent him or to give us bad advice in his name.

The Dispassionate Jesus

I was praying with a friend through some childhood traumas that left her feeling a lot of shame and vulnerability. When we invited Jesus to come, she saw a very sullen Jesus sitting to her left. He seemed very unconcerned with her, and when we asked him to respond, he began to spank her! You don't need to be St. Peter to recognize that something is amiss here. We told "it" to stop immediately and asked the true Lord Jesus to show us the real identity of this ridiculous imitation. The true Lord Jesus entered the memory in all his love and glory, stripped the unclean spirit of its disguise, and sent it away forever.

Why this experience? Apparently this demonic Jesus had somehow been introduced into my friend's life early on when she became convinced that Jesus did not care about her and all she trusted him for was punishment. This opened a door of oppression that the true Jesus was now shutting. It was insufficient to simply protect her from it or automatically cast it away. The demon was merely a symptom of some fundamental lies that she believed at some level of her heart.

Fear No Evil

Lest you worry about being easily hoodwinked by a false Jesus, I hasten to add these important points:

- Demons are *not* very good imitators of Christ! They are *nothing* like Jesus at all in either their *character* or their *message*. A false Jesus will often seem cold, harsh, distant, and religious. It only takes advantage of us when we have already believed grave lies about the character and message of the true Jesus. Someone who knows that Jesus loves them and cares about their hurts will do a major double take if they see a dispassionate or harsh Jesus.
- Jesus allows us to see false images of himself so they can be exposed and removed. It is unpleasant and annoying to run into a false Jesus, but when we do, it is only to show us that we are carrying some garbage inside that has attracted some rats. Remove the garbage (lies) and the rats (demons) will leave. Jesus is all about "cleaning house."
- The true Jesus throws in clues to warn us that we are dealing with a false Jesus. Hint: look for something black! My friend Della prayed with someone who claimed to see a vision of Jesus coming towards them. Everything seemed right, except that this Jesus was wearing a black cape. It was as though Jesus had required the spirit to expose itself through wearing a conspicuous tag!

To unmask a demonic, false Jesus:

- Renounce the religious spirit.
- Repent for any belief in a silent, uncaring Jesus.
- Ask for the true Jesus to come and act.

G. Fleshly, False Christs (Projection)

Unlike the demonic counterfeits, the fleshly false Jesus is a self-created mental projection that comes from our own judgments on others or of Jesus. In this case, our fleshly minds produce a distorted or false image of Jesus. The trouble with these fellows is that no matter how many times you try to cast them away, they just keep reappearing. When we are dealing with a demon, when Jesus sends it away to the pit, that's the end of it. It can't escape and return to oppress you over and over again. Not so with these distorted projections. They persist as long as our judgments create a filter through which we imagine Jesus to be someone he is not.

Jesus the Grey?

I was part of a prayer team that was working through a series of child-hood memories with a certain intercessor. Literally every time we invited Jesus into a memory, a grey Jesus would appear. Consistently, it would begin to act the way we expect Jesus to act, but then would do or say something uncaring, punitive or be powerless to help her. Our discovery of what was occurring and what God was up to came in stages. First, we treated the grey Jesus as a demon. But no sooner had we supposedly cast it away than it would reappear in the next "scene." Demons can't do that if Jesus is truly sending them to the pit.

When we asked Jesus what needed to happen next (our famous last resort!), he would identify some judgment the woman was car-rying towards her father. When she repented of that judgment, the grey Jesus was gone and the true, loving, and powerful Jesus in white would show up and resolve the memory. Apparently, her judg-ments against her father (as uncaring, harsh, or powerless) became filters through which she saw Jesus. To put it another way, she was "laminating" her judgments against her father onto Jesus—project-ing her dad's faults onto this false image of the grey Jesus. Through this second stage, we made headway, but it was still very troubling whenever a grey Jesus showed up.

When we complained about this recurring pattern, the Lord showed us that rather than dealing with the grey Jesus as an incon-venience, we should see it as a helpful sign that the true Jesus used to systematically reveal all of the lady's hidden judgments.

To remove a fleshly, false christ:

- Ask Jesus to lead you to the source of this false Jesus.
- Identify and repent of judgments on others that you've laminated onto him.
- Ask for the true Lord Jesus to be revealed.

Bottom Line

If we are convinced of Jesus' commitment to remove obstacles that trip us up, then hitting blocks will not scare us. We will see them as bumps and ruts in the highway to the kingdom that God wants to level out. They become a project that we work on together at just the right time. Blocks are *not* a blessing. But the ability to see them and remove them in partnership with God is a gift that deepens our communion with him.

◀)) *Tuning In* • • • • • • • • • •

Even though you are no doubt hearing and seeing the Lord by now, you needn't wait until you've bloodied your spiritual nose on a block before asking God to remove it. As an ongoing aspect of prayer, here is an excellent preventative exercise:

- Picture the Lord out in front of you. As always, he is welcoming you to draw near. Ask him, "If there are any obstacles that are preventing the fullness of relationship between you and I, please show them to me." Can you see the characters? What are they doing?
- If you see nothing, don't make an effort to create something! Just enjoy his presence. But if you see something or someone intrude into the picture, ask God what it is, where it came from, and how to remove it.

III. THE SILENCE OF GOD

This chapter would be incomplete without acknowledging those times when God chooses silence, not to expose a block, but as an act of trust. Oswald Chambers truly nailed this experience:

> Has God trusted you with his silence—a silence that has great meaning? God's silences are actually his answers. Just think of those days of absolute silence in the home at Bethany! [John 11:6] Is there anything comparable to those days in your life? Can God trust you like that, or are you still asking him for a visible answer? God will give you the very blessings you ask if you refuse to go any further without them, but his silence is the sign that he is bringing you into an even more wonderful understanding of himself. Are you mourning before God because you have not had an audible response? When you cannot hear God, you will

find that he has trusted you in the most intimate way possible—with absolute silence, not a silence of despair, but one of pleasure, because he saw that you could withstand an even bigger revelation.[1]

Teresa of Avila described one silent stage in the mystic journey as "the Prayer of Quiet." In it, the inner senses fade into silent, dark communion. We are weaned of the need for inner sights and sounds; all becomes absolute stillness. We know God is there, not by the senses but in raw faith. The spirit, unaided by the imaginative faculties of the soul, soaks in God's presence. Here is Teresa's description of a silence of God that is actually a rich, authentic state of prayer.

> This is a supernatural state, and, however hard we try, we cannot reach it for ourselves; for it is a state in which the soul enters into peace, or rather in which the Lord gives it peace through his presence, as he did to that just man Simeon [Luke 2:25–35]. In this state all the faculties are stilled. The soul, in a way which has nothing to do with the outward senses, realizes that it is now very close to its God, and that, if it were but a little closer, it would become one with him through union. *This is not because it sees him either with its bodily or with its spiritual eyes ... It is, as it were, in a swoon, both inwardly and outwardly,* so that the outward man (let me call it the "body," and then you will understand me better) does not wish to move, but rests, like one who has almost reached the end of his journey, so that it may the better start again upon its way, with redoubled strength for its task.[2]

One might wonder if such stillness is mere unproductive inactivity or how one would tell the difference if it weren't. The answer is twofold. First, in the Prayer of Quiet, although we see and hear nothing in the imaginal realm, we enjoy a strong sense of bliss in God's loving presence.

> The body experiences the greatest delight and the soul is conscious of a deep satisfaction. So glad is it merely to find itself near the fountain that, even before it has begun to drink, it has had its fill. There seems nothing left for it to desire. The faculties are stilled and have no wish to move, for any movement they may make appears to hinder the soul from loving God.[3]

Second, we experience the spiritual fruit of communion with God. Only God can lead us into the Prayer of Quiet, but when he does, look for spiritual renewal as you would with any active encounter with him.[4]

St. John of the Cross (1542–1591) looks beyond the Prayer of Quiet into a deeper, darker silence in what he called "the Dark Night of the Soul." The Dark Night of the Soul is that stage on the mystical path when,

> spiritual persons suffer great trials, by reason not so much of the aridities [dryness] which they suffer, as of the fear which they have of being lost on the road, thinking that all spiritual blessing is over for them and that God has abandoned them since they find no help or pleasure in good things.[5]

The soul is now weaned, not just from inner vision and voice but also from any sense of God's presence. This rare suspension of all spiritual senses makes possible a work of radical transformation deep in one's spirit. St. John of the Cross says that in this type of silent darkness,

> [God] puts the sensory spiritual appetites to sleep, deadens them, and deprives them of the ability to find pleasure in anything. It binds the imagination, and impedes it from doing any good discursive work. It makes the memory cease, the intellect become dark and unable to understand anything, and hence it causes the will to become arid and constrained, and all the faculties empty and useless. And over this hangs a dense and burdensome cloud, which afflicts the soul, and keeps it withdrawn from the good.[6]

The true "dark night" is not to be confused with depression, apathy or distraction. You can't snap out of it any more than a woman in labour can resist having contractions! Medication, counselling, and prayer will not break this silence. Friends and pastors may even think you are backsliding. All you can do is submit to the inner solitude and wait for God to complete his work (like a chrysalis waits for the inner metamorphosis that results in a butterfly). The end result of this silent affliction is a purification of the spirit, soul, and senses that frees the heart for ultimate oneness with God, which the mystics called "Love-Union." Once again, God's purpose here is not to wound, only to heal so he can have a closer friendship with you.

Part III

The Life of Listening Prayer

Listening Prayer In Decision Times

> *I will instruct you and teach you in the way you should go; I will counsel you and watch over you. Do not be like the horse or the mule, which have no understanding but must be controlled by bit and bridle or they will not come to you.*
>
> - Psalm 32:8–9 (KJV)

I frequently bump into two schools of thought concerning divine guidance. On the one hand, some folks expect no specific direction from God beyond basic morality, common sense, and biblical principles. They live life by their own better judgment within the boundaries of God's written word. Their attitude might be described as a sort of "Christian deism," if you will, which says that God set things up in the beginning (whenever *that* was), but has pretty much left the running of things to us, only intervening in our lives if *absolutely necessary.* Their motto is, "God can't steer a parked car." At the other extreme, many are paralyzed with indecision or fear until they receive specific direction or permission from heaven. It's sort of a "sit tight until God says something" mentality.

The model that I will propose when faced with a decision steers a middle course between the two extremes. It is as follows: *Friends of God who live by faith* (not playing it safe) *and consult the Lord* (attend to his voice) *are led by the Spirit into God's purposes* (rather than merely asking him to bless our agendas). Let's break this thesis down into its component parts so I can elaborate on it further.

1. FRIENDS OF GOD...

The premise here is that God wants to be your friend, not your psychic hotline. It stems from a concern that I have. We often critique unchurched people for neglecting prayer until some emergency inspires them to cry out to God as if he were a 911 operator. I counter that churchgoers are just as guilty of negligence and unbelief in the practice of *listening prayer* until some decision or quandary demands that they call God as their psychic hotline. I believe that the primary function of listening prayer is to maintain an intimate relationship with God *not* to get you out of a jam. When God is your best friend, you don't need to make 9-1-1 or psychic hotline calls. Knowing he is with you always, you can just ask him to take care of you, and he will. In a sermon I once heard prophet Graham Cooke preach, he went as far as to say, "If you take responsibility for your relationship with God, he'll take responsibility for your direction." [1]

In practice, I do pray for divine aid when in a crisis or at a crossroads, and I expect answers. But because my friendship with God has been nurtured through listening prayer, my requests lack the anxiety or impatience of a typical "911 prayer." Those who only listen to God during a dilemma don't know him well enough to trust him. They tend to grovel, beg, bargain, and even demand. Friends of God can make their request and then be at rest, watching what he does from a place of peace. Since they are familiar with his voice and sense his peace, they are able to step out in faith without wavering, hesitating or running ahead.

Fear of Risk

Friends of God don't fear taking risks and making mistakes. Faith doesn't require a full blueprint and ironclad warranty for every action taken. The Bible is a history of faithful people who started their journeys without an itinerary. They frequently knew only the single step in front of them, but they risked taking it.

When we began Fresh Wind, I asked the Lord, "If we begin this risky venture, can you promise that it will succeed?" His answer struck me, "I'll risk it if you will." It seemed that even God was acting in faith with no guarantees from my end. His promise was his presence, not a failsafe project. He confirmed this to Bill (Brian's successor at Fresh Wind) by saying, "Both your successes and your failures are to my glory." Because we would rather glorify God than be "successful," roughly every six months we ask the Lord, "Do you want us to shut this work down?" So far, he's still enjoying the risk.

Those who hesitate to act because they fear making mistakes betray a misunderstanding of God. They know him as "hard master" but not as friend. In Matthew 25, Jesus tells the parable of a master who commissioned three servants to make investments for him while he was away. He gives them freedom and authority to take risks and make gains. While he is gone, two of the servants follow these instructions and pull in a profit. The third merely buries his portion in the ground and waits out his time. When called to give an account for his passivity, the third servant explains, "Master... I knew that you are a

178

hard man, harvesting where you have not sown and gathering where you have not scattered seed. So I was *afraid* and went out and hid your talent in the ground. See, here is what belongs to you" (Matthew 25:24–25). Outraged, the master dismisses the man from his service. His mistaken judgment that he served a harsh taskmaster who would punish him for his mistakes became a self-fulfilling prophecy through his own faithlessness.

The Fourth Servant

At the risk of "adding to Scripture," I'd like to extend the parable to include a fourth servant. I would tell it like this:

> The fourth servant also received one talent and proceeded to faithfully invest it according to his master's wishes. Sadly, through an error in judgment, he lost the entire investment. Coming before his master, he admitted his mistake.
> The master replied, "Well done good and faithful servant! You have been faithful with a few things. I will put you in charge of more things."
> "How can this be?" asked the servant. "I lost all that you gave me! How is it that you call me faithful?"
> The master responded, "Faithfulness is not judged by one's success, but by faith and obedience. In faith and obedience, you honored my request to risk it all. Now behold, I have harvested where I have not sown and gathered where I have not scattered seed. What you believed you lost has been counted gain. Come and share your master's happiness."

I share this illustration to show you that those who truly know God's character will lose their fear of making mistakes or risking failure. They know that he works *all* things together for their good (Romans 8: 28). His perfect love has cast out their fear of punishment (1 John 4: 18). They have come to know that he does *not* require his friends to walk on eggshells around him, so they feel free to live by faith.

2. Friends of God WHO LIVE BY FAITH...

Living by faith starts with living (discerning, choosing, and acting) and continues by faith (in God's presence, promises, guidance, and protection). When I am walking in the Spirit, I *am* on the right path, led (even silently) by the Spirit. I am not just doing my own thing. I know that I am doing *God's thing,* because when I'm filled with the Spirit, my spirit proceeds where it knows to go.

Let peace be your umpire

The friend of God who lives by faith is led mainly by the Spirit's peace. Stepping out in faith doesn't always feel peaceful to our *flesh*, but peace reigns in our *hearts* before God when we are aligned with his will, even in difficult circumstances. Remember Paul and Silas praising God in prison? (Acts 16:25) If a direction I'm taking is not pleasing him or not best for me, the Spirit should convict me with a lack of peace, and, if necessary, get a message to me.

This is precisely how David related to the Lord. As a friend of God, David normally lived, chose, and acted in the faith that God was with him. By faith, he suggested to Nathan the prophet that he would build a temple for God. Nathan's default response was, "Whatever you have in mind, go ahead and do it, for the LORD is with you" (2 Samuel 7:3). But this time, David's plan was *not* God's wish, so the Lord sent him a message. That night the word of the Lord came to Nathan, saying, "Go and tell my servant David that he is not the one who should build me a house" (2 Samuel 7:4–5).

In other words, at Nathan's prompting, David had a green light to proceed. But when the light turned red, God was faithful to let him know. Apparently there *is* a time to "pull over" and put the proverbial car in "park"!

3. Friends of God who live by faith AND CONSULT THE LORD...

I am confident that God's peace will direct me as I live by faith. If I veer off God's course, he is faithful to deliver correctives to me. To ensure that I am open to hearing these messages, I typically ask for confirmations from the Word, the Body, and the Spirit. I make my requests known to intercessors and maintain contact with prophetic people. I expect God's direction beyond simple moral discernment, so I need to consult with him.

Those who simply act on their own (within God's moral bounds) without consulting him are probably not living like the apostle Paul. In Acts 16:6–10, we find Paul's team on a ministry trip in Asia Minor. Rather than "going into all the world" at random, we see their sensitivity to God's Spirit. They were *"kept from preaching by the Spirit* in the province of Asia" (vs. 6). "The Spirit of Jesus would *not allow* them" to enter Bithynia (vs. 7). Then Paul had a vision at night calling them to Macedonia (vs. 9). If the premier apostle to the Gentiles needed to consult God's Spirit in order to stay on track, then so do I—and so do you!

Consulting God includes living daily in conversation with him. Before my head leaves the pillow each morning, I like to ask questions: "Lord, what's the best use of my day?"
"Is there anything you want me to do today?"
"Is there anyone I'm supposed to meet today?"
I follow those impressions when they come. When they don't, I should not be paralyzed into inactivity or stubbornly demand a word from the Lord. I simply proceed by faith on the path of greatest peace (not the path of least resistance).

This keeps my will intact but also purposely aligns it with God's. Ignoring God is a bad idea. But so is asking him to make all your decisions for you. A maturing friendship with God means knowing more and more what pleases him. Like a football coach who knows that he and his quarterback are in sync, he increasingly trusts you to make the call. That is what "authority" means. The heavenly coach says, "You've proven that you can make good decisions with the gifts that I've given you. I'll let you run things at will a bit more, because in our friendship, you generally do what I would do. If you get off track, or I have a better idea, I'll be sure to let you know." In biblical terms, he says, "I trusted you with a city, now I'm trusting you with ten cities" (Luke 19).

4. Friends of God who live by faith and consult the Lord ARE LED BY THE SPIRIT...

As we live by the Spirit, acting spiritually and listening daily, life unfolds naturally before us. Even so, at times we still come to major crossroads. In those times I ask God, "What do you want?" Over the last few years, his first response always seems to be "Well, what do YOU want?" Part of the discernment process is learning what we want so that God can discuss with us why we want it, whether he wants it too, why we might differ on this, when we should have it, and so on. This sounds like a friendship to me. When someone tells me, "I just want what God wants," I appreciate the gesture of surrender. Yet God's desire is not to cripple our wills but to conform them to his. There may be a whiff of fear or risk in that reply, but that usually stems from the insecurity of someone who just wants to be told what to do. (Good candidates for a cult!)

Signs

Having said that, I *do* want to please God. I would rather put his kingdom ahead of my personal dreams. So when in doubt, I'm not afraid to ask for a confirming "road sign." Take note: I don't demand a sign in order to believe or obey God's voice. I commit myself to stay on the road he has given me. The role of signs is to confirm that I'm still on that road.

Gideon's fleece worked for him (Judges 6), because he was testing the spirits. He wanted to be confident that he was hearing the true God. God used the signs to confirm his call and then led him into great acts of faith and victory.

Later in Israel's history, God called King Ahaz to stand firm in his faith and stay the course he'd been given. He instructed Ahaz to ask for a sign to confirm this message. Shaken by his circumstances, Ahaz stubbornly declined. "No, I don't want to test the Lord" (i.e., "No, I'd rather flee."). Isaiah rebukes Ahaz for trying God's patience and then adds, "God will give you a sign anyway" (Isaiah 7:11–14) and foretells the destruction of Israel due to Ahaz's faithlessness.

In Matthew 16:1–4, Jesus rebukes the Pharisees' inability to read signs, rejects their demands for a sign, and then announces the coming "sign of Jonah" all at once. Their sign-seeking backfired, because they heard Jesus clearly and saw his miracles yet demanded further proof from God as a prerequisite to following in active faith and obedience (Matthew 12:38–39). Jesus refused to give it to them. God will not be controlled or cornered by our sign seeking. Signs are only meant to encourage us along the path of faith not to help us overcome our skepticism.

In Practice

We frequently experience God's confirming voice through unsolicited messengers when it's time for an important change in direction or at the beginning of a new mission. After six fruitful years of youth work at Bethel Church, I was about to resign my post to venture out into church planting. A conference was ready to back us, a local church was willing to provide a core-group, and a location was established. I had written my resignation letter and was about to hand it in. Eden and I gave the Lord a final opportunity to confirm or block our passage.

That weekend, I had a dream that I was chipping onto the sixth green of a nine-hole golf course. I noticed that the grass was knee-deep and the pins had not been placed in the holes. The course seemed unfinished. As I awoke, I realized that I was quoting aloud the Scripture, "I have fought the fight, I have finished the course." The message: I had *not* yet finished the course of ministry at Bethel. Eden also had two warning dreams, one about hidden land mines and the other about wrong fitting roller skates. (You can put two and two together.) Though we caused some disappointment by backing away, time proved that the landmines did exist (the mother-church reversed its support and opposed a church plant) and the fit was wrong (our pursuit of renewal was a problem to the conference). My course at Bethel ended up being nine years ("holes") rather than just six.

When it was finally time for us to plant a church, Eden and I trod carefully because of the first experience. First, the Lord asked us what WE wanted to do. We said we wanted to obey him, but, if we had a choice, we wanted to work with Brian West and Fresh Wind Ministries. The Lord began to speak to us through prophets, intercessors, and dreams, describing what our new work would look like. It sounded like it could *only* fit with where Brian was headed.

In boldness, not defiance, I asked for a sign. I asked that when it was time to resign, Vic Epp (a best friend of mine at the time) would tell me, "It's time for you to go." This was difficult in that I was away at a cabin in Penticton, BC for a month and was totally out of contact with him. On my final week there, the cabin owners' son came to visit. He shared something strange that had happened. "I've been working for Vic Epp this week and was surprised when he mentioned that he thinks it's time for you to go." That Tuesday, I tendered my resignation, still unsure about my future but certain that God had spoken.

I felt led to send a letter to Valley Christian Fellowship (another church in Abbotsford) and offer Eden and I to them as church-planters. One stipulation was that they would need to release Brian and Susan West from their staff to work with me (Brian was unaware of my plan). The day I dropped off my proposal at VCF, their entire pastoral team was out of town for a retreat. Unbeknownst to me, *just then* at the retreat, Brian's senior pastor approached him with the challenge, "It's time for you to go plant a church." Brian was surprised but responded immediately with, "Not unless you can get Brad Jersak to go with me." Shortly after that, we planted Fresh Wind.

5. Friends of God who live by faith and consult the Lord are led by the Spirit INTO GOD'S PURPOSES.

Recently, I received some e-mail questions about divine guidance from a Bible school student. I'll use the correspondence to sew up this chapter.

Q: *A question I have is... God's will. I have always been taught that God has a specific place, person or whatever for me to be involved with, and I can't really wrap my head around that one.*

For better or worse, here was my "gut response":

A: Don't even try. Just asking the question leads us into some sort of either/or deception. Why not just accept certain facts:

- You have a free will. Use it as a Spirit-filled person, acting in faith.
- God has a voice. Listen to it. Obey it. Follow him.
- God has a purpose for you. But don't try to find it, and don't be paranoid about missing it. Just experience it. His purpose is the thing that is happening to you AS you combine being led by his Spirit and led by his voice. It's not a destination ten years down the road that you need to know or need to make happen or measure up to or need to fear missing out on.[2] Here's a promise: If you live by his Spirit *today* (meaning acting in faith as his Spirit moves), his plan for you will roll out before you like a red carpet, one kick at a time.

Q: *Does God allow you to have something in your life if it is "second best" if you really want it bad enough or just to teach you a lesson?*

A: Ezekiel speaks to this question:

> Some of the elders of Israel came to me and sat down in front of me. Then the word of the LORD came to me:
> "Son of man, these men have set up idols in their hearts and put wicked stumbling blocks before their faces. Should I let them inquire of me at all? Therefore speak to them and tell them, 'This is what the Sovereign LORD says: When any Israelite sets up idols in his heart and puts a wicked stumbling block before his face and then goes to a prophet, I the LORD will answer him myself in keeping with his great idolatry. I will do this to recapture the hearts of the people of Israel, who have all deserted me for their idols.'"(Ezekiel 14:1–5)

If you have an idol in your heart and you want it badly enough, when you ask God for it you will hear his answer "through" that idol as a "yes." This is not because he is mean. He allows us to hear "yes," because if he says "no," the idol remains in your heart, competing with God for your loyalty and affection. It nurses resentment in you toward God for withholding it. When he allows us to hear "yes", we embrace the idol, stumble over it, and then cry out to God, who, in his grace, restores us. At that point, we will voluntarily reject the idol and re-establish our loyalty to God. This appears capricious at first, but here's the brilliance of it: it honours our free will, leaving it intact while at the same time, walking us towards repentance and relationship with God in a way that is totally our own decision. It redeems every stumble, changing it into something good in the end. It's not about "teaching us a lesson." It is about giving us what is best for us without violating our will. The whole approach is based on his lovingkindness.

◀)) *Tuning In* • • • • • • • • • •

- Ask the Lord to remind you of something that you were sure you just had to have. Did you ask God for it? Were you able to hear his "no" at the time? If you heard a "yes" *through* that idol, how did you feel?
- Do you recall the point at which you stumbled over the idol? When it became a burden to you? When it even became repulsive? When you turned from it and ran back to God?
- How did God receive you? Take time to ask him why he allowed you to experience that cycle.

Q: *"How do you tell the difference between God closing a door and Satan's opposition or life's obstacles?"*

A: This is where discernment takes practice. You need to acquire a feel for how these things differ. I am deeply indebted to Brian West for discipling me into this art. He taught me to pay close attention to what happens in my own heart as I start "pushing on the door." If Satanic or natural obstacles are barring a door that God has opened, faith, prayer, and diligence will dislodge them eventually. I should feel God's Spirit rising up within me to contend boldly with the blockage. I should have a testimony that Jesus has opened the door to me (Revelation 3:8) and that the Spirit will remove every hindrance. I will sense this within me,

> This is the word of the LORD to Zerubbabel: "Not by might nor by power, but by my Spirit," says the LORD Almighty. "What are you, O mighty mountain? Before Zerubbabel you will become level ground. Then he will bring out the capstone to shouts of 'God bless it! God bless it!'" (Zechariah 4: 6–7)

On the other hand, when the Lord begins to shut the door, the harder I try to push, the more I will sense that I am striving, manipulating, and forcing something to happen. If the Lord does allow me to wedge my way through such a door, it is to reinforce the sense of folly that is attached to self-effort.

Self-promotion is a good example of this. When Fresh Wind teams are invited to churches at the initiative of their pastors, we find a wide open door to share what God has given us. But I remember wedging our way into a particular worship "gig" in which we really wanted to participate. It felt like we were "sneaking in the back door." We made extra phone-calls to see if we were invited and how we could help. Upon arrival, our wonderful worship leader was relegated to doing overheads. The single seminar they allowed him to teach was in a cramped basement Sunday-school room with only a handful of participants. The whole experience felt "off," so we asked God what had happened. He showed us that neither he nor the church had opened the door to us. We had manufactured the invitation ourselves. He allowed us to push through in order to humble us. First, he "demoted" us from the head of the table to the servant roles. Second, he rebuked us for considering the servant roles a demotion. Point taken!

Summing Up

In this chapter, I've presented an approach to discerning God's will that is based upon friendship with a God who speaks. I've argued that *friends of God who live by faith and consult the Lord are led by the Spirit into God's purposes.* As a result, when I am unsure about my next step, I am neither immobilized by fear nor pressured to make something happen. I only want to follow Jesus through doors he has opened. And when he opens a door, I want to follow him wherever he goes. And woe to the barriers that get in *his* way. But behind those doors, behold! The purposes of God!

····· *9* ·····
Listening Prayer
With Children

The secret things belong to the LORD our God, but the things revealed belong to us and to our children forever, that we may follow all the words of this law.
- Deuteronomy 29:29

At that time Jesus said, "I praise you, Father, Lord of heaven and earth, because you have hidden these things from the wise and learned, and revealed them to little children. Yes, Father, for this was your good pleasure."
- Matthew 11:25–26

He called a little child and had him stand among them. And he said: "I tell you the truth, unless you change and become like little children, you will never enter the kingdom of heaven."
- Matthew 18:2–3

RUINED GARDENS

My son Dominic, who was four years old at the time, crawled onto my lap and leaned in close. We were sitting in the front row of the chapel at Briercrest Bible College. I had been teaching there for orientation week and was about to share my final "two cents worth." As the worship time wound down, I asked Domo, "What is God showing you about the students here?" He briefly scanned the crowd over my shoulder and replied, "God is telling me that some of them have ruined gardens." The imagery stunned me. In Song of Solomon, the garden is a specific symbol for a woman's sexuality (Song of Solomon 4:12–5:1). In that context, a locked garden represents the bride's virginity. Her invitation to the lover to enter her garden and taste its fruit is a picture of consensual intercourse. Of course, Domo knew none of this. Yet to me, the image of the ruined garden (i.e., sexual brokenness) was so striking that I followed it up, "What does Jesus want to do about that?" He replied, "Jesus wants to plant new flowers in their gardens." This spoke to me of restored innocence. At the end of my message, I related Dominic's message, but refrained from interpreting it for the students. Afterwards, several of the young women approached my wife and me, confessing through their tears that the picture was about them. It was the Father's good pleasure to reveal his word about a hidden issue through the mouth of a child.

A Parent's Job

Scripture teaches that parents are responsible to lead their children into an intimate friendship with God. More than anyone else, mom and dad must teach their children that God speaks to them.

> Only be careful, and watch yourselves closely so that you do not forget the things your eyes have seen or let them slip from your heart as long as you live. Teach them to your children and to their children after them. (Deuteronomy 4:9)

> Fix these words of mine in your hearts and minds; tie them as symbols on your hands and bind them on your foreheads. Teach them to your children, talking about them when you sit at home and when you walk along the road, when you lie down and when you get up. (Deuteronomy 11:18-19)

Children hear the Lord easier than anyone else. Virtually the only block that I ever encounter in them is their parents' own unbelief. If we will assume, as children often do, that God is *already* speaking to them, we can nurture their ability to tune in to his voice.

I woke up to this truth when my friend Phil heard his five-year-old son Richard talking to an adult male in his bedroom. Alarmed by the voice, Phil ducked into the room to see who it was that invaded their home. Richard stood there alone.

Phil looked around the room, "Who was that I heard talking to you in here?"

"God," Richard replied, as if this were normal.

Here's my point: It *is* normal. Children who *can't* hear the Lord anymore (yes, *anymore*) have usually been inadvertently shut down by an adult.

In this chapter, I hope to equip you with creative spiritual exercises and suggestions that will help you maintain and develop a "hearing heart" in your children whether they're at home, at church or another ministry setting.

1. Assume your child already hears God.

The earlier you expect your child to sense God's presence and voice, the less likely you are to shut down their spiritual eyes and ears. Remember that they will be using their imaginations (which can be pretty wild to adult ears), but that is the venue they are providing for Jesus to come. And he will. My niece Cassie meets with Jesus on a giant imaginary lollypop. Dominic meets him in a mental petting zoo. Your initial skepticism will begin to melt as you hear the profound and intimate conversations that ensue.

To begin with, you might try stating a Scripture truth and then asking your child a follow-up question. For example,

- God is in the room with us right now. Where do you see him? What's he doing? What's he look like? (Assume in faith that they know).
- God talks to us all the time. What is he telling you? What is he showing you? How is he feeling now?
- You may need to explain that even if they don't see him or hear him with their eyes or ears, they *can* see him and hear him with their hearts. So what's he doing? What's he saying in your heart?

2. Invite your child to find Jesus in a meeting place.

By now I hope you are convinced of the reality and necessity of treating prayer as a meeting place with God. I believe that every child can and should be trained to find Jesus in a variety of meeting places.

Again, assume in faith that Jesus will meet your child (and probably has already). Don't make that the issue. Start with the truth that he wants to meet them. The question is "where?" The answer: "Anywhere that they can imagine." Here are some questions to get you started:

- Jesus lives in your heart. What does it look like? If he could meet you anywhere at all, what would that place look like? What's he doing there? (Hint: It's wonderful to have the child draw or paint that place.)
- Jesus is with you in the house, the bedroom, the backyard, at school, everywhere. Where is he right now? What's he up to? What's he saying?
- Jesus meets us at church. Where is he? What's he doing? Are there any angels here today (very common)? (Hint: Let them draw what they imagine is happening during the worship.)

- Jesus wants to meet you in your favourite Bible story. Which one? Where is he? What's he doing? What's he saying? Teach your child how to "step into" Bible stories through his or her imagination.

Our second son, Justice, loves to ask, "Dad, can we do one of those Bible stories where we go into the story?" His favourite is when Jesus was asleep in the fishing boat. As I read or tell Justice the story, I pause after each sentence to ask him to describe what he is seeing. For example, "Jesus and his disciples were out at sea when a storm came up. Justice, can you see the boat? What does it look like? What does the sea look like? Tell me about the storm. What are the disciples doing?" Invariably, Justice decides that he had better go wake Jesus up. He finds him sleeping, wakes him up, and watches him calm the storm. Here's the beauty of this exercise: We then ask Jesus if there is anything else he would like to tell Justice. Consistently, Justice will see and hear the Lord speaking out promises and blessings in a flood of very pure revelation. It is so precious to hear the heart of the Lord for our sons every time we practice this.

◀)) *Tuning In* • • • • • • • • •

If you have or relate to any children, try a "stepping in" exercise with them. Ask them to choose the Bible story. Then in each case, invite the child to find Jesus, approach him, touch him, talk to him, and listen to him. This is not merely a movie for them to watch. It's a real meeting in which they participate. You might be surprised at the beautiful truths that surface.

3. Convert bedtime prayers into listening prayers.

Most parents are used to walking their children through some standard prayers at bedtime. It's not difficult to convert these rituals into three-way conversational prayers between you, your child, and Jesus. You can ask the question, the Lord can provide the answer to your child, and your child can report it back to you. This format can become a natural pattern for family prayer. Here are some starter questions you may want to try:

- Jesus, is there anything today that we could thank you for? Why?
- Is there anything that we need to say sorry for? Will you forgive me?
- Is there anyone you want us to pray for? How? (Family, friend, and missionary photo albums are terrific for this. So are atlases or missions handbooks that give children a global vision.)

- Are there any *burdens* we are carrying that you want to lift for us? If so, ask Jesus where the burden came from, what it is, and if he would please remove it.
- Jesus, do you have any *promises or blessings* for me before I go to sleep?
- Bonus question: Jesus, what was the best part of *your* day? What made *you* happy?

For years, my son Stephen was an insomniac. By the time he was eight, he was able to ruin a good night's sleep by mulling over worries with the best of them. He would commonly lie awake in bed for several hours before settling down to sleep. But on the same weekend that he had his visitation from the Lord (cf. chapter 1), he started falling asleep within ten minutes. We asked his secret. He said that he had devised a scheme in which he gathers up all the day's problems in prayer and jams them into one little knapsack. Then he walks to the Cross, finds Jesus there, and offers him the knapsack. The Lord places it on the ground and sets it on fire. The image of the living Christ by the Cross is the resting place for Stephen's anxiety and his weary head.

4. Invite Jesus into nightmares and night terrors.

Children seem to be born with their spiritual windows wide open. You don't have to look far to hear angel-stories from very young children. Our second son Justice has periodically seen angels in our house, outside in the trees, and running beside our car. Of course, children also commonly complain about "monsters" in their bedroom at night. Night terrors, nightmares, monsters under the bed or in the closet, when not a dietary or health-related issue, can often be explained as:

- Actual spiritual oppression
- Imaginary projections from real fears
- Annoying bedtime stalling tactics

In many cases, a child's own fears activate their imagination in order to delay their bedtime. Rather than rebuking them for believing in something that is not real, I find it much more helpful to invite Jesus into the room to deal with the monsters. I ask the Lord to show our kids the angels and invite them to clean house. This is very important for two reasons.

First, if the monsters are really just a projection of the child's fears, why not flush the fear out rather than repress it? And who better to eradicate fear than the Lord Jesus, who is happy to use the child's imagination to bring about peace? He loves to train them to fear no evil by "practicing his presence."

Second, if the monsters are actually unclean spirits that the child perceives through his or her spiritual windows, then the "not real" message bears awful fruit. It ignores the child's real oppression, leaving them plagued with fear. Worse, it hamstrings them from seeing the Lord or his angels come to their aid.

Diane is just one of many of my friends who bore the wounds of this message throughout childhood. She began to see monsters in her bedroom at night in open-eyed visions during her pre-school years. When she reported it to her parents, they never introduced Jesus or the angels into the problem. Instead, they would either punish her or negate what she said. The message she heard was that what she was seeing was not real. They chalked it up to an active imagination. She wondered if she was crazy and tried to pretend that the "monsters" weren't there. But she continued to see the evil images—*right into adulthood!* While the "not real" message could not deliver her from evil, it *did* create a blinding filter for good things. She now found it much easier and more common to see demonic spirits than to perceive the Lord. Prayer ministry has slowly rectified this malady. Only now in her thirties has she become aware of the presence of Jesus and his angels round about her.

In all of these cases, listening prayer is an appropriate and efficient way to resolve things. We don't deny what they are experiencing. We invite Jesus in. We ask him what the monsters are, where they came from, and what he wants to do about them. I'm not afraid to attach consequences if the trouble continues, but initially I threaten the monster, not the child. For example, "Jesus, can it come back? If it tries to come back, Jesus what will you do to it?" Then we speak a final truth over the child, "Jesus is here now and you can tuck him in with you. You're totally safe. Good night."

5. Take conflicts at school and at home to Jesus.

When our children have a rough day at school, we try to find out as soon as they get home. Whether they had trouble with the teacher or other students, we do a mini inner healing with them. The same goes for when they experience conflicts at home with their siblings or with Eden and me as parents. We come before the Lord together, finding him in the situation and meeting him at the Cross.

- What happened? How did that make you feel? Why?
- Where was Jesus when that happened? What was he doing or saying?

- Would you like Jesus to lift away the hurt and anger?
- Ask Jesus to show you the others through his eyes. Can you send these people to the Cross and leave them there?
- Is there anything you need to say sorry for?
- Does Jesus have a promise for you about this?

6. Help your children interpret their dreams.

We enjoy listening to each other's dreams in the morning. Often the kids will wake us up and sit on the bed, describing their night time escapades. These morning dreams are fun to interpret with Jesus' help. We invite him to identify the symbols in the dream and the message that he has for us that day. Asking Jesus what each object and person represents keeps us in an intuitive ("right brain") space. This type of interpretation flows much more easily than shifting into analytical dream-dictionary modes. Assume that the children will hear Jesus' interpretation without even having to think through it. The very first thought that comes to their minds when we ask Jesus a question is usually right on.

7. Incorporate listening prayer into Sunday school.

We use listening prayer in every Sunday school class at Fresh Wind. Every child is taught how to find a meeting place with Jesus, how to step into a Bible story, and is given two to three questions to ask Jesus when they get there. The children who are teaching our Sunday school classes have a lesson-planning outline that makes preparation a listening prayer exercise. Here's how it looks:

- Read the passage. Ask Jesus to highlight the verses he wants to emphasize. Ask Jesus, "What's the main point of this story?"
- Learn the story well enough to help the class step into the story.
- Ask Jesus to show you a time when you saw this main point happen in your life. Where was Jesus in that event? What was he doing?
- Ask God for questions that the class can ask him together.

Regardless of the topic, each week the children practice their skills in hearing and obeying God's voice.

My son Stephen (now thirteen) used the above lesson plan to teach the kindergarten to grade three class the story of Jesus and the ten lepers. When he read the story, God highlighted the importance of thanksgiving when asking for healing prayer. However, by the time we arrived at church, Stephen was in tears with a severe headache and ready to bail out of teaching. During pre-service prayer, we prayed for him while he focused only on thanksgiving and praise (practicing what he was going to teach). After two or three minutes of prayer, he testified that his pain had gone from a "10" to a "7." He went into the service and continued in praise for two songs, then received communion. The headache vanished completely.

After worship, Stephen went to class with a dramatically updated lesson illustration. He taught on the ten lepers, shared his experience and then brought his class into the main service. As my message wound down, the little band of intercessors roamed the room, asking Jesus who needed prayer for healing. They surrounded and soaked one person after another in prayer as God led them. No one will remember my message. But the image of children moving as one, hovering around the sick and disabled, will remain with us for a long time.

A Final Secret

As our congregation has practiced bedtime listening prayer with their children, a trend has developed: the Lord speaks to them, and then they share what he said or showed them, adding, "He also told me some secrets, but I'm not allowed to share them with you." True to his word (Matthew 11:26), Jesus is keeping the "hidden things" from us and revealing them to our little children. Only with childlike trust will we ever enter into those kingdom secrets. So here is my advice:

Your children hear God. If you wake up to it yourself, so will they. When *they* call on the Lord, he *does* answer them. For every page of revelation you read into your children's words, the Lord will write an entire journal's worth.   When you learn to hear God's voice through them, the secrets of the kingdom are just around the corner. Why? Because the kingdom of heaven belongs to them. "What is not received is not given."[1] But to those who receive, "a little child will lead them" (Isaiah 11:6).

······ *10* ·····

Listening Prayer
in the Local Church

The central question is: Are the leaders of the future truly men and women of God, people with an ardent desire to dwell in God's presence, to listen to God's voice, to look at God's beauty, to touch God's incarnate Word and to taste fully God's infinite goodness...

Christian leaders cannot simply be persons who have well-informed opinions about the burning issues of our time. Their leadership must be rooted in the permanent, intimate relationship with the incarnate Word, Jesus, and they need to find there the source for their words, advice, and guidance. Through the discipline of contemplative prayer, Christian leaders have to learn to listen again and again to the voice of love and to find there the wisdom and courage to address whatever issue presents itself to them.[1]

Henry Nouwen, *In the Name of Jesus*

WE BEGAN BY ABIDING...

When Fresh Wind Christian Fellowship was still just a gleam in the Father's eye, he created a ravenous hunger in us for his presence. We began to dream of a church where the pursuit of Jesus himself was more important than any other agenda. We sensed that if Jesus came before everything else, then the rest would flow from him.

As with the disciples in Acts 1, we did a lot of waiting. Most of our "business meetings" still involve extended times of worship, silence, and listening prayer. We insist that Jesus be the leader of the church, providing his agenda and informing our decisions. Eventually, God's Spirit breezes through (sorry, no mighty rushing winds) showing us what we need to know or do for the moment. We listen together, compare notes and act only when we've reached a consensus about what God has said. Many of these meetings convene in a cozy living room

195

where we can stretch out on the carpet and wait restfully for God to speak. After five years I'm delighted to say that hasn't changed.

In our very first official meeting, we heard Jesus say, "If you will make me your first target group, I will come. And if I come, I will bring my friends." He also directed us to scriptures that verified this message:

- "I am the vine; you are the branches. If a man remains in me and I in him, he will bear much fruit; apart from me you can do nothing." (John 15:5)
- "*Be still* and know that I am God, and *I will exalt myself* among the nations." (Psalm 46:10)
- "Heaven is my home, earth is my footstool. Where is the house you will build for me? Where will *my resting place* be?" (Isaiah 66:1)

Every six months, our intercessor friend Eric McCooeye comes to teach us again and again about "abiding in the Lord" and "being a resting place for God's presence." Over time we finally began to get it. Only by abiding in the Vine—waiting, worshiping, and listening—would we produce any fruit. By abiding in God and his Word, we developed our values first and then caught God's vision.

Abiding Leads to Values

Many ministries project what type of fruit (expected outcomes) they would like to see and identify those goals as their vision. Then they develop plans or programs that are meant to "squeeze out" that fruit. The trouble is that such vision is "fruit-focused" rather than "Vine-focused." It tends to be so forward-looking that one never arrives. The drivenness of this model typically leads to striving and burnout.

Values must precede vision. Values connect you to the Vine. They must be *who you are* and *how you live* today and every day. If you invest in your values from "day one" of the church, producing fruit becomes natural. By taking the time to marinate in God's rest, the leadership core of Fresh Wind soon arrived at some non-negotiable values:

1. Entering God's presence
2. Hearing God's voice
3. Experiencing God's grace
4. Advancing God's kingdom
5. Becoming God's family

With these values in place, God was prepared to share his vision for our fellowship.

Values Lead to God's Vision

Defining vision can be tricky. If the focus is on forthcoming fruit (expected outcomes), you end up defining vision as foreseeing what you hope to accomplish in God *someday*.[2] True vision focuses on *God's vision of who we are to be today*. It is "obeyable" today and every day that the church exists.

Jesus said, "Do you not say, 'Four months more and then the harvest'? I tell you, open your eyes and look at the fields! They are ripe for harvest. Even *now* the reaper draws his wages, even *now* he harvests the crop for eternal life, so that the sower and the reaper may be glad together" (John 4:35). He said, "The Spirit is on me to preach good news... *today* this vision is being fulfilled in your hearing" (Luke 4:18, 21). And Jesus also tells each Christian to "not worry about tomorrow" (Matthew 6:34). Would he simultaneously expect us to work out a five-year plan?

Knowing this, at first we tried to articulate our vision in some pithy mottos. Boiling it down, we thought our vision statement might read, "Becoming expressions of God's heart." We can live that vision today and if we do "fruit happens." But when we asked Jesus, he spoke out *his* vision for Fresh Wind, not once or twice but many times through a variety of people, from Haiti to Colorado to Winnipeg to Vancouver. He said, *"My vision for you is Isaiah 58: the true fast."*

> Is not this the kind of fasting I have chosen: to loose the chains of injustice and untie the cords of the yoke, to set the oppressed free and break every yoke? Is it not to share your food with the hungry and to provide the poor wanderer with shelter—when you see the naked, to clothe him, and not to turn away from your own flesh and blood?
>
> Then your light will break forth like the dawn, and your healing will quickly appear; then your righteousness will go before you, and the glory of the LORD will be your rear guard.
>
> Then you will call, and the LORD will answer; you will cry for help, and he will say: Here am I. If you do away with the yoke of oppression, with the pointing finger and malicious talk, and if you spend yourselves in behalf of the hungry and satisfy the needs of the oppressed, then your light will rise in the darkness, and your night will become like the noonday.

> The LORD will guide you always; he will satisfy your
> needs in a sun-scorched land and will strengthen your
> frame. You will be like a well-watered garden, like a spring
> whose waters never fail. Your people will rebuild the
> ancient ruins and will raise up the age-old foundations; you
> will be called Repairer of Broken Walls, Restorer of Streets
> with Dwellings. (Isaiah 58:6–12)

Pretty wordy for a bulletin cover! Apparently God didn't feel it needed
to make a good bumper sticker. But this was his vision—a foundation
upon which to build. Isaiah 58 defines who we are to be and what we are
about. It also describes our appointed mission,[3] ministries,[4] and even
the promised fruit if we're faithful.

A Wild Garden

With our values and vision coming into focus, we started asking questions about structure and programs. In response, God gave us detailed
and rather stern words from independent prophetic sources around
the theme of a "wild garden." By May 1997, Pastor Guy from Valley
Christian Fellowship, Professor Glenn Runnalls from Briercrest Bible
College, and Tracey (one of our own dreamers) delivered virtually identical messages to us.

The basic gist was that Jesus was planting a wild garden: "a
planting of the LORD" (Isaiah 61:3). He would be the seed-sower. Our
job was to watch for his seeds to sprout. He warned us *not* to run ahead
and plant tidy little rows (programs) that you might find in a domestic
garden. There may be a little watering and pruning to do, but mainly
we were to simply tend to God's plants until the fruit came (watching
who and what the Spirit seemed to be blessing and then nurturing
that). We could also make little pathways between the plants and
walking bridges over tiny creeks that wound through the garden (net-
working people in supportive relationships).

Some plants would grow to be sturdy trees that bore continuous
fruit. Other plants would be flowers meant only to flourish for a season.
He reminds us that wild gardens are indigenous and low maintenance.
If a garden is all imports or high maintenance, it's not wild. The plants
that Jesus doesn't sow in the wild garden can either become weeds that
take over the garden or they can take a lot of extra care and tending.
God warned us that he wouldn't bless what he hadn't planted. So we
were to try to do only what we saw the Father doing (John 5:19). If we
sensed that he *wanted* to do something but didn't see it happening,
we prayed until we saw him begin. If we ignored these principles, we
would doom ourselves to false starts or fruitless striving.

FOUR PILLARS

Next, God spoke to us through Trevor MacPherson, a local prophet. God showed him that once our foundation was in place (the Isaiah 58 vision), he would erect four pillars in our church. We speculated about who the pillars might be—key leaders in the church. God said, "You are completely wrong. Wait and watch." So we sat tight and waited for God to show us what he meant. It wasn't long before he revealed the first pillar.

1. The Disabled

During the first months at Fresh Wind, one of our members suggested starting a home group in a care home for people with disabilities where he worked. Brian, our fearless leader, made the now infamous statement: "You can't build a church around the disabled." God must have listened to him from heaven in amusement, saying to himself, "Just watch me."

Not much later, Brian was on a prayer walk in the local mountains when the Lord spoke to him. "You have a sister, remember?" Brian knew the sister in question was Kathy. She was severely disabled from birth and sent into an institution as a little girl. The institution recommended that the family pretend she didn't exist. Now, nearly forty years later, the Lord was saying, "Indeed, Kathy *does* exist. Do not turn away from your own flesh and blood" (Isaiah 58:7). Responding in obedience, Brian and Kathy were reunited. He was delighted to discover that not only does she know and love Jesus, she also shares Brian's passion for worship leading. Soon, she became part of our fellowship. Other people with disabilities soon followed. Brian's wife Sue invited the entire care home where she worked. Chad, a member of our leadership team, brought them from a third care home. The Lord completely blindsided us with a growing core of people with disabilities.[5] But hadn't Jesus himself predicted this?

> When you give a banquet invite the poor, the crippled, the lame, the blind, and you will be blessed. Although they cannot repay you, you will be repaid at the resurrection of the righteous. (Luke 14:13–14)

In those early months, we invited Bob Brasset to our church. He is the most unique faith healer I've ever encountered. Entirely unpretentious, Bob ministers miraculous healing in the company of his wife (a registered nurse) and children (one of whom is disabled). While some ailments were healed that morning, that was not the highlight. At one point, Bob interrupted his own sermon and pointed to Kathy.

"Who is that young lady?" he asked.

"That's my sister, Kathy West," Brian answered.

To this Bob replied, "The Lord says, 'Kathy West is a pillar of this church'!"

So we had our first pillar, not only in Kathy but also in the entire company of men and women with disabilities who were now in our midst. Now they participate in worship leading, the pastoral prayer, hosting, and even run their own home group. A sturdy pillar it is!

2. The Children

Occasionally, our disabled members become very agitated and vocal during the service. Rather than shushing or removing them, the Lord prompted some of our preschool children (Tyrel and Dominic at the time) to minister peace to them by serving them from the Lord's Table. While it may break every religious protocol in church history, I have yet to see an act of God's kingdom so authentic as when a four-year-old says, "This is his body" and places the bread on the lips of someone tormented by a disability. The first time this occurred, the Spirit came with powerful, soothing peace, and we knew immediately that we were witnessing the second pillar being erected before our eyes.

Last spring, we struggled to find Sunday school teachers. We feared that without this ministry to children, our second pillar would crumble. When the congregation spent time listening together, adults volunteered to help, but not as teachers. Meanwhile, the children were listening to God for themselves. One by one, they stepped forward. "God wants me to do it," said Justice (nine). "Me too," said Jamie (twelve). "And me," said Stephen (also twelve). "I want to as well," said Josh (age ten). Two girls were already into it. And so it happened. Children began to train each other each Sunday morning (with an adult presence for the sake of "crowd control"). The second pillar now stood firm.

3. The Prodigals

"Where's the fruit?" I demanded. I stood facing the congregation, silently challenging the Lord. We hadn't had a "new convert" or performed a baptism in over a year. We saw ourselves as a church for the "unchurched" and the "over churched," so where were they? If we were as healthy as God seemed to indicate, where was the fruit? The Lord spoke back immediately, "Ask the congregation right now: 'How many of you walked away from God and/or the church for between six months and two years but heard about this place and came to give it one last try?'" I did so, and forty percent of the congregation put up their hands. The Lord spoke again: "There's your fruit, boy, and there's your third pillar." Many of the "prodigals" have come home because either the disabled or the children won them back. Some care-workers attend only because their job requires them to bring a disabled resident. Some parents initially return to church only for their children. In that sense, the Lord has used the first two pillars to win the hearts of the third until they begin to follow Jesus for themselves.

4. The Poor

One day Brian and I visited Bruce Friesen, a prophet from Victoria, BC. We sensed that God was about to reveal our fourth pillar, but we determined not to mention this to Bruce. Personally, I went with a heavy heart. Bruce equips prophetic people, so I felt that he would tell us that the prophets were our fourth pillar. After all, Fresh Wind had become a haven for wounded prophets who needed acceptance, healing, and training. Yet in my heart, I ached for the poor. I believe God loves the poor in a special way. Isaiah 58:10 kept speaking to me, "If you spend yourselves in behalf of the hungry and satisfy the needs of the oppressed, then your light will rise in the darkness, and your night will become like the noonday." I had learned this on trips to Mexico, Haiti, and East Vancouver. I wished for the poor to be our fourth pillar.

God must have been smiling on us that day, because when we met with Bruce, all he could talk about for hours was the poor, the poor, the poor! As I listened, the Lord reminded me of Paul's experience,

> James, Peter and John, those reputed to be pillars, gave me and Barnabas the right hand of fellowship when they recognized the grace given to me... *All they asked was that we should continue to remember the poor, the very thing I was eager to do.* (Galatians 2:9–10)

At the end of the meeting, Brian and I smiled to each other. God had spoken. We had our fourth pillar.

At Fresh Wind the poor aren't that obvious. They are the "working poor" who save for months to fix a dryer switch or students who literally pray for their next meal. Some families put their final cash into the offering basket and then ask for a food hamper. And why not? You probably wouldn't recognize the poor in our midst, because they don't project an aura of poverty. They live in the confidence that God is their provider. That faith overflows into faith-filled ministry. When they "step up to the plate," it's not because we are condescending to let them have a place. They are our best musicians, best teachers, and best intercessors.

By way of review, these four pillars are not our target groups. God is our first target group. Rather, God labelled them as our pillars. These were the friends he promised to bring. We learned that the church-plant would officially be a church not when we reached our pillars but when they were activated as ministers. I see that beginning to happen now.

But this also begged the question: When the foundation is laid and the pillars are in place, what will rest on the pillars? What's the roof? We heard a clear answer from God soon after we asked that question: "My Glory." God is with us and among us, but the pillars are what provide the resting place for his glory. This was what he had asked for in the beginning (Isaiah 66:1–2). We had come full circle!

Principles and Practice

The basic premise we follow is, of course, that God's sheep hear his voice. We continually lead *every* member into the practice of listening to God. We train them how to hear, how to test, and how to share what they are hearing. We ask each other's permission to share and then we weigh what is shared together. When we conclude that God has spoken through the body, the leadership team responds appropriately by setting a direction. When the leadership team feels God has spoken to them, they present it to the people for testing. The leadership team meets monthly with "the Posse" (a lay listening group) to inquire of the Lord together and mutually share God's voice.

Prophets and Pastors: Archenemies?

When someone receives a word from the Lord for the church, we ask that they pass it through someone in leadership for testing. We tell them that when they give it to us, we will always take it seriously and weigh it but that the word is now our responsibility in terms of interpretation, application, and timing. If we don't jump to action immediately, the prophet should not take it as a personal rejection. They need to let it go, realizing that the Lord may direct us only to use it in prayer or to shelve it until further notice. If it is a word of encouragement or exhortation, leadership may ask the prophet to deliver the word to the congregation himself or herself at the appointed time. If it is a word of rebuke or correction, the leadership normally conveys it gently in pastoral terms and tones.

If the word is directional, the leadership weighs it in context with the flow of what the Spirit is currently doing and takes it into account when making decisions. When new prophets arrive, hoping for a platform from which to display their gifts, we emphasize our commitment to relationships before gifts. We encourage them to hang out with us for about six months so that we can get to know each other before giving them a microphone. About half of them stay long enough to get their chance. Even those who would abuse the prophetic gift do very little damage at Fresh Wind, because our flock knows that *any* word is only an alleged word until it has been verified by the Bible, the Body, and the Spirit.

LISTENING PRAYER: SUNDAY MORNING AND BEYOND

I'd like to conclude by giving you a glimpse of how listening prayer pervades the corporate life of Fresh Wind on Sunday mornings and beyond.

Pre-service Prayer

The leadership meet with up to one dozen intercessors who arrive early to pray. We ask them if the Lord has given them a sense of what he wants for the morning and share with them what elements we've included so far. We pray together and ask God if there is anything else he wants us to know or do that morning. If so, we incorporate it into the order of service.

Worship Time

During worship, as people hear from God, they approach me to share what they are getting. My job is to administrate the gifts during the service. I think of it as coaching. I may receive their messages as helpful direction just for me as I lead or I may feel it needs to be shared from the front. I may even choose to share it myself or I may send them up to share. We may share it immediately between songs or we may wait until after the worship set. I am always listening for God's prompting.

Pastoral Prayer Time

After worship, we carve out fifteen minutes for interactive prayer. Two or three people may share what the Spirit showed them during worship. I may ask the Lord a question or two on behalf of the congregation. They listen and are given time to respond from their seats or among themselves. We may pray corporately through a personal issue (e.g., releasing burdens to God) or join together in intercession as God brings needs to mind (whether local or global).

Listening Questions

At any point during or after the message, we may ask God to speak to us about what's on his heart. For example, at the conclusion of a recent sermon on "loving the least of these," we asked the Lord,

- "Lord, show me one person who you've put in my life that represents the least of these."
- "Lord, show me that person through your eyes. Help me to see them as you do."
- "Lord, allow me to sense your heart for them. Let your compassion for them rise up within me."
- "Lord, is there something you would have me pray or share or do for that person?"

We may leave it at that or we may follow up by sharing publicly or in groups.

Activation Exercises

We love to activate our members in ministering God's voice to one another. Teams of intercessors may drift around praying for individuals during worship. Members of the Posse speak words of blessing while serving communion. The children may sometimes lay hands on the disabled to bless them. Every commissioning service, baptism, and baby dedication includes time to share pictures, words, scriptures or songs.

Altar Ministry

We have tried to avoid assuming any one tradition for closing our services. We may end abruptly, use a closing song or prayer, minister to each other in small groups ("stand where you are and those around you can pray") or have an altar call of some sort. Our ideal for altar calls is to go to a meeting place with Jesus, receive some comfort and blessing, but leave "root work" for later prayer ministry. In effect, we invite Jesus to swab, anoint, and bandage wounds, and then book them for spiritual surgery on another day.

Small Groups

Naturally, listening prayer involving group participation works better in smaller groups. Some Sundays, we break into groups of five (this invites participation and allows for non-participation) to share and pray. We also use listening prayer questions in all our Sunday school classes. Every child is taught to find Jesus in a "meeting place." Each home group has a strong listening prayer element throughout worship, Bible study, and prayer time. It's a great place to practice and grow in these gifts.

Personal Meetings

Occasions such as marriage counselling, inner healing, discipleship, and mentoring are prime venues for listening prayer. I rarely pray or talk with anyone without inviting Jesus to speak. After all, he is the Wonderful Counsellor, the Good Shepherd, and the Anointed Teacher. I see no point in doing a lame version of his job. I may share what he's showing me or telling me, but more often, I simply lead others to hear him for themselves.

Does All of This Matter?

How important is all this to the church? To the Lord? Consider how strongly Paul states it, "What then shall we say, brothers? When you come together, *everyone* has a hymn, or a word of instruction, a revelation, a tongue or an interpretation. *All of these must be done* for the strengthening of the church" (1 Corinthians 14:26). "Everyone," "all of these," "must be done"! Activating God's voice in the life of your church matters a lot! If you do, a fresh wind may even blow your way!

Before you buy your own personal prophet's staff and don camel skin, you might want to establish a track record as someone whose prophetic messages are a blessing to your pastor and your church. Here are some good first steps that will help you to tune in to God's heart for his Bride:

◀)) *Tuning In* • • • • • • • • •

- Start praying for your pastor(s) and church regularly. Ask your church leaders how you can pray specifically for them.
- Don't be a faultfinder. Church leadership needs strengthening like never before. Ask the Lord to give you encouragement verses for

your pastor. Ask the Lord to lead you in writing an uplifting note once per month.

- Make a habit of telling your pastors what you heard the Lord saying through their messages.

- Listen for corporate words of encouragement about your church. Don't prophesy judgment or even lavish future exploits. To begin with, just ask the Lord what he's doing and blessing and pleased about, then pass that information on to the leadership. When your pastor knows that you are a safe consultant, the door may open for more directive or corrective words.

- If God gives you inspiring ideas for your church, you don't need to push those on anyone. Simply hand them in as a proposal, allow leadership to weigh them, and volunteer to help.

· · · · · 11 · · · · ·
Listening Prayer
and Outreach

"We no longer believe just because of what you said; now we have heard for ourselves, and we know that this man really is the Saviour of the world."

- John 4:42

If Jesus came to your town and made himself available in a local coffee shop, would you go meet him? Would you spend time talking to him and listening to him? Of course you would. The bulk of this book has been dedicated to the truth that you *are able to and already do* exactly this sort of thing. Apart from intimate conversation with Jesus, claims to a "personal relationship" with him ring rather hollow. And so we have learned that Christ is indeed encountered as we meet him through listening prayer.

But let's push the analogy further. If you knew that Jesus was available in that coffee shop, would you tell others about him? What would you tell them? You might say, "Jesus is alive!" If they expressed interest or skepticism, you would certainly add, "You can meet him! Come see for yourself! I can take you there! You should hear for yourself what he has to say!"

THE "WOMAN AT THE WELL" MODEL

This is exactly what the woman at the well did (John 4). Having met Jesus for herself—having tasted the living water that satisfies thirsty souls—she rushed back to town, testifying about what Jesus had done for her. Her enthusiasm was genuine and infectious, because she had an authentic meeting with the living Lord.

In contrast, while we often sing the old hymn, "I love to tell the story," our lives often model something closer to "I dread to tell the story." Why? *Because we think that evangelism is about convincing others of something we believe rather than witnessing about someone we have met.* We come across as lawyers with an argument rather than witnesses with a story. Arguments don't hook people's hearts. Testimonies do. Why? Because testimonies point to the "someone" whom our listeners have been waiting to meet all of their lives.

Going back to the woman at the well, she did not stop at telling her story, even though many of her neighbours did believe her. She said, "Don't just believe that he's quenched my thirst. You've got to meet him for yourself! Have your own drink!"

> *When the Samaritans met Jesus face to face, they said to the woman "We no longer believe just because of what you said; now we have heard for ourselves, and we know that this man really is the Saviour of the world." (John 4:42)*

So here is my thesis: *Why merely tell people about Jesus when you can also take them to meet him?* If Jesus is willing to meet with *you* for fellowship, won't he also meet with another thirsty *"seeker"*? If he has given you a meeting place you can enter any time in prayer, will he not also be immediately available to his lost sons and daughters when they want to find him? After you've told them your story of Jesus and his love, would he not also desire to *show and tell* them himself?

Evangelism is not meant to be a sales pitch trying to convince someone to marry a "mail-order groom," sight-unseen. It is more like an invitation to meet the one we've met, fallen in love with, and married. So the "woman at the well" model for outreach presupposes three truths:

1. You've met Jesus.

I don't say "met Jesus" here in the evangelical cliché sense. You've truly encountered him in the meeting place of your heart. You must *know* him, not as you know Abraham or David (biblical characters) or Jerry Seinfeld or George Bush (living celebrities), but as you know your best friend or your spouse. You would want to know Jesus intimately enough to ask: "If I bring my friend to meet with you, will you show yourself and speak to them for me?" You could make that request of any of your other friends and you can also make it of Jesus. See what he says. If you sense that he is giving you the nod, believe that he won't leave you high and dry. Expect him to show up for the meeting.

2. Others are seeking to meet him.

Perhaps you or someone you know could be called a *"seeker."* Here's a good proverb: "Those who seek will find" (Matthew 7:7). When seekers meet Jesus, they usually begin a relationship with him. Others, like the crowds in the gospels, are willing to meet Jesus (and even be fed and healed by him) but refuse to follow him. When the "crowd" types come for inner healing, Jesus will show up (because he is compassionate) even when he knows they will reject him. They receive the healing but not the healer. The third and largest group will not even receive the invitation to meet Jesus. Of these, Jesus instructed his disciple, "Shake the dust off your feet" (Matthew 10:14). In other words, let them be. They aren't ready.

3. You can lead seekers to meet him.

As a friend of God, you have the permission and the mandate to lead seekers to a meeting with Jesus. If you bring them to him, he'll be there. Why not let *him* share the gospel with them? You just need to get them there! Just watch:

Manda's Story

When Manda first came to our youth group, she didn't know Jesus, but she was desperately thirsty for living water! She struggled with her self-image and an eating disorder that was rooted in an abuse memory. She heard testimonies of other girls who had experienced healing of memories, so she asked for some prayer. I knew she did not know Jesus yet, but I could see no reason why he wouldn't show up for her.

Manda began to walk through the memory as a little girl and, sure enough, Jesus showed up. He held out his hand and beckoned her to take it and follow him. Manda hesitated for a while, so I asked the Lord if he would just take and hold her. But he continued to just stand there looking at her and waiting for her to grab his hand. When she finally did so, he scooped her up in his arms immediately and washed the stain of shame from her body. Then he placed on her a perfectly white, little dress and she was filled with his love.

Then the Lord gave me a question to ask her: "Manda, what do you think of Jesus now that you've met him?"

"I love him!" she responded.

"And how does it feel to have that stain removed?" I asked.

"Wonderful!" she said, her eyes brimming with tears.

"Would you be willing to let Jesus wash *all* of the stains of sin and shame from your heart? And would you like to be friends with him always?"

It was a no-brainer. Not only did she commit her life to him that day, so did the friend who had come with her for moral support! Later, the Lord also delivered her from anorexia. Today, she is happily married and still holding Jesus' hand.

Nicole's Story

Nicole grew up in a Roman Catholic setting but left without ever giving her heart to Jesus. She was struggling with fear and obsessive thoughts on several fronts. One of her fears related to a Wiccan co-worker who claimed to have seen ghosts in the house Nicole had just rented. Nicole asked Pam, another colleague who attends our church, if we could come and pray for a cleansing of the house. In her mind, I think she was probably imagining something like a scene from the movie *Poltergeist*.

When we arrived, Nicole invited us in. After she described some of the ghostly shadows and hair-raising incidents she had experienced, we asked her: "Do you want to be free?" She gave an emphatic YES. We asked how she felt about Jesus. Two words: cold and scary. We explained that we would invite him to speak to her. Since she appeared spiritually sensitive, we thought that maybe he would remind her of a time when he had already shown himself to her. She closed her eyes and waited.

Seconds later, she began: "He is reminding me of a dream when I was just seven years old. I am in my house looking out the bedroom window up a hill to the Cross." We encouraged her to "step into" the dream once again as if she were there now. She found this easy to do, so we asked if she would like to go to the Cross with her fears. In reliving the dream, she was able to be the seven-year-old, open the door and begin to climb the hill.

Immediately, she started to weep. "I can't believe how much he loves me. He's so tender! He's so gentle! I never knew he was like that! He's telling me that he was always with me, and the bad things that happened when I was little weren't my fault!"

Finally, we arrived at the Cross. Jesus was still hanging there. I told Nicole that he is alive and doesn't need to stay on the Cross. He might be willing to come down and hold her. Would she like that? As soon as she said yes, Jesus instantly stood before her, scooped her up, and cradled her in his arms. He held her close and poured his healing love into her soul.

When we asked what needed to happen to free her from her fears, Jesus said to her, "Surrender." But Nicole wasn't sure yet. "I only just met him. I'm not sure I could honestly trust him with my whole life all at once.

"How about just for the rest of the day?" we asked. Could she surrender and trust her life and her home to him that long? Could she give him room to begin a relationship and to build trust? She thought so. We encouraged her to tell Jesus so in her own words. Then Nicole spoke the most heartfelt sinner's prayer I've ever heard. She wept away years of guilt, hurt, and fear and received a deep touch of God's grace and love. The whole meeting took place in the memory of a childhood dream that she now beheld in vision form.

Was the dream meeting real? I believe so. Here's why: the fear and hurt were real. The love and comfort were very real. The healing was real. The conviction and repentance were real. The new relationship is real. Best of all, her new life in Christ featured the presence and voice of God from square one, and continues to do so to this day.

The Disciples' Story

Manda and Nicole are disciples of Jesus now. Why? Because they met him in person and chose to follow him. This is just how it worked for the original disciples.

Then John gave this testimony: "I saw the Spirit come down from heaven as a dove and remain on him. *I would not have known him, except that the one who sent me to baptize with water [God] told me, 'The man on whom you see the Spirit come down* and remain is he who will baptize with the Holy Spirit.' *I have seen and I testify* that this is the Son of God."

The next day John was there again with two of his disciples. When *he saw Jesus passing by, he said, "Look, the Lamb of God!"*

When the two disciples heard him say this, they followed Jesus.

Turning around, *Jesus saw them following and asked, "What do you want?"* They said, "Rabbi" (which means Teacher), "where are you staying?"

"Come" he replied, "and you will see." So they went and saw where he was staying, and spent that day with him. It was about the tenth hour.

Andrew, Simon Peter's brother, was one of the two who heard what John had said and who had followed Jesus. *The first thing Andrew did was to find his brother Simon and tell him, "We have found the Messiah"* (that is, the Christ). And *he brought him to Jesus.* Jesus looked at him and said, "You are Simon son of John. You will be called Cephas" (which, when translated, is Peter).

The next day Jesus decided to leave for Galilee. Finding Philip, he said to him, "Follow me." Philip, like Andrew and Peter, was from the town of Bethsaida. *Philip found Nathanael and told him, "We have found the one Moses wrote about* in the Law, and about whom the prophets also wrote--Jesus of Nazareth, the son of Joseph."

"Nazareth! Can anything good come from there?" Nathanael asked. *"Come and see,"* said Philip.

When Jesus saw Nathanael approaching, he said of him, "Here is a true Israelite, in whom there is nothing false."

"How do you know me?" Nathanael asked. Jesus answered, "I saw you while you were still under the fig tree before Philip called you."

Then Nathanael declared, "Rabbi, you are the Son of God; you are the King of Israel." (John 1:32–49)

Is This For Real?

Can it really be that simple? That depends on what the simple truth is. The simple truth is that Jesus is alive. As your faithful friend, he is always with you, forever speaking through the Spirit to your heart. He meets with you whenever you open the door to his knock. He goes with you wherever you go and he loves everyone that you know and meet. He also wants to meet them, talk to them, and invite them into his family. Are you with me so far?

He has planted you, like Andrew, in this world to bring others to meet him. Like John, you must admit, "I would not have known, except that God told me." But now you too can say, "I have seen and now testify, this is the Son of God." Like Philip, you can testify, "I have found him," and issue the invitation, "Come and see." You can lead others to meet him, asserting by faith, "Look! The Lamb of God!"

◀)) *Tuning In* • • • • • • • • •

Ask the Lord to bring someone across your path who is ready to meet with him. He may highlight that person for you, but, if you prefer, he will often compel them to bring up the topic of God with you. I would dare you to invite them to meet Jesus for themselves. You could tell them, "I won't speak for him, but I'm sure he'd be willing to meet with you directly." Ask them to participate in the following listening prayer exercise. Start by giving it a try yourself so you can share your own experience with them.

- Picture Jesus (or God if you like) greeting you in person at the gates of heaven. Direct all your attention towards him. Then ask him this question:
- "When we finally meet face-to-face, how will you greet me? And what is the first thing you'll say to me?" Watch and listen for his response. What does he do? What does he say?

This exercise is based on a question from the Bernard Pivot Question-naire that asks, "If heaven exists, what would you like to hear God say when you arrive at the pearly gates?"[1] I believe this question is really a subtle exercise in listening prayer. When this question was asked recently on *Bravo's* "Inside the Actors Studio," some of the answers that the celebrities gave were wonderful and insightful.[2] For example, Meg Ryan hopes to hear God say, "You big dope, I've been with you all along!" Sharon Stone would wait for the same words her father blessed her with, "You done good, kid." So many of them just hope to hear God say, "Welcome home," or "Come on in," or "We've got a table set for you." Steven Spielberg would like to hear God say to him, "Thanks for listening."

The beauty of the exercise is that it subtly brings several impor-tant truths to the foreground for meditation.

First, the things Jesus said and did in your heart almost certainly identified the greatest need (and perhaps your deepest wound) in your heart. For example, what need is he addressing if he throws his arms around you and says, "Welcome here!" Perhaps it's a need for accep-tance and a fear of rejection. Or what button is he pushing if he smiles and says, "I was with you the whole time. I never left you even once!" He could be speaking to abandonment or loneliness issues. What needs or wounds did he address through his answer to you?

Second, by addressing that need or wound, Jesus probably framed the gospel (literally the "good news") in words that apply specifically to you. For example, to some, the gospel might sound like, "It's going to be okay." To others, it's "I like you" or "I accept you." What did the good news sound like to you? Can you rephrase it in the form of a promise? When you use this question in outreach, those with whom you share will reveal exactly what the good news needs to sound like to them!

Third, Jesus' words and actions in that picture are likely *not* meant to come true only at his return or your demise. Rather, he is laying an invitation on the table to be received *today*. For example, "I accept you *today*" or "I am with you *today*."

If that is the case, during outreach, you can ask: "What was Jesus offering you? Would you like to receive it? Are there any barriers that prevent you from accepting it? How can they be removed? Don't know? Just ask him.

- As they start to hear his voice, you could take them through the friendship questions in chapter two.
- Tell them about the Meeting Place and ask them if they would like Jesus to provide one. Let them "taste and see that the Lord is good." Watch how Jesus the evangelist shares with them directly.

······ *12* ······

Listening Prayer, Mercy and Justice

*To me, faith in Jesus Christ that is not aligned with social
justice, that is not aligned with the poor—it's nothing.*

Bono

A BRUISE ON MY HEART CALLED HAITI

As the soldier played with the safety of his M-16 assault rifle, I thought
I was going to be sick. It seemed like an awful nightmare, but I was
awake—more fully awake than at any previous moment of my life.

It was November 1992. Desarmes, Haiti. After a *coup d'etat*, the
paramilitary Macoutes no longer merely terrorized the countryside;
they were actually running it. And they wielded an iron fist in this village in the Haitian outback. Groups larger than three could not meet
without a permit. Youth groups and farmers' co-ops were forbidden.
Checkpoints monitored traffic on the dirt roads.

Lares, a Haitian national serving the Mennonite Central Com-
mittee (MCC) as an agricultural trainer, had been arrested for allegedly distributing a disparaging letter against the local military chief.
The soldiers had hog-tied him and beaten him with clubs about the
head, ears, back, and thighs. Now they also declared their true intentions: "Tonight, we will get drunk and beat him to death. By morning,
he will be dead. No bribe will change our minds."

Now Ron Bluntchly, our MCC host and tour guide, stood face-to-
face with an armed guard and spoke out boldly in Creole: "God is your
judge and he is watching you! You must stand before him some day.
He sees you now and you will have to answer to him. He will hold you
to account for this! He will not tolerate this injustice. Set this man free
now!"

Questions began to race through my mind. Would they really kill
Lares? Would they kill Ron? Would they dare? What about me? Could
I escape with my wife, now six months pregnant? God? Where are you?
What are you doing? What should we do?

As I listened, the Lord spoke:

"Is not this the kind of fasting I have chosen: *to loose the chains of injustice and untie the cords of the yoke, to set the oppressed free and break every yoke?* Is it not to share your food with the hungry and to provide the poor wanderer with shelter—when you see the naked, to clothe him, and *not to turn away* from your own flesh and blood (Isaiah 58:6–7)?

God continued: "You can no longer spiritualize those verses away. This is very real, and it is *exactly* what Isaiah is talking about."

But how? How could we liberate this literal prisoner, tied as he was in actual nylon cords, from an armed, flesh-and-blood oppressor? To break this stalemate would only serve to escalate the crisis, would it not?

Silence. I watched and waited, focusing on keeping my head and my bowels together. Ron would not back down. He believed that without witnesses like us around, the Macoutes would work up the courage to kill Lares. A crowd began to gather. Mugginess and tension weighed down on us. We cried out to the Lord in prayer, but despair threatened to win the day.

Sheep or Goat?

I was beginning to see through the blindness of those who accuse Christian organizations like MCC and Christian PeaceMaker Teams of being "too political." I had heard it before and even asked it myself: "Shouldn't they be restricting themselves to relief work or channeling their energies into 'soul-winning'? Why do they have to get so political?" In the Haitian context, where life and death stand out in stark contrast every day, *souls are people.* And the people are naked, starving, and oppressed. There is no fence of ambiguity to straddle. You can walk away in silent acquiescence to the misery and evil or you can speak out and act for justice and mercy, hoping to overcome evil with good. Sometimes being a follower of Christ leaves you no choice, regardless of what the critics believe.

In the West, we don't understand this very well. Dom Helder Camara, former Archbishop of Recife, Brazil once lamented, "When I gave food to the poor, they called me a saint. When I ask why the poor have no food, they call me a communist."

Now I was getting a crash-course on kingdom justice and mercy. I was coming to realize they are not merely temporal matters of politics or philanthropy that can be isolated from one's spiritual life. They are of eternal importance and will be addressed when Christ renders verdicts on Judgment Day:

> When the Son of Man comes in his glory, and all the angels with him, he will sit on his throne in heavenly glory. All the nations will be gathered before him, and he will separate the people one from another as a shepherd separates the sheep from the goats. He will put the sheep on his right and the goats on his left.
>
> Then the King will say to those on his right, "Come, you who are blessed by my Father; take your inheritance, the kingdom prepared for you since the creation of the world. For I was hungry and you gave me something to eat, I was thirsty and you gave me something to drink, I was a stranger and you invited me in, I needed clothes and you clothed me, I was sick and you looked after me, I was in prison and you came to visit me."
>
> Then the righteous will answer him, "Lord, when did we see you hungry and feed you, or thirsty and give you something to drink? When did we see you a stranger and invite you in, or needing clothes and clothe you? When did we see you sick or in prison and go to visit you?"
>
> The King will reply, "I tell you the truth, whatever you did for one of the least of these brothers of mine, you did for me."
>
> Then he will say to those on his left, "Depart from me, you who are cursed, into the eternal fire prepared for the devil and his angels. For I was hungry and you gave me nothing to eat, I was thirsty and you gave me nothing to drink, I was a stranger and you did not invite me in, I needed clothes and you did not clothe me, I was sick and in prison and you did not look after me."
>
> They also will answer, "Lord, when did we see you hungry or thirsty or a stranger or needing clothes or sick or in prison, and did not help you?"
>
> He will reply, "I tell you the truth, whatever you did not do for one of the least of these, you did not do for me."
>
> Then they will go away to eternal punishment, but the righteous to eternal life. (Matthew 25:31–46)

When the Day of Judgment comes, what we have done or neglected to do for the naked, the hungry, the prisoner, the sick, and the oppressed will be identified with what we did or did not do for the King. He will ask: "Did you feed me and clothe me or did you not? Did you welcome

217

me, visit me, comfort me, free me, or not? You either came to me or abandoned me. If you helped them, you helped me. If not, I don't believe I know you."

On that day, whether we were "left" or "right" in our earthly politics will matter little when the divine judge beckons us to his left or his right. Whether we were conservative or liberal in our theology will flee from our minds. Even whether we said "the magic prayer" might seem shallow in that moment. But whether or not we did justice, loved mercy, and walked humbly with God will be of paramount concern (Micah 6:8). The New Testament teaches that we are saved by faith in the grace of God and not by good deeds (Ephesians 2:8–9). However, it also states that a truly living faith will not fail to reproduce the character of Christ in our lives, by which I mean our *actions* (James 2:26). It is not enough to merely listen to God. The ministries of Matthew 25 are not afterthoughts of Christian charity held in place with refrigerator magnets. They are the foundation of the very throne of God! "Righteousness and justice are the foundation of your throne; love and faithfulness go before you. Blessed are those who have learned to acclaim you, who walk in the light of your presence, O LORD" (Psalm 89:14). Once we have heard, we must follow through with action.

Lilut

Back to Haiti. As I stood there trembling, a little boy with a bright white, perfectly ironed shirt approached me. Lilut was eleven years old, with dark black skin and bright white teeth. In the middle of this moment of hell, he smiled at me and began to rub my back. I saw Jesus looking at me through those big eyes. They said, "It's going to be okay."

Ron continued to lay his life on the line, demanding immediate release of the prisoner. The guard rebutted: "We cannot release him without a court order." What an odd "justice" system. You could arrest, sentence, and punish a man without so much as a warrant or any shred of evidence, but to free him required a trial.

"Then let's go to the judge," Ron countered.

"The judge is in the next town," the guard replied.

"Then we'll go to the next town."

"We have no truck."

Ron pulled out his keys. "We'll take my truck."

Under pressure from Ron, the foreign witnesses, and now the entire village, the captors finally ran out of excuses. They loaded the prisoner and a handful of soldiers into the back of Ron's pick-up and disappeared with Ron at the wheel. We waited and prayed that evening and throughout the night. What would happen? What if they didn't return? What would happen to Ron? What if the soldiers came for us next? What if...?

The Lord eventually broke through my troubled thoughts with his peace. In retrospect, was it God who suggested I have some dry bread with avocado to settle my stomach? I don't know, but it was a good idea, because after that I was finally able to get a little sleep.

The next morning, we heard the truck returning. Villagers poured out of their homes and lined the riverbed that doubled as their main road. The whole crew was returning, but now the ropes had been removed from Lares. Our MCC friend stood in the truck-box smiling and waving at the crowds in this impromptu remake of Jesus' triumphal entry into Jerusalem. He was free. Men, women, and children began to chant in unison, "God is able! God is able!"

Justice Cries Out

That experience somehow cleansed my vision, like windshield wiper blades pushing aside a thick film of dirty drizzle accumulated through years of North American cultural dullness. I didn't ever want to forget that event. Before we left Haiti, we felt the Lord say to us, "Call the boy in Eden's womb *Justice*," and we recorded the name in my journal. Of course, this assumed she was carrying a boy. One week later in Jamaica, we asked a missionary couple to help us think of some unique girls' names. Their sixteen-year-old son spoke up: "I don't have any suggestions for a girl's name, but I wonder why nobody calls their son *Justice*. I think that would be a good name."

With that confirmation, we named our middle son Justice and committed to praying for Haiti whenever he cried throughout his first year. Of course, his first sentence was "Not fair!" and we marveled as the Lord developed in him a deep sense of compassion and justice. He is our living reminder that in the midst of poverty and injustice, "God is able! God is able!"

I. LISTENING PRAYER AND SOCIAL CONCERN

You might ask, "What does social justice have to do with listening prayer?" Ron Dart, an author and religious studies and political science professor[1] explained it to me this way: "Prophets who claim to have God's heart must find their own hearts beating for justice, or they simply don't have God's heart. We receive the word of God from the character of God—he is the well from which we fill our bucket. You cannot authentically listen to God for long without also sensing that justice, mercy, and compassion are central to his character and to his message."

Many prophets in the church today consider themselves mature because of their highly accurate "words of knowledge" or dramatic Technicolor visions. But the full-orbed prophetic gift, the tradition passed down by the true prophets of Scripture and history, entails a calling well beyond in-house personal prophecy.

The primary themes of the mature biblical prophet *always include mercy, justice, and peace—both personal and public.* Perhaps it would be best to define these terms.

A. Mercy

By *mercy* (Hebrew – *hesed*), the prophets mean the lovingkindness and compassion of God towards the poor, the oppressed, and the marginalized. Mercy refers to his *active care* for the widow and the orphan. Mercy is God's answer from heaven to those who cry out for help. Prophetic mercy spills out through God's people in humanitarian aid to bring relief and reconstruction wherever tragedy strikes. It also relates to God's patience and longsuffering for the wayward, not treating us as our sins deserve. Mercy means that God is slow to anger and abounding in love. His goodness and generosity are ever towards us, especially to those in need.

B. Justice

Justice (Hebrew – *tsadaq, ts^edaqah*, often translated "righteousness") in the prophets refers to fair treatment and active equity for all. It is quite literally "making things right." It is a shame and a sign of ill spiritual health when a society reduces the word justice into a simple synonym for punishment. Biblical justice is not only retributive, but also preventative and restorative. It is equally troublesome when the church diminishes the term to nothing more than an opposite for grace. Justice is *not* to the law what grace is to the gospel. Rather, justice and righteousness are aspects of God's character that are founded on his love for all. They are expressions of his desire to see his children treat one another with respect and without discrimination. Only a society that learns to love and care for its citizens as God does can be called a "just society." Prophetic justice advocates for the helpless and challenges the powerful.

I find it helpful to compare mercy and justice without playing them against each other as opposites: Mercy helps those who have not received what they deserve (by way of basic human rights) and relents from inflicting punishment on those who deserve it. Justice makes sure everyone gets what he or she deserves (by way of human rights and freedoms but also penalties for wrongs done). Grace adds to justice the additional blessings and gifts that we definitely do not deserve.

Mercy is like the ambulance at the bottom of a cliff, ready to help those who fall. Justice builds a fence at the top of the cliff to protect them from falling in the first place (Deuteronomy 22:8).

Mercy wipes the tears from the eyes. Justice asks, "Why are you crying?"

Mercy welcomes the hungry to gather around God's banqueting table. Justice addresses why some are under the table aching of hunger while others are sitting on top of the table aching from gluttony.[2]

Mercy seeks and saves those lost in the darkness. Justice asks, "Why is it dark? Who is keeping it dark? Who is benefiting from this darkness? Is it I, Lord?"

C. Peace

Peace (Hebrew – *shalom*) takes us a step further. More than relief from darkness, peace is the presence of light. It is that classic Hebrew blessing that includes wholeness, health, and security. It embodies a sense of spiritual and social equilibrium that is not merely the absence of war but the presence of justice and mercy. Peace is the natural byproduct of doing justice and loving mercy (as opposed to simply destroying all of one's enemies). Prophetic peacemaking is restoring *shalom* wherever it has been lost or broken:

- Between God and people (reconciliation)
- Between one person or people and another (mediation)
- Between people and themselves (healing)
- Between people and creation (environmentalism)

Thus, while the prophets heard and delivered scathing (though tearful) critiques of both individuals and society, what set them apart from the fashionable cynicism of our age was their message of peace and hope. If you examine the fruit, the cynic is a thief of hope. The prophets, on the other hand, could be brutally satirical yet somehow they also proclaimed good news. When they sound most despairing, suddenly they drop on us a vision of God's redemptive plan. Abraham Heschel explains:

> What is history? Wars, victories, and wars. So many dead. So many tears. So little regret. So many fears... The world is drenched in blood, and the guilt is endless. Should not all

hope be abandoned? What saved the prophets from despair was their messianic vision and the idea of man's capacity for repentance... History is not a blind alley, and guilt is not an abyss. There is always a way that leads out of guilt: repentance, or turning to God. The prophet is a person who, living in dismay, has the power to transcend his dismay. Over all the darkness of experience hovers the vision of a different day.[3]

Isaiah grants us one such vision:

The desert and the parched land will be glad; the wilderness will rejoice and blossom. Like the crocus, it will burst into bloom; it will rejoice greatly and shout for joy. The glory of Lebanon will be given to it, the splendor of Carmel and Sharon; they will see the glory of the LORD, the splendor of our God. Strengthen the feeble hands, steady the knees that give way; say to those with fearful hearts, "Be strong, do not fear; your God will come, he will come with vengeance; with divine retribution he will come to save you." Then will the eyes of the blind be opened and the ears of the deaf unstopped. Then will the lame leap like a deer, and the mute tongue shout for joy. Water will gush forth in the wilderness and streams in the desert. The burning sand will become a pool, the thirsty ground bubbling springs. In the haunts where jackals once lay, grass and reeds and papyrus will grow. And a highway will be there; it will be called the Way of Holiness. The unclean will not journey on it; it will be for those who walk in that Way; wicked fools will not go about on it. No lion will be there, nor will any ferocious beast get up on it; they will not be found there. But only the redeemed will walk there, and the ransomed of the LORD will return. They will enter Zion with singing; everlasting joy will crown their heads. Gladness and joy will overtake them, and sorrow and sighing will flee away. (Isaiah 35)

Broader Questions

It is one thing to notice spiritual or social darkness at the local level. It is quite another thing to ask broader systemic questions. For example, when we move from mercy to justice in the Haitian context, the mature prophet will need to ask political, economic, and social justice questions similar to those in Amos. With a listening heart, I asked myself at the time:

1. What is the relationship between Haiti's small, elite, wealthy class and the foreign interests of Canada and the U.S.A?[4]
2. Why did America prop up the corrupt Duvalier dynasty and its heirs that kept so many in grinding poverty?
3. Why did USAID oppose Aristide's labour reforms that would have raised the minimum wage in Haiti to just 37 cents per hour? What damage would that have done to the American companies who relied on a three dollar weekly wage of Haitian employees (e.g. the sugar companies).
4. Why did the Macoute jailor have an M-16? Where did an illegal chieftain who can't afford a second shirt get a Western-made assault rifle?
5. Where did the Macoute military leaders get their backing? What should I make of the General Cedras, the man who led the coup, responsible for the torture and slaughter of thousands? (We later discovered that he was trained at the "School of the Americas" at Fort Benning, Georgia and was on the payroll of the C.I.A.)
6. If we were sincere in the naval blockade around Haiti in response to the coup, why were so many cargo ships coming into port while the coast guard had no trouble turning back small rafts with refugees offshore? (We later learned that twenty-one new millionaires made their fortune through leaks in the blockade.)
7. Why did the Haitians believe George Bush Sr. was the Antichrist? Why did that seem so obvious to them? Why wouldn't he back Father Aristide, the democratically elected priest-president? (A naive question, of course; Aristide's talk of equality was construed to paint him as a communist.)
8. Why doesn't the foreign aid ever seem to help in Haiti? (We observed that much of the problem was pure stupidity: Aid agencies would dump in rice, and put all the rice farmers out of business for years. Many of them further crippled the economy by creating deeper dependency. Foreign aid improperly administered was a major contributor to unemployment.)
9. What are the cultural strangleholds that internally bind the people? (Voodoo was a chief contributor to the problem because it was so fear-ased. When MCC taught farmers to plant their seeds three inches deeper and make horizontal furrows on the hills to retain topsoil, their crops produced better yields. But the neighbors would not interpret this as a result of improved agricultural practices. They assumed MCC had stolen the spirits out of their land. Thus, they would get revenge by torching the successful grain stash.)
10. What about AIDS and other diseases? A huge epidemic! Communicable disease ripped through the slums of City Soliel. What could

be done? It certainly would have helped if the raw sewage from the wealthier sections of town didn't stream through open ditches right through the ghetto on its way downhill to the ocean).

11. Why do the people speak Creole in the streets but high French in many of the churches? Does this matter? How does it alienate or lead to elitism amongst believers? How did this contribute to a return of the common people to their deeper Voodoo spirituality in times of crisis?

12. Why do the bureaucrats seem to be people with lighter skin? Even among people of color, racism based on skin shade prevailed when it came to power and government employment.

Do such questions seem out of place in a book on listening prayer? Not if we remember that such questions were central themes in the biblical prophets. These were prime concerns whenever they came with a "thus says the Lord." How very far we in the West have watered down the prophetic ministry such that these questions are irrelevant or even threatening to the mainstream church.

The Third Heaven? (The Banana Bread Prophet)

If justice, mercy, and peace are central to the prophets' message and if the hope of redemption is ever in the prophet's vision, something very tangible will come to mind when he or she prays, "Let your kingdom come, let your will be done on earth as it is in heaven." The Lord spoke to me concerning this one Sunday when I was speaking in another church. He said, "Tell them not to look for the mature prophets in the third heaven. You won't find them there. You'll find them at the native reserve, ministering mercy to those overwhelmed by grief."

I knew he was comparing our fascination with extraordinary prophetic phenomena (cf. 2 Corinthians 12:2) to the harsh reality of a tragic accident where a carload of teens from a local reservation had all perished. The darkness of grief had descended on the village. The entire community was reeling. God was weeping with them, waiting for the prophets to come with a word of hope and a grace gift for the families.

As the church service I was visiting that morning proceeded, I found out why the Lord had brought up the topic when a young woman shared her testimony concerning listening prayer.

"I was watching the news this week, and when the television cameras showed the site of that fatal car crash near Chilliwack, I recognized the place. And the Lord said, 'Go there and pray.' I didn't want to. I resisted God because of past issues that I have with the First Nations people. But he wouldn't drop it so I eventually drove past there, slowing down momentarily to pray. He said, 'No. I want you to go back there and pray at the site.' Grudgingly, I went back and prayed and then returned home.

"Then the Lord spoke again and said, 'Bake banana bread for the families and take it to the village.' After fighting about this with the Lord, I gave in and made the banana bread. I hoped to make enough for all of the families and to drop it off for them at the community centre. But when I went to the village, I couldn't find the centre anywhere no matter how long I drove around. The Lord said, 'I want you to give it to the families.' I soon saw a family standing out on their lawn and approached them to ask where I might find people whose loved ones were involved in the accident. Sure enough, these were relatives of one of the deceased. They showed me to the home of the immediate family. I hoped that I could drop off the banana bread for all of the families at that one home without entering. No way. They invited me in. The darkness of grief there was stifling. The family was not coping well at all. I handed over the loaf and then before I realized what I was doing, I found my arms open and extended to the mother of one of the teens. She melted into my arms, clinging and sobbing. Before I left the village, they made sure I handed the bread to each family personally in their own home."

Those families needed a prophet. She came. She came because she listened. She sensed the heart of Christ and followed him into the needy world. And so must we.

Dirty Hands and Dirty Mouths

If listening prayer is about friendship with God, then we should not be surprised if God begins to confide in us about his sorrow over the world's agony or his anger over its injustice. As I listen to God about his love for the world, I hear him say: "It is hard for me to share my grief about the misery and injustice I see in this world with the church. This is because you nearly always assume that I'm putting you on a guilt trip. It's a sign that our relationship is still all about you and that it's not a friendship yet. I don't want to paralyze you with guilt trips. I want you to feel my grief, experience my comfort, share my hope, and follow me into action."

How will this look? God's answer is no ivory tower idealism. It is intense, specific, and highly practical.

Defend the cause of the weak and fatherless; maintain the rights of the poor and oppressed. Rescue the weak and needy; deliver them from the hand of the wicked. (Psalm 82:3–4)

Religion that God our Father accepts as pure and faultless is this: to look after orphans and widows in their distress and to keep oneself from being polluted by the world. (James 1:27)

The prophets have dirty hands (and mouths too sometimes), because you'll find them wading without apology through the mess of life. Their target audience begins with the church and its religious leaders but extends to nations and heads of state and to corporations with their economic power brokers. They have unabashed social agendas and are not afraid of being perceived as political. Their concern is for the oppressed, the poor, the widow, the orphan, and the enslaved. The mature prophets call for both personal righteousness and social justice. They retreat inward in contemplation then explode onto the public scene as spokespersons for God's heart and as advocates for the downtrodden.

The Isaiahs of today may look and sound like documentary director, Michael Moore (*Bowling for Columbine*) or the late Henry Nouwen, author and advocate for the disabled, or rock star Bono pressing the nations for AIDS relief and debt forgiveness in Africa. Deborahs of today may sound alarmingly like comedienne Janeane Garafalo challenging the idolatry of might or Rosa Parks of the civil rights movement confronting racism. The church at large may not accept them—they, we, you, I may even stone them. But before we do, perhaps we should listen. God may be using them to speak to us.

But never mind the celebrities, the mature prophets are also ordinary people doing extraordinary things because they listen to God. They are young people like Jenni, accompanying police on brothel raids in Bangkok and rescuing children from slave-prostitution *because she listened.* Or Darla in Zambia, running an orphanage for children victimized by HIV *because she listened.* Then there is Rodney, who developed the first Christian AIDS hospice in Winnipeg, Canada *because he listened.* There is also Linda, who organized the feeding of 100,000 people in Mozambique for four days with one million pounds of food *because she listened.* And there is Greg on the Thai/Burmese border, teaching and helping Karen refugees daily *because he listened.*

Here at home, there is Lisa, gently holding Allison's convulsing limbs as she goes through her third grand-mal seizure of the evening *because she listened.*

The mature prophets will not only talk about justice and mercy from the safety of tabernacles on the mount of transfiguration. They live these themes as they follow Jesus back down into the valley to touch today's lepers or pray with today's demoniacs.

God's Preference

Again and again, God makes clear his preference for mercy and justice over self-absorbed religious ritual, including listening prayer that never comes out of the prayer closet. He calls into question any liturgical or sacrificial system that fails to express the heart of God for justice and mercy beyond the temple walls. He rebukes the prophets who would thin out or shrink down the prophetic message into an ingrown spiritual subculture. Frankly, such "religion" annoys him:

> "Stop bringing meaningless offerings! Your incense is detestable to me. New Moons, Sabbaths and convocations— I cannot bear your evil assemblies... They have become a burden to me; I am weary of bearing them... Seek justice, encourage the oppressed. Defend the cause of the fatherless, plead the case of the widow." (Isaiah 1:13–17)

> With what shall I come before the LORD and bow down before the exalted God?... He has showed you, O man, what is good. And what does the LORD require of you? To act justly and to love mercy and to walk humbly with your God. (Micah 3:6, 8)

> "Away with the noise of your songs! I will not listen to the music of your harps. But let justice roll on like a river, righteousness like a never-failing stream!" (Amos 5:23–24)

II. DISTILLING THE PROPHETIC VISION

You've read about my seminal experience with social justice, and I've shared briefly from the biblical prophetic tradition. But what did Jesus himself teach? If Jesus is the perfect representative and living manifestation of God's heart and mind, what place do these themes have in his vision of the kingdom? I would argue that the passage known as the beatitudes represents the absolute core of Jesus' kingdom message.

In that core, justice, mercy, and peacemaking are the predominant seeds:

> Blessed are the poor in spirit, for theirs is the kingdom of heaven.
>
> Blessed are those who mourn, for they will be comforted.
>
> Blessed are the meek, for they will inherit the earth.
>
> Blessed are those who hunger and thirst for [justice],[5] for they will be filled.
>
> Blessed are the merciful, for they will be shown mercy.
>
> Blessed are the pure in heart, for they will see God.
>
> Blessed are the peacemakers, for they will be called sons of God.
>
> Blessed are those who are persecuted because of [justice], for theirs is the kingdom of heaven.
>
> Blessed are you when people insult you, persecute you and falsely say all kinds of evil against you because of me. Rejoice and be glad, because great is your reward in heaven, for in the same way they persecuted the prophets who were before you.
>
> You are the salt of the earth. But if the salt loses its saltiness, how can it be made salty again? It is no longer good for anything, except to be thrown out and trampled by men.
>
> You are the light [out there in] the world. A city on a hill cannot be hidden. Neither do people light a lamp and put it under a bowl. Instead they put it on its stand, and it gives light to everyone in the house. In the same way, let your light shine before men, that they may see your good deeds and praise your Father in heaven. (Matthew 5:3–13)

The beatitudes are not to be reduced to today's inspirational thought-for-the-day. Ron Dart explains: "This text represents the distillation of the entire Jewish prophetic vision and supplies the ethical core and centre for all Christianity. We must not ignore, domesticate, sanitize, or censure this Magna Carta of our faith."[6] In fact, every claim to revelation should not only be strained through the written Word of God.

It should also pass through the narrow gate of these ten verses before we appropriate it as a truly Christian message. The beatitudes act as a perfect litmus test for prophetic purity.

III. PROPHETIC RESPIRATION

The beatitudes show us a type of "prophetic respiration" in which the disciple inhales the fullness of the Spirit in contemplative prayer then exhales justice and mercy into the community. They step into the meeting place of the heart and then emerge as lights into the darkness of a world-gone-mad. Inhale and be filled. Exhale and be merciful. Inhale and be purified. Exhale and bring justice. Inhale and receive peace. Exhale and be peacemakers. Inhale and be illumined. Exhale and be light.

Spirituality that only inhales is nothing more than pietism. It becomes bloated and useless (salt that loses its savor). Listening prayer that does not lead to a lifestyle of compassion can actually lead to the sin of Sodom: "Now this was the sin of your sister Sodom: She and her daughters were arrogant, overfed and unconcerned; they did not help the poor and needy" (Ezekiel 16:49). On the other hand, the activist who only exhales becomes winded, burned out or bitter (no longer pure in heart). Activism that is not rooted in listening prayer becomes ineffective and even dangerous if it leads to the fundamentalist terrorism of the zealots.

In the beatitudes, Jesus teaches us how to breathe properly. He shows us both inner and outer spirituality—contemplation and social action, mysticism and mercy. Retreat to the mountain, the heart or the throne room. Then return to the city, the crowds, and the lepers. From this discovery emerges the beginning of prophetic maturity.

◀)) *Tuning In*

Ask the Lord these questions:

- Would you please take me deep enough into your heart to sense your concern for justice, mercy, and peace?
- As I tune in to those themes, is there some grief in your heart about an area or people group or issue that you would like to share with me? Let me see it how you see it. Let me feel how you feel.
- What is the darkness that is prevailing there? Why is it there? What needs to happen there? What promise do you have for them?

- What do you want me to pray? What do you want me to say? What do you want me to do? If you need a spokesperson, I am available. To whom should I go? How shall I deliver this message? What is the word of hope? What will redemption look like?

If this is your first time doing such an exercise, I would suggest writing out your message and then praying (and perhaps fasting) over it until peace comes. Then ask the Lord what action you can take with a pure heart.

Listening Prayer for Inner Healing

My heart lies before you, O my God. Look deep within. See these memories of mine, for you are my hope. You cleanse me when unclean humors such as these possess me, by drawing my eyes to yourself and saving my feet from the snare.

- Augustine, Confessions, 4.6

MEET ME IN THE LOBBY

My brother-in-law Alan and I were harnessed to the exterior wall of an enormous apartment building, dangling like spiders looking for their next footing. We were trying to find the right window, one of identical hundreds, to penetrate a very specific room in the high rise. We were frustrated and bewildered. Where would we even start?

At that moment, Jesus opened one of the windows and poked his head out. With a puzzled look on his face, he asked, "What are you doing out there? Why not just meet me in the *lobby*, and I'll lead you directly where you need to go from there! That's why I created it for you."

At that moment, I woke up. The dream was my answer. Allow me to set up the question for you.

This chapter is for those whom God is calling and equipping to do what we call "prayer ministry."[1] This may be your first introduction to this amazing realm. Or perhaps you've already been well trained in a number of approaches to this ministry. Your mind may even brim with mental filing cabinets full of information. I strongly value the many insights gleaned from various schools of inner healing, but, to be honest, I've also found it overwhelming. The more I learned, the more complicated the issues became. The more analytical I became, the less I knew where to start. Rather than seeing people's lives as a simple house (as Jesus did, see Matthew 7:24; 12:44), they began to look like the gigantic apartment blocks of my dream. Attending more classes and seminars just added more windows to choose from when trying to pray *into* that person's life. As someone sat across from me for prayer and looked into my calm, confident eyes, on the inside I felt like I was swinging by that harness, struggling for a window through which I could peek into their hearts.

Alan and I were grumbling about this one evening after a difficult prayer session. What had happened to the simplicity of depending on Jesus? When had we started to lean on our own understanding? We had slipped from, "Oh God, we need you to come into this house!" to "Well, from our extensive training, we know it could be this window or this issue or this one or this one or ... Wow, this is confusing." It was only when we finally asked, "God, could you please boil it down for us?" that I had my dream about the lobby.

The central message of the dream was that rather than sorting out for ourselves which window of a person's soul we must enter in order to invite Jesus, why not just find Jesus first and ask him to lead us there? The lobby that Jesus had already provided was a "place of refuge" or "meeting place" (cf. chapter five). By showing us this, Jesus was saying, "Before you worry about people's issues and try to track their problems, wounds, behaviours, and demons through the endless mazes of inner corridors, first give them a lobby. When they have their own place of refuge, I'll meet you there and lead you into the healing work that I deem necessary for that session.

Why the Meeting Place First?

While I am going to lay out a proven, effective model for prayer ministry in this chapter, let me hasten to add that if God has already given you a fruitful approach, stick with it. But also let me just suggest that you experiment with adding a place of refuge to the *front end* of what you're currently doing. Here's why:

- Everyone—even the most wounded or fragmented soul—has a safe place in his or her heart in which to meet Jesus. God has graciously preserved a place of refuge for himself in even the most broken or bound up of his children. Count on it.
- A meeting place enables you to find Jesus in a safe place rather than searching frantically for him in the middle of a traumatic memory. It becomes a safe home base for all forays into healing.
- In the meeting place, Jesus prepares us to enter painful memories. He provides comfort, courage, reassurance, and promises before we enter the scary places. If things in a memory get "hairy," you can always retreat to the lobby for more clarification or courage.
- A meeting place allows you to get acquainted with how each person personally hears, sees or senses Jesus. You can get the hang of what

three-way conversation looks and feels like for that person while still in a peaceful context. In this chapter, whenever I say, "We asked Jesus and he told us ...," hear that in the context of the inner healing triangle, which includes you, the person you're praying for, and Jesus. In this model, I ask the question, Jesus gives the answer to the one I'm praying for, and he or she reports Jesus' answer back to me.

Three-Way Conversational Prayer

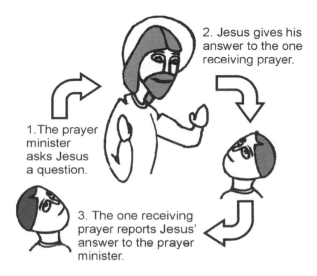

2. Jesus gives his answer to the one receiving prayer.

1.The prayer minister asks Jesus a question.

3. The one receiving prayer reports Jesus' answer to the prayer minister.

- A meeting place allows you to discover any blocks to hearing God that need to be removed up front. Jesus will show us what they are, and he is willing to remove them.
- A meeting place establishes the permanent agenda for intimacy. This is a higher priority to God than healing. Only healing *plus* intimate relationship leads to transformation. This is where the subject learns to "abide" in God even after the healing work is done.
- A meeting place establishes Jesus as the leader of every prayer ministry time. Whenever you feel lost, you can simply ask, "What needs to happen next?" As Trevor Walters, a wise Anglican priest, once told me, "The less you think you know, the more authority you'll have." That's because you leave more room for Jesus to work rather than assuming you know how to fix the problem.
- A meeting place enables those with repressed or dissociated memories ("windowless rooms" to use the apartment analogy again) to find Jesus in a safe place where he is able to open a way into otherwise inaccessible memories.

Overview of Our Model

The model as it stands today includes a journey with Jesus through three major meetings.

I. First, we find Jesus in a place of refuge (the lobby). Our agenda in the place of refuge is threefold.

> A. Intimacy: We ask Jesus for a safe place to commune with him, and remove any immediate blocks that prevent us from hearing his voice or experiencing his love.

> B. Comfort: We ask Jesus how he sees us and how he feels about us. We draw near to behold him and to be held by him. We ask the Lord for blessings and promises, for strength and courage.

> C. Recognition: We ask the Lord to identify issues that he wants to address and to open our eyes to recognize where we are bearing or experiencing bad fruit (spiritual, emotional, behavioural, mental, or physical).

II. Second, we follow Jesus to the "root wound." We ask him to lead us back through the years from the place of refuge to the moment when the initial seed that bears this fruit was first sown into our hearts. Normally, he takes us to a narrative memory. But as we'll see later, God may surprise us with another destination. In any case, his major agenda in the root wound is healing. This healing includes four elements:

> A. Confession: A brutally honest confession of our pain and/ or sin in that scenario.

> B. Revelation of Jesus: A revelation of where Jesus was in the scene.

> C. Healing: A removal of each painful emotion (1. exposing lies and 2. removing burdens).

> D. Revelation of others: We ask Jesus to show us each character in that scenario through his eyes (the offender, the victim, other people or spirit-beings involved).

III. Finally, we meet Jesus at "the Cross," where the agenda is freedom. Again this meeting includes up to four elements:

A. Forgiveness: Leaving our offenders at the Cross.

B. Repentance: Repenting and receiving forgiveness for reactive sins and putting to death unholy habits.

C. Renunciation: Cutting off judgments, curses, vows, and ungodly soul-ties between our offenders and us.

D. Deliverance: Removing any legal right for the enemy to stay and if there are demons, sending them to Jesus for removal.

The remainder of this chapter will expand on the above outline, illustrating how this model looks in practice and what type of questions we would typically ask Jesus at each stage. Rather than claiming, "This is the right way to do it!" I intend simply to testify to what Jesus has done and is willing to do through this approach.

ONE PREREQUISITE: DO YOU WANT TO BE FREE?

When we first started inviting Jesus into memories, it seemed that we could do no wrong. But eventually, we ran into some cases where the person receiving prayer would shut down the session before healing could come. Puzzled, my friend Tyler asked the Lord for an explanation. He was told very directly, "It was not 'the Day of the Lord' for them." Over time, we began to understand that "the Day of the Lord" was when someone was ripe and ready to receive healing and freedom. Tyler was intrigued. He prayed, "Lord, you need to show me how to discern whether it's the Day of the Lord for someone. I don't have the time or energy to do it by trial and error." Jesus responded, "Before launching into prayer ministry with anyone, ask this point-blank question, 'Do you want to be free?'"

Do you remember Jesus asking the crippled man in John 5:1, "Do you want to be made whole?" Why would he ask that? Could it be that some people are not ready to be healed? Exactly. We may cling to our wounds as a comfortable identity, a protective formula, or as a convenient excuse. God will only set us free when *we* are *willing* to be free.

Jesus explained, "Only proceed when they give a straightforward, emphatic 'yes'." This was to be our God-given sign that they were ripe for healing: Christ's promise to set them free at this time *no matter how resistant they might become during the session*. On the other hand, Jesus said, "If they are not really ready for ministry, they will answer the question by talking in circles or repeating their complaints." For example, if they say, "Well yes, but you just don't know what my mom was like," that person is not ready. When a person is in this frame of mind, we will invariably run into their will at some point, thus shutting down the session, *no matter how desperate they seem to be at the outset.* In such cases, we ask them to call us again when they know they want to be free.

Whenever I have *not* followed these instructions (I can count three times in the last decade), I have regretted it. The person has left frustrated and disappointed. It's as if I've inoculated them from further prayer ministry, because they now live under the impression, "Well I tried that before and it didn't work!" So again, the million-dollar question (sorry, Tyler, it'll have to be an IOU): "Do you want to be free?"

I. FIND JESUS IN A PLACE OF REFUGE

There are three main elements to this first stage of prayer ministry.

A. Intimacy

In chapter five, we learned in detail how to find Jesus in a safe meeting place. Leading people into a personal place of refuge is my first and last order of business with those who need prayer ministry. As soon as they'll let me, I pray to ask Jesus, "Thank you for creating and preserving a safe place in every human heart where we can meet with you to begin the healing process. Please show us now what that place of refuge looks like in this person?" Most often, he will paint them an idyllic setting or take them to a familiar place. Once there, he invites them to be intimate with him.

B. Comfort

When we ask Jesus how he sees us, the most common picture is that of a child with a loving parent. As we draw near, a deep sense of comfort may overtake us. Please note the important difference between comfort and healing. Comfort is akin to plucking bad fruit off the tree. Healing happens when the tree is removed, roots and all. When someone feels the comforting love of God in the place of refuge, they may feel such relief that tracking this fruit to a root wound might seem superfluous. Usually that is not the case. The same fruit, now plucked, will tend to grow again if the root wound is not healed.

For example, one young man with issues of inadequacy continually heard an inner tape playing—"I'm not good enough. I can't do it"—whenever he faced a challenge. Facing a speaking engagement he turned to the Lord for comfort and, in his place of refuge, Jesus reassured him, "You can do all things through me. I will give you strength." Heartened, the young man rose to the occasion and overcame his fears. The message went off without a hitch.

However, the Lord only seemed to provide comfort for the moment. Weeks later, the young man faced another test. The old feelings of inadequacy started to rise again and the familiar "not good enough" message came to assault his mind. After repeating this cycle for a number of years he was desperate enough to take the next step. He wanted healing, not just comfort. The Lord showed him that to receive healing they would need to meet not in the place of refuge but back at a root wound. When the Lord healed him in the context of his root wound (a series of painful childhood memories), the inadequacy *never came back.* The inner tapes were erased and he was set free. Rather than simply lopping off more bad fruit, the young man finally allowed Jesus to take the axe to the root of the tree.

The point is that God's comfort is available, not merely to strengthen us for the moment but also to prepare us for the next stage of our healing. He grants blessings and promises, strength and courage so that we will follow him deeper into root level healing.

C. Recognition

We ask the Lord, "Would you please show us what issues you want to address? Open our eyes to recognize where we are bearing or experiencing bad fruit." At this stage, I may ask what someone's felt needs are (i.e., "What's 'in your face' right now?"). But I find it more helpful to ask Jesus what is most in *his* face. Our felt needs and our real needs frequently differ. I may feel that I'm hard done by and need a break in life while the Lord may know that I'm actually a narcissist ("It's all about me!") who needs to be freed from selfishness and whining. He knows and will share with us what the real issues are.

The negative fruit (symptoms) in our lives *may* have originated in a "root wound"—defined as a seminal experience in which we embraced lies, received burdens, and/or made choices that continue to trouble us. On the other hand, the original "domino" may have been physiological (e.g., misfiring neurons), chemical (e.g., substance abuse), or viral/ bacterial (e.g., encephalitis). In *theory,* inner healing should work 100 percent of the time on "root wound damage" and zero percent when the problem is medical. But in fact, in *either* case inner healing may bring about complete healing *or* it may need to be part of a therapeutic "cocktail" of conventional counselling, medication or traditional deliverance.

Regardless, the following five categories tend to present themselves as symptoms of a root wound:

- Emotional symptoms: fear, anger, anxiety, depression, loneliness
- Behavioural symptoms: sinful patterns, addictions, compulsions
- Mental symptoms: confusion, paranoia, delusions, flashbacks
- Physical symptoms: stress-based diseases like ulcers, heart disease, some asthma[2]
- Spiritual symptoms: spiritual malaise, demonic oppression, obsession with the occult

Once Jesus has established a place of refuge and used it to prepare us for the journey, we are ready to follow him back to the root wound.

II. FOLLOW JESUS TO THE ROOT WOUND

Narrative Memories

When God begins to lead us back to a root wound, we find it is usually an early, painful memory or an obvious, specific trauma. At such times, wounds are inflicted and messages are imprinted on our hearts. Even when the memory itself is long forgotten, we read and respond to life through the grid of those hurts. Thus, we normally learn to be angry, or fearful, or despairing at a very early age.

If the Lord leads us to a memory from later on, I like to check in with him, "Lord, is this the memory where you want to meet with us or do we keep going?" He may walk us through a series of memories before he stops and says, "This is the one." The purpose for the "tour" is either to demonstrate a life-long pattern *or* to help the person gather enough emotional momentum to follow Jesus back as far as he or she needs to go. I've also seen over a dozen memories accumulate in no particular order. In such cases, we just lay all of these memories down on a spiritual table before the Lord and ask, "Now Lord, which one would YOU like to highlight so that we can meet you there?"

We prefer to follow Jesus into root wounds rather than casting people into their painful memories and then hoping Jesus will show up. Sometimes he will actually take them by the hand and lead them through a door from the place of refuge into the place of pain. Other times, he will go before them to let us know when it's safe to enter. Most often, Jesus sends them into the memory, assuring them that he will be there even though they may not see him immediately. The rationale is that they must first experience the event as they *have been* remembering it. They need to realize what lies they've embraced, what hurts they carry, and what reactions they gave. Connecting with those events at an emotional level allows them to witness the origins of their bad fruit. This is much easier if Jesus has already spoken a promise of his presence beforehand in the place of refuge.

As I hinted earlier, God is not limited to our narrative memory. He may instead take us to pre-memory events or show us a symbolic memory. Jesus can take us back to wounds experienced in infancy, in the womb, and even in our family tree![3] He often verifies the work done there by (a) curing the resulting symptoms and (b) through an external witness, such as one's parents.

Let's take a brief survey of some of these atypical memories in which we encounter God to receive healing.

Infant Memories

A young woman came for prayer concerning the suicidal thoughts that haunted her every year during her birthday. The temptation to take her own life only came at that time of year, but it was compelling enough to alarm her. When we asked the Lord to take us to the root wound, I was not surprised when she wound up in the delivery room. At her birth, complications threatened both her life and her mother's. The baby was blue and not breathing; the mother appeared to be hemorrhaging to death. The doctor made a quick judgment call, "Let the baby die! It won't make it anyway." He turned from the baby to save her mom. Her father intervened and, through his persistence, both lives were saved. Nevertheless, somehow the message was imprinted in the child's heart (subconscious): "Let the baby die!" Thus, every year on the date of her birth, the message resurfaced as suicidal thoughts like, "I should be dead." When Jesus entered that memory, he took the form of her father. He picked up the baby and spoke to everyone (but especially to her), "Let the baby live! She's going to make it." He spoke words of blessing over her, welcoming her to abundant life in this world. Since then, six years ago, she has never struggled with suicidal thoughts on her birthday or on any other day for that matter.

Pre-natal Memories

The most amazing pre-natal memory that I witnessed came to a fellow I'll call Bob. Bob wanted to get to the root cause of his rage, which was accompanied by a very powerful death wish. When these two forces worked in tandem, let's just say you wouldn't want to cut him off during rush hour traffic!

Following Jesus, Bob found himself floating in the womb alongside something very dark. When we asked the Lord if it had a label, the word that came was simply "death." What came out later was a double-whammy. First, Bob's mom had lost a prior baby. Second, when she found out that she was pregnant with Bob, she chose to abort him. She went to the clinic and was on the table before she changed her mind. Suffice it to say that there was a major "spirit of death" assailing Bob, even in the womb, which gave rise to both his rage and his death wish. After we dealt with the grief of the lost baby and the threat of the abortion, the spirit of death left rather easily, but the death wish remained. In his spirit, the vow had formed, "I don't want to live."

Next, Jesus took us to the moment when Bob was about to be born. Before my eyes, his face started turning blue and his head snapped back with his chin cranked up and to the left. His body went rigid and completely straight, toes outstretched as far as he could reach. While I did a quick mental scan of my insurance policy, I asked Bob, "What's happening?" He was angry. "I won't," he gasped, "I'm not coming out. I don't want to live!" What was going on?

Bob's mom was able to verify that when he was born, it was as if he didn't want to come out. Aside from being very late, he also came out feet first (hence the stretched out legs and toes). But what blew us away was the position of his head and chin. His mother explained that he had nearly suffocated because his *chin had got caught and stuck in her cervix.*

Now here is the brilliance of God. As Bob relived his delivery, he opened his eyes and looked up at the nine-foot ceiling in terror. I asked what was wrong. He said, "It's Jesus. He's here in the delivery room. He's bigger than the room!" I wondered if we had bumped into a false Jesus. I expected a gentle Jesus that would take the baby in his arms and love it to health. But Bob was terrified. In this open-eyed vision, he cowered as if Jesus were a monster. He cried out, "Don't kill me! Don't kill me!" I heard God's Spirit ask through me, "Why not?" To which Bob exploded—here's the kicker—*"I want to live!"* In that moment, the fear of the Lord flipped on Bob's survival switch. The death wish was broken.

Family Memories

Tom is a well-known professional counsellor who specializes in treating dissociative disorders (DID) through listening prayer. He's seen and heard it all—at least he used to think so. Then one day a man who had suffered for decades with chronic, clinical depression came to Tom for counselling. Medication, counselling, and prayer had so far been ineffective, and the man was now hopeless and suicidal. Though he had not been diagnosed with DID, Tom consented to pray with the man. Together, they asked the Lord to trace the man's depression back

240

to its root, the very moment when it was seeded into his heart. As they waited on the Lord, the man began to relive a memory of a rape. Mysteriously, the memory was not his own. He was aware of experiencing it as a woman—and he "just knew" that it occurred roughly two hundred years ago! Tom was perplexed. Should he shut down this counselling session? Were the past-life people right after all? Or was it all a delusion? Tom decided to invite Jesus into the memory.

Jesus appeared in the memory and performed a rescue. He brought emotional healing to the memory and removed the effects of trauma. He explained that the client was burden bearing for a female ancestor who had been sexually assaulted many generations ago. By stepping into her place, the man was able to carry her burden and deliver it to the Lord on her behalf. Now here's the *really* weird part: When Tom's client came out of the memory, his depression was *completely* lifted! This session occurred three years ago, and while the man has experienced the normal highs and lows of a healthy life, the client has never once slipped back into his familiar depressive state.

We know that this man received a mental and emotional healing. I wonder if the Lord also delivered grace to his foremother in her day through the prayers of her descendent. I can't know that nor can I explain it. I'm only telling the story as I heard it from Tom's mouth.

Recovered Memories[4]

The topic of recovered memories[5] is far too large and loaded to tackle in this book. I will virtually skip through it with a few brief definitions. Yet, to be truthful, when tracking bad fruit back to a root wound, we land in previously unrecalled memories far too often to ignore this phenomenon. Again, our criterion for authenticating an allegedly recovered memory is the verification of healing fruit and a credible witness. Since we can't be sure of either until we invite Jesus into the memory, we *always* do so in the humility that the memory may not be exactly the way things were. (Are they ever?) Whether the picture in the person's mind is an accurate memory, a symbolic ideation, or a total fabrication of the flesh, my only course of action is to invite Jesus to bring truth, light, and healing into the situation. I must refrain from suggesting *any* images or encouraging accusations. I simply introduce Jesus into whatever is presented without making judgments, assumptions, or conclusions about it.

Recovering a Memory and a Sister

One tremendously fruitful recovered memory came to my friend Colleen. She was asking God, "Why am I constantly stressed? I wake up in knots, full of anxiety, but I can see no cause for it in my present life circumstances." The Lord answered, "It's your sister." Colleen pictured her three sisters and asked, "Which one?" He responded, "None of them." What was *that* supposed to mean?

The Lord took her into a memory from her toddler years. She vividly recalled sitting on the kitchen floor in her diaper while her mom discussed something serious with another lady. She couldn't understand what was being said. (She was two years old at the very most.) But at the time, she knew it was scary, and it involved a great loss. The moment had traumatized her, because even at that age, she was aware that they might be talking about her. Fear of abandonment entered her heart and remained there for forty years as a constant backdrop of anxiety even though she had completely blanked out the memory. What she saw now was that her parents could not care for another child, and were planning to give up the baby her mother was now carrying for adoption.

Jesus' first order of agenda was to enter the memory and heal Colleen of her fear of abandonment. He came into the room and sat cross-legged on the floor. The little girl backed up towards him until she plopped into his lap. From there, with Jesus at her back, she played and watched the room without fear. She could see the conversation but remained at perfect peace. Jesus held her and assured her that he would never abandon her.

Next came the process of verifying the existence of this alleged sister. After several months of digging, one of Colleen's aunts indirectly hinted at the adoption by discretely passing Colleen a newspaper clipping—an ad from an adult woman searching for her family. After that, finding this sister became one of Colleen's top priorities. Success again! The sisters found each other through the adoption reunion channels. After exchanging letters for a year, they chose to meet. But God wasn't done yet. It took another year before Colleen was finally able to introduce her newfound sister to their mother. An enormous load of guilt was lifted from her mother's life and, even in her senior years, she's become like a new person. Not only is she much more easygoing, she has also chosen to receive Christian baptism. All of this came by believing God's voice and following him into a recovered memory.

False Memories

Speak of recovered memories and the topic of false memories will flare up immediately—usually with a lot more heat than light. The whole area is a lawsuit just waiting to happen. On one hand, advocates for children who have suffered abuse urge us to believe the children. On the other hand, reports of abuse stemming from recovered memories are *sometimes* proven false. The polarization between accuser and accused is often nothing less than vicious. Because I've encountered so many verifiable recovered memories, I don't expect or need to have a hearing with the false-memory-syndrome movement. However, I might presume to offer a few suggestions to those genuinely willing to sort recovered memories from false.

- Just because someone recovers a vivid, detailed memory does not mean that we *know* the events occurred in exactly that way. Memories are subjective by their very nature.
- Just because we've done due diligence to avoid suggestive or leading questions does not guarantee that false memories cannot arise through other means.
- Please consider the power of the flesh and the enemy to generate false images, fantasies, and delusions in the mind.
- Please consider the possibility that symbolic mental images might be mistaken for literal events.
- Please consider the possibility that freshly recovered memories may overlap like stacked overheads (e.g., an angry dad memory may be superimposed over an abusive stranger memory, suggesting an abusive dad memory).
- Just because we don't *know* the events occurred in exactly that way does not mean we cannot invite Jesus into the picture. If he is aware that someone is living in a deluded fantasy, he will still enter that place, first to heal them of their pain and then to draw them out of the lie. We ask him to remove all deception, illusion, and delusion. But Jesus may *show* us the false images first so that we can identify and remove them.

Symbolic Memories

When we ask God to take us to a root wound, he sometimes opts for the symbolism of a vision or a dream rather than a literal event. This is a gracious concession to those who cannot face the actual memory, a provision of God's gentle heart. The Lord may also use a vision or dream because it symbolically represents an ongoing life pattern that encompasses *many* memories. I still call these vision and dream scenarios "memories," because while the narrative is non-literal, it reflects real life, real hurt, real lies, and real burdens. Mostly, Jesus will use such a vision or dream as a springboard into memory work, connecting us with our emotions before taking us to the narrative.

Whenever I do prayer ministry with Colleen, she typically has a diagnostic dream the night before we meet. Her dreams act as a tool for discovering what emotions are stirring inside. For example, she often dreams about a house beside an ocean in which the characters represent aspects of her heart. The state of the house shows us the state of her heart. The dynamics of the ocean symbolize the source of her fear. Jesus will often come directly into that area to do "root work," but he also springs back from there into old narrative memories that need healing.

In all of these types of memory, Jesus' major agenda is healing. Healing a root wound includes four elements: confession, a revelation of Christ, healing, and a revelation of others through Jesus' eyes.

A. Confession

A brutally honest confession of our pain and/or sin in that scenario: Whenever we find ourselves in a root wound, the first rule of thumb is to find Jesus as soon as possible. But whether or not we see him immediately, he wants to hear an honest confession of all the emotions we are feeling. He doesn't want us to play games, keeping emotional cards up our sleeves. In his kindness, he may not speak or act until it's all on the table. But once we're brutally honest, I find that he rushes in to help.

B. Revelation of Jesus

A revelation of Jesus in that scenario: We ask, "Lord, your Word says that you never leave us or forsake us. You promise to be with us always. Would you now open the eyes of our heart? Please enable us to find you in this memory." Then his presence transforms our perspective. Encountering him in our dark times brings light and truth. Many lies and burdens just vanish when he enters the picture. He truly was there the whole time: only now we are aware of it. He has come to cleanse that memory of *all pain.*

In making that statement, my friends tease me of being a very generous absolutist. But reflect on the truth that he came to bear *all* our sins *and* our sorrows (Isaiah 52:4). At the Cross, Jesus provided a place to cast all of our guilt (of sin) and all (not most) of our pain (sorrow). We are invited to cast all (not 80 percent) of our cares and anxieties on the Lord (Psalm 55:22, 1 Peter 5:7). We hear that he is able to save completely (utterly) those who come to him (Hebrews 7: 25). He sprinkles our hearts clean (how clean?) and washes our bodies with pure water (Hebrews 10:22). This doesn't happen some day in "the sweet by and by" but *now, today,* in each and every event of our lives where we carry the residue of guilt and grief. What can wash away my sins? And what can *make me whole* again? Let us not undersell the power of the gospel to both wash *and* heal the broken heart. As Andy, a friend and veteran in ministry says, "Yes, we carry lifelong scars. But scars are *not* wounds. They are the sign of a past wound, now healed. Rather than disfiguring, they become golden stripes where God's light shines through most brightly." How does God do this?

C. Healing

The removal of each painful emotion: When we ask someone to confess painful emotions stored in a particular memory, we find that every one of those emotions fits into one of two categories: truth-based burdens and lie-based pain. Jesus approaches each one differently. He lifts burdens away to the Cross and he removes lies by showing us the truth.

1. Truth-based Burdens

These are appropriate emotional responses to real events. However, we still need them to be lifted away by Jesus, because carrying them on our own becomes too heavy and too costly. The most common truth-based burdens are:

- Hurt (pain or trauma). For example, someone hurt us verbally, emotionally or physically. This includes insults, physical or sexual assaults or accidents that caused us real hurt.
- Anger (hate, resentment). Perhaps we are angry because of an actual offence, whether towards us or not. Even righteous anger, if carried overnight, spoils into the poison of malice or bitterness.
- Grief (loss or disappointment). We may mourn when we lose a loved one through death or separation. We may also grieve for unfulfilled needs and neglect where there should have been love. We may feel it as a vacuum or a deep ache.
- Guilt (unresolved sin). When we actually sin, we will feel the weight of guilt until we give it to God and experience his forgiveness. This is in contrast to shame, which is rooted in a lie that we are not forgiven, not worthy, dirty, tainted, etc. (more on that below).
- Burden bearing (carrying the hurts of others). When we feel someone else's truth-based hurts, we are actually carrying them and need to deliver that burden to Jesus.
- Embarrassment (as opposed to humiliation). Embarrassment seems to be a real burden that someone puts on us and must be lifted away. In my case, I usually end up embarrassing myself. It is a hurt based in a real situation. Humiliation, by contrast, involves

a false message about who we are. It is a form of shame that Jesus treats as a lie.

While I'm not sure that Ed Smith[6] regards truth-based burdens as a category unto itself, I learned how Jesus removes truth-based pain by listening to his wife's testimony. For eleven years, she could physically feel the grief of losing one of her children. She constantly carried that ache right in her sternum. During a prayer ministry session, the Lord lifted that grief away in such a way that she could actually feel it leave. The burden of grief and its physical sensation, were borne away to the Cross. Now what she felt was literally a "loving memory."

I could hardly believe this, but I started experimenting with the Lord to see if he was willing to lift pain like this for everyone. Jesus gladly obliged the first twenty times in a row on all types of truth-based burdens. I began to trust that the removal of burdens is *always* his will, just as it is with the removal of sin or demons. The questions that we ask Jesus concerning truth-based burdens are:

- "Jesus, what is the burden that they have been carrying?"
- "Jesus, where do they carry that burden in their body?" Most people have a physical sense that corresponds to the emotion (if not, that's okay, but nine out of ten do). They may carry it in their heart, their head, the pit of their stomach, their back and shoulders, their jaw, their fists, and so on. Jesus usually allows them to feel where they are carrying it as you pray together.
- "Jesus, what does that burden look like in the spirit?" This is usually an unpleasant picture. Recently, I met someone who carried anger like a spiked iron bowling ball in her stomach. She also carried grief like a ball of ugly darkness in her heart.
- "Jesus, what has carrying this burden cost them?" The Lord will show them that however appropriate the feeling was at first, carrying over time has cost them dearly. They often answer, "It has cost me my life/joy/peace," or "It's cost me so many relationships."

These questions serve to loosen our grip from our burdens. Too often we befriend our burdens, believing that they somehow comfort or even protect us from further pain. In truth, they allow and even cause further hurt in our lives while filtering out nothing but love, joy, and peace.

Ed Smith asks, "If Jesus were willing to take this burden from you, would you let him?" Most answer "yes," but when he follows up with "are you sure?" up to half of his clients are *not sure*. They believe a lie that somehow they need this burden. Maybe they believe their anger protects them or that their grief proves they really cared for their lost loved one. Maybe they believe that carrying guilt protects them from sin, when really it drives them to it. Smith refers all such objections to the Lord, who shows or tells them the truth. Even then, some clients are reluctant to relinquish the burden, because they've known nothing else. In such cases, we follow up with:

> "Jesus, with what would you replace this burden?" If we have been using a burden for protection, Jesus may give us a shield of faith or a sword of truth in its place. Or he may just replace it with an emotion like love, joy or peace.

When all their objections are satisfied, the person will be willing to pray, "Lord, if you'll take this burden from me, I'll let you take it." Then I pray, "Lord, would you now lay your wounded hand on that burden and lift it away to the Cross. Draw all its poison into your own wounds and remove it completely." I instruct them, "Now just let him take it. Let me know when it is all gone or if it plateaus at some stage." If they get stuck at some point, I just ask the Lord where the remaining hurt is coming from. Once he shows them, I ask if it's okay for the Lord to remove it. (Again, if they have objections, refer them to Jesus.) We continue this process until it's *all* gone—utterly removed.

Your Guilt Is Removed

Imagine carrying the guilt of a woman who had killed not one, not two or three, but five of her own children. I met such a woman. During her younger years, she had used abortion as a method of birth control and would now have been the mother of five children between the ages of twenty and thirty. When she became a Christian, it dawned on her that she had taken the lives of her own healthy kids. The weight of guilt that came upon her was so strong that she sank into a long-term, clinical depression and suffered from chronic fatigue syndrome (CFS). It was totally debilitating. Sadly, the church at large normally reinforces guilt rather than relieving it. All the "sorries" in the world could not dislodge the burden.

Finally, she went for prayer ministry with an acquaintance who invited Jesus into her memory of the abortuary. Jesus came and received each baby into his arms and welcomed them into the kingdom of heaven. He showed her that they were safe and happy with him, that it was okay to release them. He allowed her to name each one and she held a service in their memory. Best of all, Jesus spoke his forgiveness to her. As he removed her guilt, the rush of divine power began flowing into her physical body. She shook with energy for about thirty minutes, and when it was over, she was healed of her depression and the CFS. Jesus gave her a promise that each little "flower" that had been cut off was now replanted in heaven. He also promised that for each one of them, she would reap a thousand more on earth. As it turns out, she has become instrumental in the child sponsorship of multitudes of orphaned children in Africa. If we can believe what Jesus showed her, I expect she'll break the five thousand mark before she's through. The awesome healing power of God has redeemed her life from the pit and crowned her with love and compassion (alluding to Psalm 103).

Thanks, Ed

The body of Christ owes Ed Smith a huge debt of gratitude for redis-covering the power of the gospel to remove hurt, anger, grief, guilt, and other truth-based burdens. For centuries, we've allowed the wounded to carry burdens all the way to the grave rather than to the Cross. We hoped that time would heal instead of believing that Jesus would. I no longer fear the exceedingly strong anger and grief of rape and sexual abuse victims nor the guilt and self-hatred of rapists and abusers. Why not? Because I know that wounded hand of love, capable of bearing the entire weight of any burden all the way to the Cross.

2. Lie-Based Pain

This is the other category of emotion that needs to be removed from our memories. The most common lie-based emotions we encounter are:

- Fear/anxiety/panic
- Shame/worthlessness/dirtiness
- Rejection
- Abandonment
- Loneliness/isolation
- Hopelessness/despair
- Helplessness/powerlessness

Many of these emotions dissolve as soon as we find Jesus in a memory, because he is truth and love incarnate. In his presence, the lies behind these emotions do not feel true anymore. However, Jesus would also have us bring each of these lies before him to hear and see his truthful reaction. Here's how he does it:

- We ask the person *why* they feel that emotion. This exposes lies that energize the emotion.
- We also ask the person what messages they received about them-selves (e.g., "I'm a loser"), others (e.g., "Adults are liars"), life or the world (e.g., "Life sucks"), and even God (e.g., "He doesn't care"). This question shows us what judgments they have made which

248

now reap consequences in their daily life. Even true judgments, if made in bitterness, will rebound to punish us. We often become what we judge or else turn into the extreme opposite.

- We ask what decisions they made as a result of those judgments. We sometimes call these "inner vows" (i.e., "I will never ..." statements). When we vow as children that we will never _____, the vow, if rooted in bitterness, takes on a life of its own. It binds our emotions and actions much more powerfully than any demon.
- Having coaxed out each lie, judgment, and inner vow, we ask the person to approach Jesus and verbalize them to his face one at a time.
- We pray, "Jesus, part of their heart really feels that way, what do you want them to know about that?" I never personally contradict lies, judgments, and vows with reason or even with Scripture. Such answers only enter the mind as data without removing the lie and resultant emotion from their hearts. However, Jesus' answer *does* effectively demolish lies so that it no longer "feels" true. And therefore, the energy behind the emotions and actions is totally drained. With the root gone, the fruit withers, falls off, and dies. For example, someone who knows that they are never alone *cannot* feel lonely. Someone who knows that Jesus will never leave them *cannot* feel isolated. Someone who knows that Jesus will watch over them as a Good Shepherd *will not* feel anxious. The truth defeats the lie, and the emotion it generated simply vanishes.

The Spelling Test

I used to suffer from severe bouts of anxiety. At times, I would become so anxious about "getting it wrong" or getting behind or being late that I would have panic-attacks. It could happen as I stressed over my to-do list or even in a slow grocery store line-up. It was so ridiculous that I booked some time alone with Jesus to track the problem to its root.

The Lord took me to a grade one spelling test. The teacher said the word "of" and I spelled it "uv." I knew it didn't look right, so I began to erase it. She said the next word, "and." I tried to print it out and go back to "uv." I thought to myself, "I can't figure it out. I'm getting it wrong!" Before I was done she said the next word. And the next. I lost track. "I'm getting behind. I can't remember. I can't catch up!" I panicked to the point of wetting myself.

As I relived the memory, I knew that I had made a big mistake. I should *not* have been working this through by myself at a public coffee shop! Cornered, I was trembling violently, crossing my legs in a vice for fear of again losing bladder control!

Then I saw Jesus, standing up front as the schoolteacher. He was patiently waiting for me. I said, "I'm getting behind. I can't keep up." He said calmly, "It'll wait." I wondered about the other students. He spoke again, "They can wait too. We'll go at your pace." Forty percent of my anxiety melted away.

I looked down at the spelling test. There was the word: "uv." It was so frustrating. I felt Jesus at my left shoulder now acting as a tutor. He said, "It's okay. Take your time. You can't fail this test. If you make a mistake, we'll just erase it and try again. I'll help you with it 'til you're comfortable. Then we'll go on to the next one." Another forty percent of my anxiety disappeared.

I scanned the classroom. What was the source of the remaining 20 percent? The bell rang and Jesus announced, "Recess!" I reacted, "I don't want to go to recess. I want to get rid of the last twenty percent of my anxiety." Jesus responded, "Twenty percent of your anxiety comes when you don't take recess."

Since then, I've never had an anxiety attack. When my schedule threatens to overwhelm me or people pressure me for time, I hear his voice inside assuring me, "It'll wait." When I "get it wrong," I hear him say, "It's okay. We can erase it at the Cross. Let's try it again until you get it right." And why I sense panic knocking at the door of my emotions, I just book some "recess" time.

Concerning Depression and Confusion

Depression is one of the most common negative emotional states, at least in the West. Yet you'll note that I have excluded it from the above lists. This is because *non-medical* depression—that is, depression that has no physiological cause—is virtually always caused by a repressed emotion. If we are being brutally honest with God about our feelings, we are no longer repressing. The door marked depression is opened and out comes the "real" emotion, whether truth-based (anger turned inwards, unresolved guilt) or lie-based (stuffed down anxiety, hopelessness or despair). When those burdens are lifted or the lies are removed, depression is displaced with peace and love. But I have *no* trouble honouring the medical profession when they assist those trapped in depression or anxiety with medications. My experience is that they help us get at the real issues for inner healing rather than hindering us.

Confusion also has its non-medical sources:

- Some people are confused because they believe a lie. When Jesus speaks the truth, the confusion gives way to clarity.

- Others may experience confusion while under the oppression of a demonic spirit. Binding that spirit and sending it to Jesus brings that type of confusion to an end.
- Those who have been wronged at a young age may not know why what is happening is wrong, so they experience it as confusion. The clearest example is of those who were sexually abused or aroused before they understood what it meant. The child's question is, "Why is this happening?" Even an adult who returns to a childhood memory of abuse may feel the confusion, because that's how they experienced the abuse *at the time* (it didn't "hurt," but it didn't "feel right"). In this case, the Lord usually treats the confusion as a burden to be lifted.

To deal with confusion, we walk with Jesus through one emotion after another until the perfect peace of Christ (Isaiah 26:3) reigns supreme in the memory. Every burden is lifted, every lie is removed, and all pain is gone from that memory. Having dealt with each emotion, we now turn to each character in the memory.

D. Revelation of Others

A revelation of each character through Jesus' eyes in that scenario. We ask the Lord to lend us his eyes and show us his perspective on each character that played a role in that memory. This includes:

- *The person receiving prayer:* "Jesus, what do you see when you look at me?" This is especially healing for those who have seen themselves as unworthy, unlovable or spoiled through sin (either their own or a sin that has been committed against them). Jesus often shows them an innocent child washed clean and clothed in white. Once, I prayed with a woman who had just fled prostitution to enter a halfway house. When we asked this question, she laughed herself into tears of joy saying, "I see myself in a spotless white wedding dress!" Men often see the Lord clothing them in the gleaming armour of a royal warrior. You can imagine how these images would heal someone whose self-worth has been crushed!
- *Other people in the memory:* This may include the person's offender(s) or their victim(s), someone they are bearing a burden for and/or any accomplices or witnesses. Jesus may simply dismiss everyone but himself from the memory. But more often, he wants us to see others from his perspective. We may see the offender as

a broken child in need of compassion. Or we may see that they are now impotent and unable to hurt us anymore. We may see the Lord restoring the victims of our sin or carrying those we're burdened for. His purpose is to unhook any emotional chains that bind us to others. He is preparing us for our trip together to the final meeting place: the Cross.

- *Spiritual characters in the memory:* The Lord may also open our eyes to angelic or demonic characters involved in that event. Any demons seen there should be bound immediately and sent on ahead of us to the Cross. Then later at the Cross, they must leave without an argument.

- *Dissociated parts:* Without expanding on debate over the reality of dissociated parts, I want you to be aware that you may stumble into some "little ones" and/or their "protectors" in traumatic memories. These are distinct identities or personality states that are actually "part" of the person you are praying for. You can distinguish them from demons by asking Jesus, "Does this part have a human heart?" If he says "no" then it's just a demon and you can send it to the Cross for disposal. But if he says, "Yes, it has a human heart," *never attempt to cast it out!* This is a fragment or projection of the person's own heart. You should simply ask Jesus to minister his healing love to that part. If more is required, I'd recommend referring the person on to someone experienced in this area.

III. MEET JESUS AT THE CROSS

We know we have reached this stage when Jesus has thoroughly cleansed the memory of all pain and shown us that we are ready to go to the Cross. While the place of refuge was about *comfort*, and the root wound was about *healing*, the agenda at the Cross is *freedom*. When we come to the Cross, we begin by finding Jesus. He is not usually on the Cross but somewhere waiting for us nearby. Again, this meeting includes up to four elements: forgiveness, repentance, renunciation and deliverance.

A. Forgiveness

This is absolutely critical to fulfilment of the healing journey. Jesus taught us to include it in our daily prayers (Matthew 6:12). He warns that those who do not forgive will not be forgiven (Matthew 6:15). We must forgive even repeat offenders (Matthew 18:22) and not only begrudgingly, as through gritted teeth. It doesn't count unless it's *from the heart* (Matthew 18:35)! Jesus even says we must love, bless, and pray for our enemies. In Christ's kingdom, forgiveness is non-negotiable!

On the other hand, the Christian party line has often re-abused victims by (1) wrongly defining forgiveness or (2) making forgiveness a prerequisite to healing rather than it's result.

My working definition of forgiveness is "taking our offenders to the Cross and leaving them there to God's mercy."[7] Forgiveness does not excuse sin ("Oh, that's okay") or the sinner ("Well, he didn't know better"). It does not demand reconciliation with someone who is still unrepentant or unsafe. Rather, forgiveness releases the sinner from our judgments, curses, and sentences and into the hands of a righteous Judge. When we hand them over to God, we acknowledge that they, like we, deserve judgment, but we appeal for mercy. We pray on their behalf for the blessings of repentance and forgiveness.

This forgiveness will be sincere only when it is a natural outcome of healing. Consider this contrast: On the one hand, we have a victim who tries to forgive while they can still feel *all* their pain and still fear their offender as an evil monster. Picture them trying desperately to forgive while still buried in burdens, lies, and bondage. And feel their condemnation as they consider Christ's demands (nay, threats!) concerning forgiveness. Now on the other hand, imagine someone who cannot feel *any* of the emotional pain that had oppressed them. It's *all* gone, replaced by the perfect peace and the healing love of God. Moreover, when they picture their offender, they see a pathetic little human in deep need of mercy rather than a scary monster. Their heart is stirred to compassion. How will THEY respond to the question, "Do you think you could send that person to Jesus and release them to his mercy?" Allow me to illustrate the extreme contrast.

You'll Have to Get Through Me First!

Reg was seeing red! We were in a violent memory with his physically abusive father. I asked him to give an honest confession of his pain. He exploded in rage, "If he were here right now, I'd kill him! I could never ever forgive him for what he did!" He was shaking with anger, fists and jaw clenched, his face turning red as capillaries threatened to burst. Inwardly, I was cheering! Reg was being brutally honesty, and he wanted to be free. We only had one emotion to deal with, and Jesus was in the room. This was going to be a good day!

We walked faithfully through the steps for lifting away the *entire* burden of anger. Then, seeing his dad through Jesus' eyes, Reg's heart melted. He resigned as judge and released his father (who he now saw as an abused child) over to Jesus. We looked to Jesus for a response. Instead of seeing him as a gentle healer, Christ looked at Reg's dad with a flash of anger in his eyes! He drew a sword and approached Reg's dad as if to strike him down in judgment! Immediately, Reg stood in the way. He stared down the King of Heaven and shouted, "You'll have to get through me first!" Then he burst into tears and began pleading for mercy for his dad with *all his heart!* Jesus relented and embraced both of them with fatherly love. Reg had moved from one extreme to another, from murderous rage to heart-rending intercession in less than twenty minutes!

Here is what we can learn from this episode: when walking through the healing journey, find Jesus as early as you can along the way, but save forgiveness and deliverance until all the healing work is done. The presence of Christ and the completion of healing takes forgiveness and deliverance much deeper, but it also makes it much easier.

B. Repentance

The next step is to repent of reactive sins and receive God's forgiveness. Even if the offender was completely at fault, my righteous anger can easily turn into resentment, bitterness, malice or vengeance. Unforgiveness and hardness of heart are reactive sins for which we need to be forgiven. Rather than saying sorry, sorry, sorry (regret is not repentance), we boldly pray, "Lord, in my anger, I have sinned. I will not excuse it and I cannot fix it. I deserve judgment but I ask for mercy. Will you please forgive me?" His resounding "Yes!" settles the issue. Please wait on the Lord, expecting to hear his answer. Once given, the enemy's attempts at accusation will ring hollow in your heart.

In addition, I may need to put to death unholy habit patterns that were formed as a result of the wound I received. To illustrate this problem, imagine a bad tree growing up and bearing bad fruit (For example, a child is sexually abused—the root wound. Her worth is shattered and she feels dirty—the bad fruit). Now that fruit ripens and goes to seed. It falls to the ground and begins to sprout independently (Looking for comfort, she gives herself over to promiscuity and substance abuse—the fruit gone to seed and sprouting). The new sprouts develop and produce their own fruit (such as STDs and addictions). As you can see, dealing with the initial root wound is not sufficient. We must also attend to the resultant habits that sprang up as a consequence. We do that by bringing them to death, daily if necessary, at the Cross. (And that's exactly how we pray it!)

Now here is a common lie that I'd like to challenge: "God will forgive your sins, but you have to live with the consequences" (Hesitations 3:16). I suspect this is not *always* so; in fact, it may *only* be so if we believe it is so! The gospel is powerful to forgive sin, bring inner healing, *and* remove consequences. We've seen it enough to at least ask, "Lord, restore ALL that was lost!" (Joel 2:17–27).

Saved, Delivered, and Healed

June, a pastor's kid, was neglected by her busy father and then fell prey to an abuser. Shattered, she looked for comfort in the arms of one boy after another, looked for life in one substance after another. The lifestyle brought with it multiple STDs and addictions. The tough love approach drove her deeper into her pain and her self-medication. She moved out. Work was sparse—life seemed hopeless.

As she went for a drive one night, the car broke down. That was the proverbial last straw. She got out and walked and walked and walked. Her journey took her right by the open door of a church in San Diego where Brian West, a youth evangelist at the time, was leading a renewal meeting. June stumbled in. She looked such a mess that we wondered whether we should welcome her or fear her! She sat and listened to Brian's message of a God who meets the broken with his love. At the end of the service, she made a beeline for him and got right in his face. She glared him down, demanding to know if Brian and his message were authentic. With the authority of God's Spirit in his eyes, Brian asked her to hold out her hands and wait. He spoke from God's heart to hers, and, as he did, demons manifested themselves and then began to leave. Brian kept blessing June. When the Holy Spirit had flushed out the demons, Brian continued to pray. June began to feel God's undaunted love for her. She felt God's Spirit filling all those empty places inside. She wept healing tears, and her face became radiant. Brian kept praying: forgiveness of sin *and* removal of consequences, freedom from addictions *and* healing of STDs. Her body shuddered with the power of God, and then it was done. She left that night, saved, delivered, and healed. She kept in touch with Brian by e-mail, sharing the happy news that her addictions *and* her STDs were gone.

I'm not saying things always work this way, but I do think examples like this should be an encouragement to those who've suffered the consequences of their sin to go back to the Cross and ask for mercy.

C. Renunciation

Another aspect of repentance is renunciation. We repent of playing judge and cursing our enemies. We renounce every vow or judgment made in bitterness. We cut ungodly soul-ties (e.g., co-dependency,

manipulation, and control) and sinful one-flesh bonds (1 Corinthians 6:
16; e.g., anyone that we've had sexual encounters with outside of marriage, including abusers) between others and ourselves. Any emotional
hooks we've planted in each other are removed, any chains binding us
are broken. We place the Cross of Christ as a filter for all these relationships. All communication must flow through it, releasing blessings
and obstructing curses. Henceforth, we will only relate through that
cross.

D. Deliverance

I am assuming that any demons we ran into along the way, whether
exposed or not, will be waiting at the Cross for their final boarding call
to the pit. We used to interrogate demons as to their name, function,
legal right to stay, and so on. Finally, a friend from Vancouver Island
challenged me regarding this: "What's the fruit of conversing with
demons?" He asked, "Would you please ask the Lord about that?" We
listened together. The conversation with God went as follows:

> Brad: Lord, I find it helpful to interview the demons. How
> do you feel about that?
> Jesus: Maybe it is. But it's *more* helpful to get that informa-
> tion from me.
> Brad: You mean you're willing to tell me everything I was
> trying to pry out of them—their name, function, and legal
> right to stay?
> Jesus: Of course. And you'll never need to pry it out of me.
> I'll tell you everything you need to know. Also, remember
> that all demons are liars. But I'll never lie to you.
> Brad: And if you won't tell me?
> Jesus: Tell me what's wrong with this sentence: "If Jesus
> won't reveal what I think I need to know, I'll consult with
> the demons."
> Brad: I see your point.

Since then, I've never needed to ask a demon a question. Anything
I ever needed to learn from them, I'm able to ask Jesus (and so are
you). Actually, I ask Jesus the question, then he gives the answer to
the one we are praying for in the Cross scene, and they relate it to me.
I lay down kingdom laws for the demons (no talking, no manifesting,
no body pain, just stay under Jesus' feet) and establish consequences
for breaking those laws (if you don't obey me, Jesus will deal with you

directly). But I don't ask them questions or respond to theirs. If they break a kingdom rule, they are defying the God whom I represent, so I immediately turn to Jesus and ask him how he feels about that. I ask Jesus to deal with them directly, and he does. The only questions we need to ask the Lord for their disposal are:

- "Jesus, if there were any unclean spirits attached to this memory, would you please retrieve and restrain them? I ask you to bind them together and cause them to kneel at your feet."
- If the person sees demons in the Cross scene, or feels them in their body, we ask: "Jesus, is there anything we need to know or do before you remove these demons permanently? Do they have any legal right that we need to deal with? What needs to happen?" Jesus may tell the person, "Everything is done. They need to go now." Or he might say, "There still needs to be repentance about _____." We keep checking in, "Jesus, is that everything?"
- When Jesus gives the "all clear" we ask: "Jesus, how would you like to remove these critters, and to where?" Ninety percent of the time, Jesus is willing to remove the demons by himself. We may see him consume them in fire, dropkick them into the pit or provide some other creative imagery to represent the deliverance. The remainder of the time, he will tell the person who needs deliverance to command the demons to go (to drive home the truth of their own authority in Christ) or he'll let me do it (my payday of vengeance for the bruises I've taken along the way).

A FINAL BLESSING

When the Lord says we're done, we may return to the place of refuge to enjoy a final word of blessing and promise. The last taste in our mouth should be the sweetness of the Lord's peaceful presence.

At this time, we may share some of the pictures that God has been giving the prayer team along the way. Allow me to emphasize that the words and pictures that the prayer team gets along the way are meant to affirm and confirm what the one receiving prayer is hearing. They are *not* meant to get us out of jams when someone is blocked. It's tempting to jump in with, "Can't you see him? I can see him! Look over at the bed!" But remember that removing those blocks is part of God's agenda in the healing journey. We do a disservice when, in our impatience or frustration, we use a prophetic word to bypass them. In so doing, we are short-circuiting a critical healing process for the person for whom we're praying.

On the other hand, when we save what we saw for the end, it is *very* reassuring to the one who has been struggling to believe that they are really hearing God's voice. When other credible witnesses can say, "That's what I saw, too!" or supplement the session with additional revelation, it greatly reinforces their faith in God's voice.

◀)) *Tuning In* • • • • • • • • •

If you have never invited Jesus into a memory for healing before, there are some simple, safe beginning exercises:

- First, practice finding Jesus in a memory. Ask the Lord to remind you of a pleasant memory where you felt full of love, joy or peace. Then ask Jesus to show you where he was then.
- Next, practice removing a simple truth-based burden. Remember a time when you felt a disappointment that made you hang your head or slump your shoulders. Ask the Lord to show you what that heavy disappointment looked like. Invite him to draw near in the memory to lift the burden off. Practice allowing him to remove that burden.
- Finally, practice removing a simple lie-based pain. Recall an incident where you were anxious about a "first time" (at a new school, job, public speaking, etc.). Find Jesus in that memory. Tell him that you're afraid and why you're afraid. See how he responds. Feel what that does to your anxiety.

These three spiritual tools are sufficient to tackle nearly *any* root wound memory. Remember: They are *not* mere techniques; they are the presence of Jesus in every memory, the Cross of Christ for every burden, and the truth of Christ for every lie.

On the following page, I have concluded this chapter by adding a summary outline that some of our prayer ministers at Fresh Wind keep on hand when following Jesus through an inner healing. The key is remembering that we are following Jesus, not a formula. In the midst of a prayer session, we don't typically ask, "What does the chart tell us to do next?" Rather, we lean on the Lord himself, knowing that he is with us and asking him directly, "Jesus, what needs to happen here?"

MEETING PLACE PRAYER MINISTRY
Q: Do you want to be free?

1. FIND JESUS IN A "PLACE OF REFUGE"
(a Biblical image, familiar place, vision, or memory)

A. Intimacy - Ask Jesus for a safe place where you can meet with him. Ask him to identify and remove any blocks to hearing his voice or seeing his face.

B. Comfort - Ask Jesus how he sees you and feels about you. Draw near to behold him and be held by him. Ask him for blessings, promises, courage, and strength.

C. Recognition - Ask Jesus to identify issues he wants to address: bad fruit we experience or produce (spiritual, emotional, behavioral, mental, or physical).

2. FOLLOW JESUS TO THE "ROOT WOUND"
(an experience, dream, vision, pre-natal)

A. Confessions - A brutally honest confession of each painful emotion and/or offence (by you or against you) in that scene.

B. Revelation of Jesus - Ask Jesus to show you where he was.

C. Healing - Ask Jesus to heal each painful emotion.
Ask him to expose each lie and answer it with truth.
Ask him to identify each burden and bear it to the cross for you.

D. Revelation of others - Ask Jesus show you how he sees each character in that scene (offenders, victims, spirits).

3. MEET JESUS AT "THE CROSS"

A. Forgiveness - Take each character (offenders or victims) to the cross and leave them to Jesus' mercy.

B. Repentance - Repent and receive forgiveness for any reactive sins. Put to death any ungodly habit patterns.

C. Renunciation - Renounce and cut off judgements, curses, inner vows, and soul ties between yourself and each character.

D. Deliverance - Remove any legal right that unclean spirits have to stay and ask Jesus how he would like to dispatch them.

· · · · · *Epilogue* · · · ·
Do You Want to Start a Fire?

So [Samson] went out and caught three hundred foxes and
tied them tail to tail in pairs. He then fastened a torch to
every pair of tails, lit the torches and let the foxes loose in the
standing grain ...

Judges 15:4-5

I was in a foul mood, feeling self-absorbed and self-condemning. I found
myself journaling my complaints to God and recording his responses.
As I attempted to verbalize my woes to him, he completely interrupted
my spiraling train of thought with a question.

"Do you want to start a fire?"

What? Somehow I sensed that he was referring to the listening prayer teaching that I was developing. "Sure," I replied, and then
returned to my grumbling.

A few months later, I was doing prayer ministry over the phone
with a woman. She was in a pond-like meeting place with Jesus,
receiving some spiritual cleansing from damaged emotions. When I
asked Jesus what needed to happen next, the person receiving prayer
said, "Jesus has a question for you." This was unusual for a healing
session, but I said, "Shoot." She said, "Jesus is asking, 'Do you want to
start a fire?'"

When I asked God about this on my own, he led me directly into
the story where Samson tied torches to the foxes' tails and released
them into the enemy's fields.

> So he went out and caught three hundred foxes and tied
> them tail to tail in pairs. He then fastened a torch to every
> pair of tails, lit the torches and let the foxes loose in the
> standing grain of the Philistines. He burned up the shocks
> and standing grain, together with the vineyards and olive
> groves. (Judges 15:4–5)

Samson certainly started a fire. Then Jesus reminded me of how he
had sent out the disciples two by two into the spiritual harvest fields,
taking the fire of the gospel and the Spirit with them. He then applied
it to this teaching.

261

"From now on," he said, "whenever you teach listening prayer, it will be like tying torches to foxes' tails. Among those who hear this message will be foxes who run with it immediately. They will in turn spread this fire by teaching others to listen to my voice. The fire will move quickly through the fields and many whom it ignites will not even know you started it."

Sure enough, since then, whenever I have shared this message, someone invariably testifies, "I tried this with my children last night and they all got a meeting place" or "I called my parents and taught them the whole lesson over the phone. They both heard God!" Others have begun listening prayer home groups in their local churches. One youth group in Kelowna, BC took the fire on a missions trip to Africa and trained a church there how God speaks to them.

Now I share this final exhortation with you. I am no one of consequence, a messenger at best. This torch has always belonged to the church, to God. This fire has always burned, though dimly at times. But if, after reading this book, you smell smoke from your own tail, run with it! Begin to teach others how to hear God's voice. Show others how to find Jesus in a meeting place. Give away what you've learned. In fact, find a dry field and light it up!

····· *Testing All Things* ·····
Further Reading

"TUNING IN" CLASSICS

Dark Night of the Soul by St. John of the Cross
Descent in Hell by Charles Williams
Experiencing the Depths of Jesus Christ by Jeanne Guyon
Mysticism by Evelyn Underhill
Revelations of Divine Love by Julian of Norwich
Spiritual Canticles by St. John of the Cross
The Cloud of Unknowing by Anonymous
The Dialogue of Saint Catherine of Sienna by St. Catherine
The Healing Light by Agnes Sanford
The Holiest of All by Andrew Murray
The Imitation of Christ by Thomas A Kempis
The Interior Castle by Teresa of Avila
The Labyrinth of the World and the Paradise of the Heart by
John Amos Comenius
The Practice of the Presence of God by Brother Lawrence
The Way of Perfection by Teresa of Avila

"TUNING IN" CONTEMPORARIES

Developing Your Prophetic Gifting by Graham Cooke
Experiencing God by Henry Blackaby and Claude King
Hearing God by Peter Lord
Intercessory Prayer by Dutch Sheets
Listening Prayer by David and Linda Olsen
Listening Prayer and *The Healing Presence* by Leanne Payne
Listening to God in Times of Choice by Gordon Smith
The Prophets by Abraham J. Heschel
Surprised by the Voice of God by Jack Deere
The Shattered Lantern by Ronald Rolheiser
The Voice of God by Cindy Jacobs

····· Endnotes ·····

Chapter 1 "My Sheep Hear My Voice"

[1] I hope that my emphasis on the "human face" of Jesus will cultivate a deep spiritual intimacy with him. But this should not be misunderstood as minimizing his divinity in favour of his closeness. I believe this Jesus *is* the Christ, the only divine Son of God and one mediator between God and humanity (the "God-man"). I have concluded that he is more than an incarnation of his Father: Jesus Christ remains the first, last, and only incarnation of God in human history. When I refer to the voice of God and then elsewhere to the voice of Jesus or Christ, I am talking about one and the same person.

However, believing this is *not* a prerequisite to hearing the voice of Jesus. His own disciples spent time relating to him and following him as a teacher before coming to the conclusion that this was the Christ, the Son of God (Mark 8:27–29). Readers who "aren't there yet" need only keep listening and watching for what God reveals about himself.

[2] I co-wrote this section with Colleen Taylor, a friend and professor at Briercrest Bible College.

[3] Words and Music by Christine Dente, Scott Dente and Charlie Peacock, Sparrow, 1991.

[4] Francis Thompson, *The Hound of Heaven* (accessed Dec. 30, 2002) available from http://www2.bc.edu/~anderso/sr/ft.html; Internet.

> But with unhurrying chase,
> And unperturbed pace,
> Deliberate speed, majestic instancy,
> They beat - and a Voice beat
> More instant than the Feet -
> "All things betray thee, who betrayest Me."

[5] Douglas Coupland, *Life After God* (New York: Pocket Books, 1994) 357-360.

[6] Jeromey Q. Martini, *Of Magic and Technology* (Caronport, SK: Unpublished Essay, 2002).

[7] *America's Great Revivals*, Bethany House Pub.: Minneapolis, MN, reissued ed. 1994.

Chapter 2 Awakened Hearts: How We Hear and See God

[1] R. Paul Stevens, *"Poems for People Under Pressure: The Apocalypse of John and the Contemplative Life"* in *Alive to God.* Ed. by J. I. Packer and Loren Wilkinson (Downers Grove, IL: IVP, 1992) 88.

[2] I recommend Kevin J. Conner, *Interpreting the Symbols and Types* (Portland, OR: City Bible Pub., 1992). Conner gives us an extensive summary of biblical symbols. This is helpful as long as we don't assume that "this" *always* means "that."

[3] This is an example of what Carl Jung called "synchronicity." Inner and outer world messages coincide. The simplest type of synchronicity would be when an acquaintance phones just as you've been thinking about them.

[4] Exodus 20:5–6: "You shall not bow down to them or worship them; for I, the LORD your God, am a jealous God, punishing the children for the sin of the fathers to the third and fourth generation of those who hate me, but showing love to a thousand generations of those who love me and keep my commandments." If family sins and curses can affect three or four generations, then family blessings can extend indefinitely.

[5] When I shared this at the Marek family reunion, my father pointed out that my great uncle Joseph Marek was actually a well-digger: a neat little "coincidence." He also discovered in my grandfather's personal sermon notes (he was a lay-preacher) a hand-written lecture entitled *Jan Comensky: Teacher of Nations* (dated 1936).

[6] John Donne, *Sermons,* 7.13.346.

[7] Words and tune by Helen H. Lemmel, 1922.

[8] Words and music by Paul Baloche, Integrity's Hosanna! Music, 1977.

[9] Cf. David Hunt, *Beyond Seduction: A Return to Biblical Christianity* (Eugene, OR: Harvest House Publishers, Inc., 1986).

[10] Evelyn Underhill, *Mysticism* (New York, NY: Penguin Books, 1910) 315.

[11] R. Paul Stevens, *"Poems for People Under Pressure,"* 90.

[12] Andrew Murray, *The Holiest of All* (New Kensington, PA: Whitaker House, 1996) 65, 76, 103.

[13] Anonymous, *The Cloud of Unknowing*, trans. Clifton Wolters (Markham, ON: Penguin Books, 1961) 46.

[14] Ronald Rolheiser, *The Shattered Lantern* (New York, NY: Crossroad Pub. Co., 2001) 21.

Chapter 3 God, Is That Really You?

[1] Obsessive-compulsive disorder.

[2] "Schizophrenia is a chronic, severe, and disabling brain disease ... People with schizophrenia often suffer terrifying symptoms such as hearing internal voices not heard by others, or believing that other people are reading their minds, controlling their thoughts, or plotting to harm them." Leonard Holmes, "Schizophrenia," *Mental Health Resources*, (accessed 4 October, 2002) available from http://mentalhealth.about.com/library/mh/blschizoph.htm.

[3] "The essential feature of Dissociative Identity Disorder is the presence of two or more distinct identities or personality states that recurrently take control of behaviour. There is an inability to recall important personal information, the extent of which is too great to be explained by ordinary forgetfulness. The disturbance is not due to the direct physiological effects of a substance or a general medical condition. In children, the symptoms cannot be attributed to imaginary playmates or fantasy play." DSM IV-American Psychiatric Association Staff, *Diagnostic and Statistical Manual of Mental Disorders* (Washington, DC: American Psychiatric Press, 1994), 300.14.

[4] Jacob Boehme, *Dialogues on the Supersensual Life*, (London, 1901) 56.

[5] Teresa of Avila, *The Way of Perfection*, trans. the Benedictines of Stanbrook (Rockford, IL: Tan Books and Pub., Inc., 1997) 162, ch. 28.7.

[6] Ibid, 184, ch. 31.9.

[7] Cf. Anonymous, *The Cloud of Unknowing* (New York, NY: Image Books, 1973) ch. 4.

[8] Teresa of Avila describes this. "The soul is here like a babe at the breast of its mother, who to please it, feeds it without its moving its lips. Thus it is now, for the soul loves without using the understanding. Our Lord wishes it to realize, without reasoning about the matter, that it is in his company. He desires that it should drink the milk he gives and enjoy its sweetness while acknowledging that it is receiving a divine favour, and that it should delight in its own happiness." Teresa of Avila, *The Way of Perfection* 182–183, ch. 31.7.

[9] Briercrest Bible College, Caronport, SK.

[10] Cf. The philosophical arguments of Alvin Plantinga. Esp. Alvin Plantinga, *Warrant and Proper Function* (New York, NY: Oxford University Press, 1993). In his works, he demonstrates the possibility of knowledge apart from the myth of objectivity. He puts reason and scientific method in its proper place alongside other methods of knowing, including testimony, experience, intuition, faith, etc. None of these are truly objective, but their inter-subjectivity accumulates to provide sufficient warrant to make "I know" statements.

[11] Summary of Glenn Runnalls' thoughts on Agora, an Internet newsgroup.

[12] I am indebted to author Gordon Smith for his influence here. I was particularly inspired by a lecture he taught at Regent College entitled, "Three Voices; One Tradition: The Congruence of Ignatius Loyola, John Wesley, and Jonathan Edwards" in his course, *Divine Guidance and Spiritual Discernment* (Regent College, Class notes, Fall 2002).

[13] Jonathan Edwards, *A Treatise Concerning Religious Affections in Three Parts*, 1776, Sept. 18, 2002, I.2 (accessed 4 Oct. 2002) http://www.ccel.org/e/edwards/affections/religious_affections.html.

[14] John Wesley, *The Journal of John Wesley*. Ed. by Percy Livingstone Parker (Chicago, IL: Moody Press, 1951), ch. 2, May 14, 1738.

[15] Ignatius Loyola, *The Spiritual Exercises of St. Ignatius of Loyola*, trans. Father Elder Mullan, (Christian Classics Ethereal Library; accessed 20 Dec. 2002) available from http://www.ccel.org/pager.cgi. (Rules for Perceiving the Movements Caused in the Soul - Third and Fourth Rule).

Chapter 4 Was That Just My Imagination?

[1] Abraham J. Heschel, *The Prophets, Volume I,* (New York, NY: Harper Torchbooks, 1962), p. x.

[2] "Is this the voice of the Spirit or the voice of the flesh?" (Paul's version-Romans 8:5-8). Or "Is this the Spirit of God or the spirit of antichrist?" (John's version-1 John 4:1-4). Or "Is this the voice of the Shepherd or the voice of the stranger?" (Jesus' version-John 10:1–10).

[3] Tesla Coil: A device for producing a high-frequency high-voltage current. It consists of a transformer with a high turns ratio, the primary circuit of which includes a spark gap and a fixed capacitor; the secondary circuit is tuned by means of a variable capacitor to resonate with the primary. It was devised by Nikola Tesla. Tesla coils are commonly used to excite luminous discharges in glass vacuum apparatus, in order to detect leaks. Cf. About Inc., *Tesla Coil*, 2002 (accessed 1 October, 2002) available from
http://physics.about.com/library/dict/bldefteslacoil.htm.

[4] John J. O'Neill, *Prodigal Genius, Life of Nicola Tesla.* (New York, NY: Ives Wasburn Inc., 1944).

[5] Oswald Chambers, *My Utmost for his Highest* (New York: Dodd, Mead & Co., 1935.), 2/11. It interests me that the modernized (literally!) editions of Chambers book replace the word "imagination" with "mind" at this stage.

[6] Leanne Payne, *Healing Presence* (Grand Rapids, MI: Baker Books, 1989) 163.

[7] Cf. Beulah Karney, *Mary of Agreda and Her Extraordinary Excursions into Multidimensional Consciousness, 2001*, The New Mary Agreda Page, (accessed 1 Oct. 2002) available from http://www.murray creek.net/elliott/agreda/index.html. Cf. also Armadillo's WWW Server, The Lady in Blue (accessed 1 Oct. 2002) available from http://www.rice.edu/armadillo/Projects/ladyblue.html. Cf. also C.F. Eckhardt, *The Mystery of the Lady in Blue* (accessed 1 October, 2002) available from http://www.sanmarcostexas.net/eckhardt/ladyinblue.htm.

[8] George MacDonald, *Lilith: A Romance* (Grand Rapids, MI: Wm. B. Eerdmans Publishing Company, 1895) 251.

Chapter 5 The Meeting Place

[1] John Comenius, *The Labyrinth of the World and the Paradise of the Heart*, trans. Howard Louthan and Andrea Sterk (New York, NY: Paulist Press, 1998) 188-189.

[2] The fellow who shared this with me was Todd Bentley, a flamboyant evangelist with an authentic healing gift. He's quite an enigma.

[3] Page Wise, *Austin Miles' Methodist Hymn: in the Garden*, 2001 (accessed 1 Oct. 2002) available at http://akksands.com/Religious/Christian/hymnsreligiong_yuu_gn.htm.

[4] John H. Sailhamer, *The Pentateuch as Narrative* (Grand Rapids, MI: Zondervan, 1992) 289.

[5] Revelation 22:18. Cf. also the hymn *Whosoever Will May Come* by Philip P. Bliss and the classic sermon by Methodist Sam Jones.

[6] U2, "When Love Comes to Town," *Rattle and Hum*, 1988.

[7] Bruce Cockburn, "Dweller by a Dark Stream," *Mummy Dust*, 1981.

[8] "Hail Mary, full of grace, the Lord is with thee, blessed art thou among women, and blessed is the fruit of thy womb, Jesus. Holy Mary, Mother of God, pray for us sinners, now at the hour of our death. Amen." The "Hail Mary" was never meant to be an act of worship to Mary, but rather as a blessing (Luke 1:42) and an invitation that this great intercessor would join with us in our prayers to Jesus. She is one of the living cloud of witnesses that cheers us on from their place with Christ in the heavenlies (Hebrews 12:1). While acknowledging this, we need not also give ascent to Mariolatry nor replace Jesus as the one Mediator between God and mankind (1 Timothy 2:5).

[9] "Glory be to the Father, and to the Son, and to the Holy Ghost; as it was in the beginning, is now, and ever shall be, world without end. Amen."

[10] "O My Jesus, forgive us our sins, save us from the fires of Hell; lead all souls to Heaven, especially those who have most need of Thy mercy."

[11] Cited in *Divine Mysteries of the Most Holy Trinity* (New Lisbon, WS: J.M.J. Book Company, 1973), Introduction.

[12] Ignatius Loyola, *The Spiritual Exercises*, Second Week, The Fifth Contemplation.

[13] Teresa of Avila, *The Way of Perfection*. 150–151.

[14] Ibid, 151.

[15] Prader Willi Syndrome: "PWS is a complex genetic disorder that includes short stature, mental retardation or learning disabilities, incomplete sexual development, characteristic behavior problems, low muscle tone, and an involuntary urge to eat constantly, which, coupled with a reduced need for calories, leads to obesity." Prader Willi Syndrome Association (USA), *Prader Willi Syndrome*, 1997 (accessed 18 December, 2002) available from http://www.thearc.org/faqs/pwsynd.html.

[16] St. John of the Cross, *Spiritual Canticle,* trans. E. Allison Peers (Garden City, NY: Image Books, 1961) stanza i. 7,8.

[17] Teresa of Avila, Stanbrook, 163, ch. 28.9.

[18] Julian of Norwich, *Revelations of Divine Love*, trans. Elizabeth Spearing (Toronto: Penguin Books, 1998) 33. Translation copyright © Elizabeth Spears, 1998. Used by permission.

[19] Ibid. 174.

[20] Archbishop Anthony Bloom, *Living Prayer* (London: Libra Books, 1966) 108.

[21] Teresa of Avila, Cant. 7:10, 149.

[22] Julian of Norwich, 158-159.

[23] Comenius, 188, ch. 38.1.

[24] Archbishop Bloom, p. viii.

[25] E. A. Hoffman, "Leaning on the Everlasting Arms," Public Domain, 1887.

[26] Craig Musseau, "Arms of Love," Mercy/Vineyard Publishing, 1991.

[27] Augustine of Hippo, *Confessions.* 5.2.2.

Chapter 6 Meeting God to Intercede

[1] Elijah House, Inc., *Training for the Ministry of Prayer Counseling, Section III* (Post Falls, Idaho: Elijah House, Inc., 1989, 1997) 135 ff.

[2] Teresa of Avila, *The Way of Perfection*, XXVI.4.

Chapter 7 Overcoming Blocks to Meeting God

[1] Oswald Chambers, *My Utmost for his Highest*, Special Updated Edition, ed. James Reimann (Grand Rapids, MI: Discovery House Publishers, 1995), 10/11.

[2] Teresa of Avila, Stanbrook, 163, ch. 31.2.

[3] Ibid, 31.3.

[4] Cf. Also, Jeanne Guyon, *Experiencing the Depths of Jesus Christ.* Library of Spiritual Classics, Vol. 2.(Sargent, GA: Seedsowers, 1975), chapter 21, "Silence-In the Depths."

[5] St. John of the Cross, *Dark Night of the Soul*, trans. E. Allison Peers (New York, NY: Image Books, 1990), X.1.

[6] Ibid, XIII.15. Here follows John of the Cross' poetic description of the Dark Night, given at the beginning of the text.

Stanzas Of The Soul

1. One dark night, fired with love's urgent longings
—ah , the sheer grace!—
I went out unseen,
my house being now all stilled.
2. In darkness, and secure,
by the secret ladder, disguised,
—ah , the sheer grace!—
in darkness and concealment,
my house being now all stilled.
3. On that glad night,
in secret, for no one saw me,
nor did I look at anything,
with no other light or guide
than the one that burned in my heart.
4. This guided me
more surely than the light of noon
to where he was awaiting me
—him I knew so well—
there in a place where no one appeared.
5. O guiding night!
O night more lovely than the dawn!
O night that has united
the Lover with his beloved,
transforming the beloved in her Lover.
6. Upon my flowering breast
which I kept wholly for him alone,
there he lay sleeping,
and I caressing him
there in a breeze from the fanning cedars.
7. When the breeze blew from the turret,

as I parted his hair,
it wounded my neck
with its gentle hand,
suspending all my senses.
8. I abandoned and forgot myself,
laying my face on my Beloved;
all things ceased; I went out from myself,
leaving my cares
forgotten among the lilies.

From *The Collected Works of St. John of the Cross,* translated by Kieran Kavanaugh and Otilio Rodriguez Copyright (c) 1964, 1979, 1991 by Washington Province of Discalced Carmelites ICS Publications 2131 Lincoln Road, N.E. Washington, DC 20002-1199 U.S.A. www.icspublications.org. Used by permission.

Chapter 8 Listening Prayer in Decision Times

[1] Prophetic Conference at New Life Church, Kelowna BC, 2001.
[2] This is the major danger of personal predictive prophecy. If it strengthens our faith and resolve to obey God, if it encourages us to stay the course, then fine. But I've had to clean up a few prophetic messes where the destination foretold created fear, striving, burnout, and bitterness. Prophetic people should consider focusing on teaching people to hear what God has for them today, and then confirming those messages with encouraging promises about what God will do (not what they will do).

Chapter 9 Listening Prayer With Children

[1] Henry Nouwen, *Adam, God's Beloved* (Maryknoll, NY: Orbis Books, 1997) 31.

Chapter 10 Listening Prayer in the Local Church

[1] Henry Nouwen, *In the Name of Jesus* (New York, NY: Crossroad, 1989) 31.
[2] This is a critical error. Fruit-focused vision perpetually defers the harvest into the future-the carrot on a stick with which to drive the flock. The sheep become weary and then bitter.
[3] Many churches look to the Great Commission (Matthew 28:18–20) for their mission. But we err if we pare down Jesus' command to "make disciples" as simple evangelism and discipleship. "Teaching them everything I've commanded you" included more: "Preach the gospel to

the poor, heal the sick, and cast out demons" (Matthew 10:7–8). Jesus said, "As the Father sent me, so I am sending you" (John 20:21). This recalls Jesus' own great commission:

> Jesus said, "The Spirit of the Lord is upon me, because he has anointed me to preach good news to the poor. He has sent me to proclaim freedom for the prisoners and recovery of sight for the blind, to release the oppressed, to proclaim the year of the Lord's favor." (Luke 4:18–19)

Seeing this caused us to adopt Jesus' mission statement as our church mission statement.

[4] Our Ministries correlate to our values:

Values	Ministries
1. Entering God's Presence	Worship Ministry
2. Hearing God's Voice	Speaking Ministry
3. Experiencing God's Grace	Prayer Ministry
4. Advancing God's Kingdom	Outreach Ministry
5. Being God's Family	Fellowship Ministry

[5] On the one hand, since Brian and I were both experienced in youth ministry, we expected to gather a following of "Gen-Xers" as they were labelled at the time. But since we treated God as our first target group, we hadn't boxed ourselves in.

Chapter 11 Listening Prayer and Outreach

[1] A ten question survey originally used on the French series, "Bouillon de Culture" hosted by Bernard Pivot. Ryan Marcin, *Bernard Pivot's Ten Questions*, 2002, (accessed 4 October, 2002) available from http://home. uchicago.edu/-rpmarcin/10questions.html.

[2] Bravo Home, "Inside the Actors Studio" (accessed 20 Dec. 2002) available from http://www.bravotv.com/series/actorsstudio/frames/index_ad.html.

Chapter 12 Listening Prayer and Social Justice

[1] Ron currently teaches Religious Studies and Political Science at the University College of the Fraser Valley in BC. He has also served in a number of coordinating roles with Amnesty International. He has been a guiding light in the integration of spirituality with justice. It

was he who initially pointed this glaring omission in the first edition of this book.

[2] Jean-Bertrand Aristide, *Aristide: An Autobiography* (Maryknoll, New York: Orbis Books, 1993) 201–202.

[3] Abraham Heschel, *The Prophets,* p. 185.

[4] Facts pertaining to the following twelve questions are well documented in Paul Farmer, *The Uses of Haiti* (Monroe, ME: Common Courage Press, 1994) and Amy Wilentz, *The Rainy Season* (New York, NY: Touchstone / Simon and Schuster). I don't wish to sound partisan or anti-American here. Indeed, I believe God has blessed America and I would exhort Americans to "fear no evil" because God's rod and his staff are still with you! These are but examples of the questions that prophets in the biblical tradition must ask as they stand before God and the nations he loves.

[5] Traditionally, translators render this word to read "righteousness." This would be fine except that in modern English theology, we equate righteousness with personal piety, whereas historically, this Greek word has stronger social connotations, much more akin to "justice."

[6] Ron Dart, *Spirituality and Justice: the Vision of the Beatitudes* (St. Matthew's Anglican Parish, Abbotsford, BC: Diocesan Synod, 2003).

Chapter 13 Listening Prayer for Inner Healing

[1] Others have called it "prayer counselling," but that carries legal snags around the label "counsellor," and it doesn't reflect our emphasis on listening versus telling. We've also heard it called "inner healing" or "healing of memories" (too narrow?) and "listening prayer" (too broad?). Some have copyrighted a name for their particular approach (e.g., Ed Smith's "theophostic") or their approach has eventually been named after the group (e.g., Elijah House) or author (e.g., Neil Anderson) that developed it.

[2] Cf. Henry Wright, *A More Excellent Way* (Thomaston, GA: Pleasant Valley Pub., 2000). This is a fascinating, experiential report on the spiritual roots of many physical diseases.

[3] Cf. John H. Hampsch, *Healing Your Family Tree*, 2nd Ed. (Huntington, IN: Our Sunday Visitor Books, Inc., 1989).

[4] Cf. Daniel Brown, Alan W. Scheflin and D. Corydon Hammond, *Memory, Trauma Treatment, and the Law* (New York, London: W. W. Norton & Company, 1998. Esp. ch. 13: "Phase-Oriented Trauma Treatment." This is the most comprehensive and up-to-date treatment available addressing the complexities of repressed, dissociated, and false memories. It also critically analyzes the conflicts surrounding the debate.

[5] I run into two types of recovered memories. The first type is "repressed memory." In these memories, the person does not want to remember and so, through effort of will, they gradually shove it away into a corner of the mind. They probably remembered the event for a day, a week, or perhaps even several months. But eventually, they are able to erase it from their conscious history. The second type is "dissociated memory." In these, such a strong double bind is established (e.g., "I can't leave, I must leave" or "Daddy loves me, daddy is hurting me") that the mind splits into parts, some which live in denial for the purpose of function and others that carry the memory and experience the pain. I currently follow Tom Hawkins's approach, whose main agenda is not initially pushing for integration but rather bringing Jesus in to resolve the double bind (Tom Hawkins, Restoration In Christ Ministries, Grottoes, VA).

[6] Ed Smith is the developer of theophostic prayer ministry. The technique I share here is found in Ed Smith's basic training seminar, *Beyond Tolerable Recovery* (Campbellsville, KY: Theophostic Ministries, 1997).

[7] This from friend and prayer minister, Brian Headley.

BRAD JERSAK

Brad Jersak lives in Abbotsford,
British Columbia, Canada with
his wife Eden and three sons:
Stephen, Justice, and Dominic.

He is a pastor at Fresh Wind
Christian Fellowship and a
teacher with Listening Prayer
Community, a ministry that
helps churches hear God better.

To contact the author or to get information on his Listening
Prayer seminars, email him at info@freshwindpress.com.

BY THE SAME AUTHOR

FRESHWIND PRESS
www.freshwindpress.com

Children, Can You Hear Me?
by Brad Jersak
Illustrated by Ken Save

Rivers from Eden:
40 Days of Intimate Conversation with God
by Brad Jersak and Eden Jersak

Fear No Evil:
Breaking Free from the Culture of Fear
by Brad Jersak